Rangers de

Jake Je

JAKOVENKO

JAKOVENKO

FROM THE STEPPES OF
UKRAINE
TO THE US ARMY RANGER HALL OF FAME

Jake Jakovenko, Son Tay Raider

with Cliff Westbrook

WITH A FOREWORD BY DREW DIX, MEDAL OF HONOR

PALMETTO
PUBLISHING
Charleston, SC
www.PalmettoPublishing.com

Copyright © 2024 by JakovenkoBook, LLC (V. Jakovenko and C. Westbrook)

Hardcover ISBN: 979-8-8229-1601-2
Paperback ISBN: 979-8-8229-1602-9
eBook ISBN: 979-8-8229-1603-6

"Over the past decades, I've regularly come across people who tell amazing stories about their time with Jakovenko. Born under the terror of Stalin, becoming a US citizen, and dedicating 30 years serving America as a Green Beret in unimaginable combat situations. He is a stud, a legend. At last, we have a book about his incredible life."

-John Stryker Meyer, MACV-SOG, author of…

SOG Chronicles Vol. 1,

Across the Fence, and

On The Ground

Dedication by Jake

To my wife, Sandy L. Jakovenko, who made this book possible. Hundreds of hours of capturing my stories over a ten-year period. To my children and their children. You fill my heart.

To my mother and to my stepfather, "Pop," who did what was needed to survive and to get us to America.

To the memory of my father, my grandparents, my aunts and uncles, and the millions of other Ukrainian people who died at the hands of Joseph Stalin and his Marxist/socialist government.

To the people who are willing to fight to protect and defend the Liberties enshrined in the US Constitution, even at the risk of laying down their lives.

Dedication by Cliff

To my father and all the others who carried out the Son Tay Raid. Our POWs are worth it.

To my mother and all military spouses. You sacrifice so much in order that our country may field the greatest warriors.

Table of Contents

Foreword

May God bless America and the 'warrior class.'

We are a great country made up of people from every ethnic background, every religion, and every belief. We have the liberty to pursue happiness, any occupation or lifestyle, no matter how personally offensive some may find it. These freedoms are often taken for granted. Many never think about the sacrifices made to earn these freedoms. We have people in government and in business who benefit from the blood and sweat of others, showing no appreciation. This is their choice!

Though we use the words 'upper,' 'middle,' and 'lower,' we are not a 'class' society—except for the 'warrior class.'

This book is about the warrior class. Every American should read it. I see no better way to explain this magnificent, underappreciated class of people, than to tell the life story of Jake Jakovenko.

I've known Jake for many years in the classroom and in the field during our time in the US Army Special Forces. The men in SF were there for the camaraderie of being part of the best. Living off the land, going into a war zone with only the limited resources already in theater, we were truly force multipliers. There were many with the vision that America could help at-risk countries fight the spread of communism. We would not do it for them. We would help them develop the ability to fight for their own country. That vision became reality under President Kennedy, and in 1961, he awarded these warriors a distinctive head gear, the Green Beret.

Jake and I knew we had an obligation to keep the legacy of the warrior class alive. As it has from the beginning of time, it will always take audacity and courage to meet the demands of unconventional warfare. Insurgencies and counterinsurgencies are not scripted. It requires flexibility, commitment, and independence not found in conventional forces. You are always fighting outnumbered. When in those situations, you excel, or you die!

In the early days of our SF careers, we occasionally wondered what the average citizen thought about what we were doing. Our conversations ended with "…the poor bastards don't get it and never will." This statement remains as true today as it was 60 years ago.

When reading *Jakovenko*, you won't need to read between the lines as it is so descriptive, but I ask you to think about and appreciate the kind of person it takes to do this work…the Warrior Class.

-Drew Dix, Major, USA (retired), Medal of Honor
Author of *The Rescue of River City*

PREFACE 1

How to Savor a War Story

Smoke arose from the crackling fire pit into the desert's cool midnight air. Overhead, the stars blazed in the clear dark, this November in 2020. A saguaro cactus dutifully stood guard with a stark silhouette. Every now and then, the nocturnal chirping was broken by raucous laughter. Fifteen warriors had been drawn to Scottsdale for cigars, whiskey, and war stories. Among us were Green Berets, SEALs, Rangers, and Air Force Special Ops, with a broad range of specialties and ranks. The fire had been burning for a very long time—millennia if you will. Each storyteller had a glint of that fire in their eyes. It had been passed down to us from our fathers, our grandparents, great grandparents, or some combination of a hundred distant ancestors of centuries past who fought against or alongside Pershing, Wellington, Charlemagne, Alexander the Great, Xerxes, the Sumerians, African kings, Sun Tzu, or native tribes of prehistory. The stars held that flame. They were watching and listening, never complaining that they'd heard every story before, many times over. They'd witnessed the actual events.

That November night was the 50th anniversary of the Son Tay Raid. We were listening to the men who'd lived that Special Ops mission, now legend. We had worked all day in the filming of a documentary with hundreds of live rounds fired from our helicopters' miniguns and grenades launched into the recreated enemy barracks. The next year, we'd be commemorating the anniversary of a mission from a different conflict, and we'd be hearing the legends of that combat told by those who'd lived it.

You're about to experience some great legends. Some of these were first told just as we came back in from the operation. They were told at the NCO Club, or at the Officers' Club, or at a watering hole downtown. Telling the stories is a way that we decompress. These missions always rattled some nerves, and it takes time—sometimes years. But at the club or at the fire pit, time is what we've got, and you are welcome to listen in.

This storytelling has been a noble institution for countless generations. Have a look at these gentlemen below (some of my ancestors), upholding the tradition.

Image 1. War stories.

Are these the kind of people you regularly have as company? Maybe not, but that really doesn't matter. If you'll choose to listen to their stories for a while, they would more than likely offer you their friendship.

You're about to read about some great bar fights. You're also going to hear about fierce combat and SCUBA Teams and Parachuting and Vietnam and Ukraine and Legendary Soldiers and Military Aviation and Weapons and Rangers and Special Forces. All of this can easily be found through the Index provided at the end of the book.

My buddies know me. Where there are verbatim quotes, they know that I've tried my best to recall how the conversation went, though I'm sure I'm not getting the quote exact. Some stories from the old country rely upon details told to me by my mother and my stepfather.

PREFACE 2

On a 20th Century Battlefield

I run around the perimeter toward Lieutenant Kubit's commo position. From 50 feet away, I can tell he's been hit and he's lying flat on his back.

Right as I reach him, a gunship comes in over my head just above the trees on a loud, heavy, full-auto gun run firing straight outward from above us. Hovering right over our heads, he's letting loose with the M60 machine guns and his 2.75-inch Folding Fin rockets. The terrible thought does pass through my mind. *That gunship is the enemy's prime target at this second. The right shot could bring it crashing down upon us.* But the actual feeling in me is one of security, of power, and of trust. These helicopters have only a single, spinning, steel rotor mast holding them up. They are standing up beside me, tall, taking the blows to the face and dealing the same to the enemy. They are shoulder to shoulder with us in the fight. They have the horsepower to escape to safety, yet they have no interest in running. They want to be here with us in this fight. They know us, even though we've never met.

I check Lt Kubit. Yes, he's been hit in his left side. He's still conscious but looking like he's going into shock. I open his jungle camo shirt and pull up his T-shirt, which is soaking up blood from the left front to the left back. He keeps asking, "How bad is it?"

That's a lot of blood. I grab his left hip and pull him forward so I can see if there's an exit wound on his back. (There is.) The round entered from the front and exited his back, zipping by his left kidney. "Nothing but a scratch," is my answer. I start giving him first aid. I rip open one of the packets of gauze in my medical kit hanging on my LBE. I shove some into the dirty mess of a bullet hole. It went right through him, and most of the blood is coming out the back. Keeping the lieutenant balanced on his right side, I push a wad of gauze into his exit wound trying to apply pressure to stop the bleeding. He's still talking to me.

An indigenous troop has brought the bigger medical kit, full of bags and needles that I need. I try to give Lt Kubit some blood expander. The blood expander is a pressurized canister with an I.V.-type of hose with a needle. In the dirt and sweat and combat noise, I'm kinda fumbling around with the needle and hose and have a hell of a time spotting any vein I can stick. I worry that the round might have damaged his kidney or intestines. But the gauze seems to be holding back the blood (they're not drenching through now), so I bandage him up and tape it off securely. I take the cap off the needle and eventually find a vein in his left arm, just below the elbow and secure it with tape.

I pick up the radio. The frequency has just a lot of static. "Gators, come in!" No helicopters. Nothing but static. It dawns on me that I've not been hearing any chatter on the radio since I landed. I check the frequency. It's the right freq. My concern is to get Lt Kubit MEDEVACed to a hospital. He keeps saying, "I can't feel anything." (*Is that a bad thing? Maybe it's better than the alternative.*) He's shaking slightly, kind of all over his body. He's turning gray in his face. His lips are blue. He's fully into shock now. I call on the radio, but no one is replying. I feel like Lt Kubit's life is in my hands. It's a hell of a feeling. Make all the right decisions learned in training and he may live.

Someone pops green smoke about 25 meters away from me at the tree line. A helicopter is coming in. It's now steadying to land about 100 meters from us. I start dragging Lt Kubit toward the helicopter even before it lands. I see the two pathfinders getting ready to board. It's clear that they're not even aware of Lt Kubit's situation. I realize now that they must have gone to a backup freq.

The fire fight is raging. A lot of fire is directed at this helicopter, which is facing to the right as I'm looking at it. I'm dragging the lieutenant at a running/limping pace. My left hand has a death grip on his LBE at his left shoulder; my right hand is trying to hold on to all my gear and my weapons. I hear rounds over my head and sometimes kicking up dirt nearby. It feels like a hundred bullwhips chasing me. The louder the crack, the closer the bullet. I can tell that they're not shooting at me. They want to bring down the chopper. I hear explosives, but I can't tell if it's incoming RPGs (rocket propelled grenades) or our gunships' suppressing rockets.

This is the purpose for all those years of grueling P.T.

I'm still 50 meters from the helicopter. *Dammit! Do they see me?* I wave my rifle trying to get their attention while still trying to make progress dragging Lt Kubit. Dammit, it looks like the pathfinders just got on board. *Come help here!* I think the helicopter is going to leave. A thought crosses my mind.

[*If they try to leave, I'll let go of the Lt and shoot the tail rotor off with full-auto. They'll be able to set it down. No one will be injured. They have plenty of firepower to keep the enemy out of the LZ. A lot of priority effort would immediately be made by other helicopters to rescue the crew and pathfinders...and Lt Kubit.*

--but on the other hand, that right-side door gunner with the M60 machine gun would instinctively cut me in half with one sweep before I put more than a few bullet holes in his sheet metal.]

The helicopter engine noise changes to more a power-ful sound. *He's lifting off?* I'm shouting vulgarities at them with a cursing anger, "Don't leave without Lt Kubit! Lord Jesus, stop them!"

Right then, I witness a hallowed moment.

But first, I want to give you some background of how I got here.

[You'll notice that, sometimes, in the moment, I'll change to the present tense. Bear with me.]

CHAPTER 1

Holodomor

1940 AND BEFORE

I was born Володимир Яковенко (Volodymyr/Vladimir Jakovenko) on July 15th, 1940, to Кузьмо Яковенко (Kuzmo/Cosmo Jakovenko) and Варвара Яковенко (Varvara/Barbara Jakovenko) in a peasant village in the countryside not too far from the city of Kharkiv on the eastern border of Ukraine. The Donets River flows nearby, beautiful, scenic, and historic. Along the river's broad watershed, cliffs overlook pristine forests. Thousand-year-old towns gather around the onion-dome-topped towers of Orthodox churches like worshipers gathering around flame-topped candles. The river originates in the Central Russian Upland, north of Belgorod, flows south through Ukraine's Kharkiv, Donetsk and Luhansk regions and then returns to Russia to join the river Don, which flows into the Black Sea.

Our home was a humble wooden structure with an outhouse in the back, a work shed for implements, a cow, a few goats, and chickens. We'd get our water from a nearby well down the dirt street. Immediately behind our house, we grew a cash crop such as corn or wheat in the acre that sloped down a small hill over which we could view a couple of other homes with similar small fields. Just outside the back door, my mother kept a vegetable garden. My father had a tendency to go to the tavern in town too often. My mother therefore got into the habit of hiding his bicycle. She (with me in trail) would sometimes have to walk around in the cornfield for a while, trying to remember where she had hidden it.

My mother's maiden name was Варвара Харіна Бабенко (Varvara Harina Babenko) and she was from the picturesque and historic city of Poltava, which is much more toward the center of Ukraine. She was born on July 22nd, 1916. Her father's name was Прокопі Бабенко (Prokopi Babenko). She had a brother, Василій (Vasyliy).

Both Kharkiv and Poltava are near the region called the Donbas Coal Basin.

And this was the Soviet Union.

But let me start by telling you the very sad story of my mother, Varvara, and how she lost her parents when she was a teenager.

In 1933, the terror of Joseph Stalin had set upon the Ukrainian people. The "Holodomor" (Starvation Death) of 1932—1933 was Stalin's orchestrated famine of Ukraine.

Now, I'm about to get very graphic, but this is the reality of living under the Marxists/socialists. The following was told to me by my mother. I trust her description of this. She witnessed it. She lived it. Something this graphic lodges in the mind, never to be forgotten.

Image 2. Starved peasants on a street in Kharkiv, 1933

My mother, Varvara (aged 17), her brother, Vasyliy (about 21), and their parents were scratching out a pauper's starvation diet in their desolate village outside Poltava.

Desperate neighbor began to turn against desperate neighbor. Vasyliy was accused of having a pistol. The terrorizing Bolsheviks came to the home to investigate because it was illegal for any civilian to have a firearm. There was no firearm. The Soviet socialists were all about terrorizing their own people. This is how they made sure that everyone in their society got the message about the state's power. They tortured him for hours, trying to find the pistol. But there was no pistol. Then they brought his father to make Vasyliy watch them beat his father. They asked, "Where is the pistol?!" But there was no pistol. They beat his father with clubs. They would stop and ask, "Where is the pistol?!" But there was no pistol. They beat his father to death. Then they brought his mother before him. They asked, "Where is the pistol?!" But there was no pistol. They took them both outside and tied a rope around her legs and hitched the rope to a horse. They would stop and ask, "Where is the pistol?!" But there was no pistol. They dragged his mother down the road and came back to him. They would stop and ask, "Where is the pistol?!" But there was no pistol. They repeated, dragging her again and again. Her clothes were shredding off. Her skin was shredding off. Eventually, you couldn't identify her body as human.

They never found a pistol. They killed Vasyliy, leaving him lying there as he breathed his last on the street in front of their house. Then they walked over to Vasyliy's sister, Varvara, my dear mother, who was made to watch everything. She was so distraught that she'd decided in her mind that she was ready to die. She was so emaciated, so close to death by starvation. She had been propping herself up on the front yard fence. One of the Bolsheviks put a gun to her head. My mother remembered another Bolshevik saying, "Why waste a bullet? She'll be dead before the sun goes down."

They rounded up the other villagers and told them that this is an example to warn others. They gave orders that the three bodies must be left there in the street.

Neighbors took my mother in that night.

The next morning, due to the birds and the starving dogs, there was just about nothing left but bones. A neighbor eventually raked the remains into a blanket and buried them nearby in a shallow grave.

(And what was it that prompted the communists to focus their horrific evil on these relatives of mine? A loaf of bread. The Bolsheviks had offered a loaf of black bread as a reward to anyone who would turn in neighbors possessing a gun.)

This was genocide, the annihilation of seven million Ukrainian people. This period was unprecedented in the history of Ukraine, the breadbasket of the Soviet states. The socialist government had confiscated and collectivized all household foodstuffs. They restricted any movement of the population into or out of the region. They rejected outside aid. The US Congress sent a delegation to Ukraine at the invitation of Joseph Stalin. He took them on guided tours and showed them silos full of grain and corn. They were shown plenty of livestock. The Ukrainians that the congressmen saw were well-fed, with no sign of famine. The US Representatives came back and told the American public that Stalin was taking good care of the Ukrainian people.

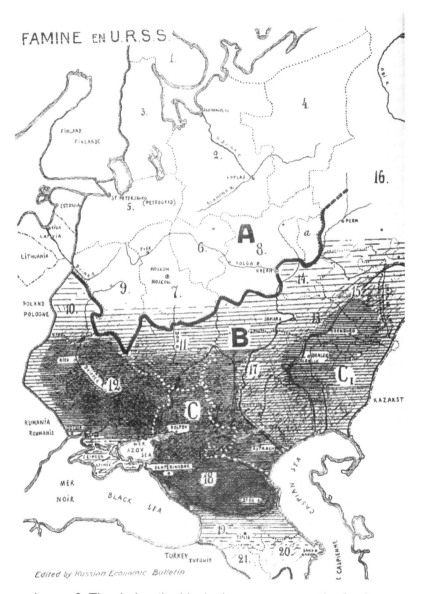

Image 3. The darker the black, the more severe the famine of 1932—1933. I was born where you see the number 12.

Now on her own, my mother found work in a coal mine near Kharkiv. At first, my mother drove a machine that hauled coal up from out of the mine shaft.

Image 4. Girls arrive to work the mines in the Donbas region in the early 1930s.

I don't know much about the background of my father, Kuzmo Jakovenko. I know he was born in 1913 and was a painter on construction sites when he met my mother. They married in 1939.

By early 1940, she was becoming large, pregnant with me. The Commissar allowed her to switch to being the above-ground operator of an elevator that transported miners down into the coal mine. In July of 1940, Mom's water broke, and the Commissar got another woman to help mom walk to our village. I was brought into this world by a midwife in the midwife's home.

World War II was being fought in the neighboring country of Poland, but that was almost 1,000 miles away. It really didn't affect our daily peasant life.

2

Nazis vs Soviets

1941

But then, in 1941, the German army invaded the western states of the Soviet Union and quickly advanced into Ukraine. We, the Ukrainian people, actually welcomed them. In our minds, these were not conquerors, but liberators, freeing us from communist socialism. The German army enlisted two million Ukrainians to fight the communists. They even had a Ukrainian S.S. division. Many Ukrainians were in support units helping the German army defeat the Soviets. My father became part of a police auxiliary under German command. Some of the Ukrainian police became overly zealous in prosecuting and beating former communist supporters. Some became as ruthless and vicious as the communists had been. Seething for revenge, atrocities were committed.

Image 5. German tanks heading to a
Soviet village in October 1941.

The constant Soviet propaganda steadfastly told the
Ukrainian people that the Germans were invaders and that
we must join the partisans and fight the Germans. Many
Ukrainians did and they were very effective as partisans.
The Germans sent in S.S. troops to any area recently won
by the regular army and would shoot captured partisans
on the spot. Any suspected sympathizers had their houses
burned to the ground. It seemed that the whole Ukrainian
countryside was burning.

The regular German army infantry hated the S.S. In
many cases, they would actually help the Ukrainians
around them. Many of us stayed close and moved with the
German regulars, finding some measure of safety.

By 1943, the war was going badly for the Germans
on the Eastern Front. By June, they started to retreat. We

who found our refuge alongside them had no choice but to follow them. If we had stayed, it would have been certain death. The Russians labeled us traitors and collaborators.

It was warm when we packed up all our belongings in a covered wagon drawn by our horse. We headed into the unknown alongside the retreating German army with the war raging around us. Some of the German soldiers shared food with us, even though they had little themselves.

We kept heading west to Poland. There, we entered our first "Displaced Persons" camp.

We were interrogated by the Germans and segregated by nationality. Our horse and our wagon were taken from us, never to be seen again. We could immediately see the distinct cruelty the Germans had toward the Jews in our group. So many Jews in Ukraine had already been brought here to this camp. The German S.S. ran this camp which primarily had Ukrainians, Czechs, and Poles. We had become friends with some Jewish families while on the road. After about 24 hours, the Germans put us on a freight train in a cattle car.

…but we realized that none of the Jewish families were aboard.

Rumors started to circulate about what had been done with the Jewish families.

They thought they were escaping persecution and instead ran into the jaws of death.

Among the endless thousands of refugees streaming out of Ukraine, there were hundreds of children who had lost their families in the chaos of war. Some children attached themselves to other families, but most had to survive on their own wits. All of us were in a survival situation. Death and starvation were just one step behind us day after day. Sometimes, the Germans would round up those children with no families. When we saw that, all we could do was pray for them.

The train took us through Poland to another camp. This camp also had many Jews. We again were segregated. We were stripped and they fumigated us with DDT dust. We bathed, our first time in many weeks.

After a short time there, they again loaded us into box cars and our journey continued until at last we reached our final destination, Berlin.

There, we were again segregated, this time with men in one group, the older boys and girls in another, and then women and smaller children in another. My father was assigned to be part of a German fire brigade and was taken away to another city. Mom ended up working in a factory sewing buttons and epaulets onto German officer uniforms. We were assigned a small apartment and, each day, I was in some kind of daycare system.

[This is a good place to pause and give you a brief behind-the-scenes summary of what is now known about what the Nazis were doing with us. This was Operation Barbarossa, named for the twelfth-century German king Frederick ('Barbarossa' or 'Red Beard'), who ruled the Holy Roman Empire, the first 'Reich' ('Realm'). This operation, started on June 22nd, 1941, and implemented the Nazis' plan for removing people from the western Soviet Union (and putting those people into slavery) and then re-populating it with Germans. In this way, the Nazis would take over the agricultural lands and the coal and oil reserves.]

My father came home on leave once in a while. I so looked forward to my father's visits. He would always bring me things. I distinctly remember his arrival one day when he gave me something very special, a toy duck. I was so proud of my duck. I felt like I was the only kid in the world who had a wooden duck. We had a photo taken with my father in his fire fighter's uniform, my mother in her nicest outfit, and me holding the toy duck, radiating my joy. We spent the day together and my father showed a great deal of affection to me and my mother.

My father could stay only until that afternoon, and I did not want him to leave. I remember crying so much. He cried and held me. My mom walked him to the trolley car. I stayed in the apartment holding and hugging that duck. It was made of thin plywood, and I was hugging it so hard. Suddenly, the head snapped from my hugging! I ran out to tell my father that I broke the duck! But he was gone.

I was heartbroken. Nothing else mattered to me. I cried all night. My mom tried to fix it. She told me my father would get me another duck when he came home. It was the saddest day of my life.

That night, the allies conducted a bombing raid on Berlin. We rushed to a bomb shelter. We were being bombed all night. Many buildings were destroyed. Everyone feared the bombing. Stories were told of phosphorus incendiaries landing on buildings and burning clear through to the bottom, creating fumes and heat that killed people even inside the bomb shelters, a horrible death of suffocation and extreme heat. In 1944, all major cities were being burned: Berlin, Hamburg, Frankfurt, Hanover, Dresden, Stuttgart, Leipzig and other smaller cities. It seemed we were being

Image 6. Kuzmo, Volodymyr, and Varvara
Jakovenko in Berlin, early 1945.

bombed 24 hours a day. The Germans would broadcast how many allied planes they had shot down.

Any aircrews who survived would face German wrath. I remember the first American that I ever saw. I was with my mother. It was the headless body of an aircrew member suspended, still in his parachute, from a streetlight. There was a large crowd. As we got closer, he looked huge. He must have been shot down and his body must have been hit by anti-aircraft fire. The Germans put a sign on him. "*This is what happens to those who bomb our cities and kill our women and children.*" That poor aircrew man hung there a long time.

This nightmare was endless. We spent a lot of time in our air raid shelters and came out when the bombing was not so intense.

I had not seen my father in months. My mother was home because her factory had been bombed and almost completely destroyed. Then, rumors said that the war was almost lost and that the allies were close to Berlin. The bombing was replaced with the sound of artillery and small arms. Berlin was surrounded.

On May 1st and 2nd, 1945, everybody was hanging white sheets out their windows. White flags were everywhere.

3

Hunted Refugees

1945

Any happiness was short-lived. Conversations turned to horror. Apparently, the Americans, British and French were not coming. They were going to let the Soviets take this part of Berlin!

My father was back, and we were a family again. Now was the time to flee to the West, another escape as desperate as any we'd already experienced. The underground rail system was the way out of Berlin. So, that very day, taking little with us, we hurried to the nearest subway station. There were thousands of people packed in the station and logjammed out on the sidewalk. You couldn't even get near to where the stairway starts leading you down to the underground platform. My father got information that another way to leave was by canal on a coal barge. We went immediately. There, hundreds of people were boarding, climbing inside empty coal barges that were setting off to the West.

[We learned later that the subway system flooded that day, May 2nd, covering 25 stations, a quarter of the system. Hundreds of people died.]

Image 7. Occupied Germany and Berlin

We rode the coal barge for a couple of days and the sounds of gunfire around Berlin became more distant. We were traveling west on the canal and the coal barges were crowded well over capacity.

Except for the weather, lack of food, and the over-crowded conditions, we were out of danger. We were anxiously putting miles between us and the Russians. We were free of the Nazi socialists, but we knew the horrible fate that awaited all those who were trapped by the communist socialists.

After a couple of days on the canal, a beautiful warm sun combined with the cooking fires inside the barge to make temperatures inside overbearing. People climbed out topside. The barges were marked with big Red Crosses identifying them as civilian. These were in no way military targets. Some small aircraft appeared out of the east.

They made a pass over the barges and people started to wave. Then, the people noticed the red star on the fuselage. These were Soviet attack aircraft turning to make another pass on us. People scrambled back into the hulls. Then came the unforgettable roar and high pitch whine of a diving attack. People started to panic. The fighters opened up with machine gun fire on these Red Cross marked coal barges, an unconscionable slaughter of men, women and children. They then disappeared in the direction they came from. The dead were thrown into the canal, and you could see them floating behind and along the sides of the barges. There were wounded in the water, but there was no stopping the barge. My mother and father and I were not hurt. Many decided to leave the barges. They would take their chances on land.

At last, we came upon the allies. We found a refugee camp established by the Americans, treating the wounded, feeding the starving, and trying to reunite families. There were hundreds of children that had been separated from their parents. Everyone wanted to be under the care of the Americans because they provided the best care and more than enough food.

But then a rumor arose. "Don't trust Americans, they take good care of you and then turn you over to the Russians." The Soviets were allies and the post-war agreements required Ukrainians to be returned to their homeland. For us, returning would mean slavery and death.

The Soviet trucks would come at night.

I guess the Americans were under orders to cooperate when the Russians came into American-controlled camps. The Americans allowed them to load the trucks even though people cried and begged not to go. In some cases, people would fall under the wheels of the trucks rather than go with the Soviets.

The Ukrainians held a meeting to propose a plan. A certain church in that neighborhood had a distinctive, electric-lit cross. When the Soviets came, all women and children would flee to that church, and the men would try to fend off the Russians. But it was futile. Our clubs and stones would be no match for the Russian guns. It was decided that we'd leave this refugee camp and take our chances trying to make it to the areas controlled by the British. It was known that they would not allow the Soviet units to enter their camps.

So, for the remainder of 1945 and 1946, we moved from one camp to another. Would we ever find a place we could call home? We knew we would never go back to our birthplace, for it would mean certain death. Through the spring and summer, we moved further and further away from the Soviets and farther and farther away from Ukraine.

Then, in the cold fall, my father got sick. He had tuberculosis. At that time, we were in Bad Munder, Germany. He was only 33 years old. I was six. His condition worsened slowly day after day. My mother did what she could, given the poverty of a refugee camp in a country with a wrecked economy. On November 6th, 1946, my father passed away.

He provided for us. He was our strength, and he never gave up and told us, "Life is precious. Trust in God and stand up for the liberties He has given us."

How would we survive now? That day, I thought my life was ending.

There were about a dozen people at the funeral led by a priest. I literally tried to jump into the grave with him. I had to be restrained. I cried, "Daddy, I love you! Don't leave me!" The wind was blowing bitterly, a heavy snow was coming down, and it was getting dark. Everyone was freezing and started to leave. My mother told me, "Vova (a nick name for Volodymyr), we have to go. There's nothing more we can do. He is in God's hands now. He would want you to go." I cried even harder and didn't want to leave the grave.

It took both the priest and my mother to make me leave. As we walked away, I kept looking back. Snow was already piling up on the grave. It seemed wrong that we didn't even have one flower on it. I think it had just a wooden cross with maybe something simple like, "In memory of Kuzmo Jakovenko, born 1913, died 1946."

Through the snow and my tears, I could hardly see where we were going. But I couldn't stop looking back. The grave seemed to grow higher and whiter. I remember it clearly. I heard my father's last words, "Respect your mother. Love your country. Remember how much I love you."

My loving parents took great care ensuring that I have, to this day, the following message from my father. After it is the translation.

22-/X 1946р.

Шпиталь. (Госпиталь)

Заповіт Синові моєму Володимирові від хворого батька. Сину мій дорогий. Я тебе залишаю на чужині ще малим, коли тобі тільки шість років. До батьківщини далеко та й чи зможити до неї повернутися. Заповідаю тобі, Сину, ніколи не забувай Бога і молися йому щоденно. Не забувай своєї рідної матчи, слухай і шануй її, то й люди тебе шануватимуть. Як виростеш, увесь час пам'ятай про другу свою рідну Матір Україну і дбай про її щастя й волю. Не будь її зрадником, а будь вірним Сином своєї сьогодні окупованої московським наїзником батьківщина. Прощай для її щастя й волі. Будь здоровий і щасливий, Сину! Шкода міні тебе покидати, але розлучає нас воля Божа. Молис за мени, Сину, а я за теби молитиму Бога, щоб тобі дав кращу ніж міні долю. Твій батько

К. Яковенко

Image 8. The final letter from my father, Kuzmo Jakovenko, to me.

Here's the translation of my father's letter.

October 22, 1946.

Hospital Testament to my son Volodymyr from his ill father.

My dear son,

I leave you in a foreign land while you are but a six-year-old child. Our Homeland is far away, and it is unknown if you will be able to return. I urge you, my son, never forget God and pray to Him every day. Do not forget your mother; listen to her and respect her. Then people will respect you. As you grow up, remember your other dear mother, Ukraine, and care for her happiness and freedom. Do not be her traitor, but be a faithful son of your homeland, which today is occupied by the Muscovite invader (Farewell to her happiness and freedom.) May you be healthy and happy my son! I am sorry to leave you, but this is the will of God to separate us. Pray for me son, and I will pray for you that God will give you a better end than mine.

Your father,
K. Jakovenko

My mother was desperate. She worked in the fields during harvest picking vegetables, fruits, and berries. Some could only pay her by giving her some of what she had picked that day. She'd then go to the market and sell or trade it for something to bring home to feed me. Sometimes I went with her and helped pick in the fields. I liked that. It meant I would not be hungry through the day.

It was cold and I didn't have a coat. One day, my mother came back from the market and had a beautiful blue coat. It was really fancy; but after a few moments of looking at it, I figured out that it was a girl's coat. I had a big decision to make. Would I stay warm and get laughed at by other kids for wearing a girl's coat? I chose to stay warm.

I got laughed at, alright. I got called names. I began to get into fights. And in those fights, I tended to whoop 'em. I even whipped some kids that were older than me. Word got around, "Don't mess with that kid wearing a girl's coat. He can fight."

The year 1947 was especially hard on me…
not only because of the fights…
and not only because I had lost my father.

My mother started seeing other men.

I cried when they would come over. I asked my mother how she could do this. "Have you already forgotten him?" She would cry. She hugged me and told me that she still loved my father and missed him so much. She'd never forget him. No one could ever take his place.

It was always a different man, and these were not good men.

Looking back now, I know what was going on.

She was selling herself to provide for me.

4

Living in the Rubble of WWII

1948

People started to immigrate-to South America, to Australia, to North America. We made our way to a big Displaced Persons camp in Hanover. The Red Cross helped displaced persons immigrate, but we ran into a problem. Countries were willing to accept families but were less willing to accept a widow and child. So, my mother explained to me that I was going to have a new father. I'd seen him with my mother, and I didn't like him. I didn't hate him, but it was not so much a marriage of love, but rather of necessity.

They went to a German court and got married. Her new name was Kolosha. She kept my name as Jakovenko.

My stepfather, Jakiv Kolosha, was working for the British Army, part of a labor battalion. I later found out from my mother that my stepfather was from Kiev. In Ukraine, he had worked for the Germans, so when the Soviets re-took Ukraine in 1943, it was no longer safe for him. It wasn't long before the Bolsheviks arrived at his front door. At that moment, he was in the back, by the barn and heard them asking his wife of his whereabouts. He hid in the tall corn until they left. It was decided that he must flee that moment.

On our immigration request, we picked three countries in this order: America, Canada, and Australia. As our wait turned from weeks to months, we began to worry. It was now the summer of 1948. We wondered if the war might start again, this time with the Soviet Union fighting against all the western countries. We were constantly hearing the terrifying sound of what we thought were bomber aircraft at all hours of the day and night. But this time, the planes were much lower. Every few minutes they would pass over our camp, heading toward Berlin. This was the Berlin Airlift.

Image 9. An Avro York C. aircraft, G-AHFI of the Skyways Company taxiing at Wunstorf aerodrome near Hanover during the Berlin Airlift, November 1948.

Americans now clearly understood that they could never trust the Soviets. Socialist governments will not hesitate to starve their people who defy them. The Americans and allies broke the Soviet land blockade by airlifting food, medicine and necessities into West Berlin, the free areas of Berlin. These missions kept flying 24 hours a day as one front of the Cold War. The Berlin Airlift lasted a full year as I went to school at our displaced persons camp there in Hanover.

The city had been bombed back to the Stone Age, but the rebuilding was amazing. And the allies had a way for the people to earn money as they rebuilt their cities. Groups of families or groups of individuals would sign up to work on a bombed-out building and, as if it was a mining operation, they would separate the valuable materials from the ruins. Copper and brass were the most valuable, then lead, zinc, and iron. You would separate the unbroken bricks, clean them off, and stack them. Selling the materials would bring enough money to live on. German salvage companies would come around and pay you the going rate. Also, you were free to keep any valuables you found, like clothes, dishes, or furniture. I don't know if there might have been some things that you were supposed to report to the government. To this day I still have a ceramic cup we salvaged from the rubble.

The work was hard and dangerous. I remember that British demolition experts would defuse the many unex-ploded bombs. Sometimes undiscovered bombs would det-onate as people worked on a demolition site. There were cave-ins. Sometimes people were killed when a part of a building would collapse.

Many dead bodies were still in the buildings. Medical teams would come in and check for disease. The govern-ment would come and account for them and give them a decent burial. The Germans definitely took care to account for their people.

The British also helped unite German families and establish places for the thousands of children who were separated from their parents. They kept good records of all children and their locations. They had an excellent record of reuniting families even after years of separation. Those children who could not be reunited were provided shelter, food, and education until they could stand on their own. This was the norm all over West Germany.

Image 10. "Ukrainian people's school, teaching year 1948-49 in Hanover." Volodymyr Jakovenko is standing behind the first row of seated teachers, peering over the left shoulder of the third teacher from the left. This is a school for displaced Ukrainians in Hanover Germany.

We were thankful for what we had in Hanover. We were assigned an apartment to live in during these months. Now, this was a damaged neighborhood, so there was no running water in our apartment. And we shared this apartment with three or four other families. A family's living space was separated from another's by blankets that hung down to provide some privacy. One of my chores was very important—to keep a certain 5-gallon zinc pail full of drinking water. In the winter, the water outside would sometimes freeze, so you always kept it filled to the brim, just in case. Mom cooked with a small electric stove with one burner. We also had a round tub that was for our weekly bath and for washing clothes.

We used an outhouse that was a 30-seater. It was a small wooden building with a wall dividing it in half, one side for females and the other for males. Literally, you were just sitting there with 14 other guys. To think about it, that's not a bad place to have a meeting of important issues facing us displaced persons. I'm not sure who cleaned the building, but I do know who came every week to pump it—the local farmers. I know why the fields were so green and the harvest so plentiful. We thought life was good and looked forward to an even better life in America.

But things were very different in East Germany under the Soviets. There, people barely could survive from day to day. The communist socialists were dismantling whole factories and sending them to Russia. It was a continuation of looting, raping, and killing, just under new management.

By January of 1950, with the dawn of a new decade, West Germany clearly was getting back on its feet. That decade of horror was over.

But on the other side of the country was the reminder of the war years, a permanent mark of history like a time capsule. East Germany still looked like 1945. While West Germany turned its energy toward rebuilding and peace, East Germany constantly talked of war, robbing its people's resources to centralize all power in Mother Russia.

5

Ocean Crossing

1950

Happiness at last! We were called by immigration. We were on the list to immigrate! It was jumping, hugging, crying, screaming! Our dream had come true. We were going to America.

Processing through, we were given a medical examination and were told to pack only what we could carry. We brought some housewares, the round washing tub and the 5-gallon zinc pail that we used for drinking water.

We got on a truck in our neighborhood which took us to the Hanover train station. When our train arrived at the port city of Bremerhaven, we were herded into large warehouses where we would spend the next few days. We were checked and asked a few questions, our paperwork was processed, and our goods were inspected and tagged for shipment.

At last, we were told that we would start our journey to America tomorrow. Everybody was so excited. Tales and dreams about America were all we heard. I, too, was excited. I couldn't sleep, dreaming about our new life.

But I remember that my happiness then turned to sorrow. I was 10 years old. I thought about this world I was leaving forever. I thought about so many who would never go anywhere, those who had died so horribly during the war, and all those children lost or separated from their parents and my friends who were still in the camps.

I was leaving my father. I vividly remembered that cold November afternoon when we buried him.

In that Bremerhaven warehouse, I fell asleep. My sleep had dreams about the promise of America, but with an open, aching sadness.

The next morning, Monday November 13th, 1950, everyone was hustling to get ready for embarking. The ship was gigantic. It was all gray, like a battleship without the big guns. It was a converted troop ship, the USS *General Samuel D. Sturgis*.

Walking aboard, we were guided below deck. It was very crowded. Each of us carried one or two suitcases, but we still had our washtub and pail. It was many hours later that they let us go on deck. I remember there was no sign of land. Following the ship were hundreds of seagulls, which I had never seen before.

At times, over the coming days, the Atlantic Ocean was rough, and many people became seasick. It was a mess. I tried to stay on deck as much as possible, but during storms, they wouldn't allow any of us up on deck. The smell of people throwing up made everyone else sick. It seemed to be everywhere. My mother was so sick that she could not

Image 11. Stock photo of refugees boarding the USS *Sturgis*.

stand up. I tried to help however I could. I got her a lemon from the crew. They would pass them out to help people who were sick. Mom was right; I seriously doubt she could have made it through a 30-day voyage to Australia.

The food aboard ship was actually very good. I was 10 years old and had never had white sliced bread. I thought it was some kind of cake. It was so delicious, and I put sugar on it. I couldn't get enough of it! There was plenty of everything for everyone. And each family got a box of Hershey bars! That was like gold! We accepted the discomforts, the smells, the crowded conditions; most of us had been through so much worse. There was laughter and singing. Yes, it was a long journey. It took twelve days to cross the Atlantic.

And then, there she was, the Statue of Liberty. We had heard stories of her, the most beautiful lady in the world.

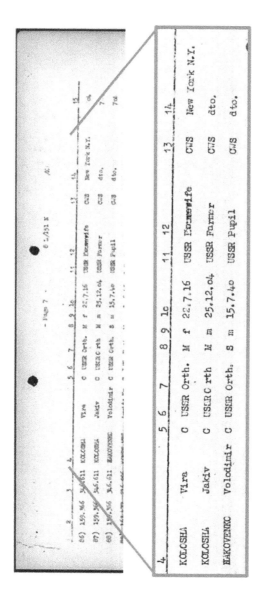

Image 12. The manifest as we departed Bremerhaven.

She was majestic. We knew we were finally free. She seemed to say, "Welcome to America. You're safe now." Then, as the morning mist cleared, the most spectacular city came into view. Skyscrapers, docks, bridges, and the Empire State Building.

Image 13. New York City, 1950. Ellis Island is the next island beyond the Statue of Liberty Island.

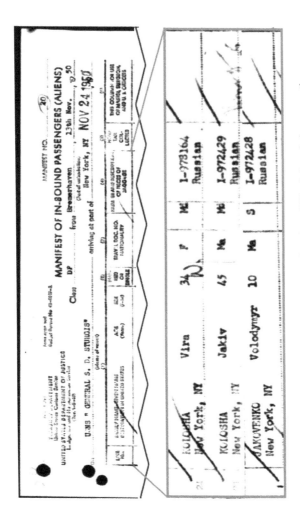

Image 14. The manifest as we arrived at Ellis Island. I guess they called everyone from the Soviet Union 'Russian.'

6

Crossing America

1950

Coming ashore on Friday, November 24th, 1950, we were processed by the American Red Cross. I remember us wearing these Red Cross buttons. We were sponsored (Americans paid travel fees from NY to parts of the country based on the skills that they needed). We would work for them to pay those fees back. Our sponsoring family was in Ashton, Idaho. They were ranchers. My stepfather had listed that as a trade, having worked with cattle. We were given thirty-five dollars, the first American money we had ever seen. We thought we were pretty well off. In those days, you could live on a dollar for a week. We were put up in a New York hotel room for the night to await someone who would put us on a train for our trip to Idaho.

Everything was wonderfully strange to us. You could simply pull a string or flip a switch, and a light would come on. We stood for a long time, trying to figure out the different items in our hotel room. Everything was a mystery. Controlling the water temperature for the sink and the tub. Flushing the commode. At first, we worried for the people in the hotel room below us, because we could not imagine when the commode was flushed, where it went. My step-father seriously didn't want to use the commode. He said, "Even pigs don't defecate where they sleep."

[Bless his heart, the first thing he did when he finally built us a house, was to build a very nice one-seater outhouse. Yes, he built a bathroom in the house, but he personally would never use it. I tried to tell him he can't put an outhouse on his property. There are building codes and health standards! For 30 years, he used that outhouse. My mother also used it, but only occasionally.]

Our stay in New York City was just a few days. My father did some shopping. We ate in our room. We could not read or speak English, so going to a restaurant was completely out of the question. He bought us some sausage, bread, onions, and some cans of sardines. We had 7 Up and loved it. For years later, that's all we had in our house, 7 Up. This was real living to us.

A Red Cross representative came up to our hotel room. She could speak Polish, and that was sufficient to get the point across. She explained to us details about our upcoming journey to Idaho. We would have to change trains in Chicago. Someone would meet us at that station to help us get to the right train. It was totally confusing, and we were not at all convinced that this could ever succeed. Would someone really be able to find us at a train station halfway across the United States?

As we stepped off the train in Chicago, we certainly stood out from the crowds, the way we dressed, the fact that we had name tags on us written in English in case of an emergency, the zinc tub and the 5-gallon pail clanking around our bodies. People figured out immediately that we were not locals. (Some probably wondered if we were from another planet.)

This was 1950 and people were kind and helpful. The Red Cross people found us. They had sandwiches for us, another first for us in America. Sandwiches just were not something we'd ever had. It seemed so novel and was a welcome break from the dark loaf bread, sardines, and onions. I had milk. My parents had coffee for the first time in a long time.

As the train pulled away from the station, an epic was presented to me, not on a movie screen, but rather at the window of the train. Over the hours, cities gave way to towns. Towns gave way to forests. Forests gave way to farmlands. And it continued day after day—America, with all its beauty and riches. Farmlands gave way to ranches and to the Great Plains.

Eventually there came the massive mountains, piles of white. As we rose in elevation, ranch homes had snow on their roofs, smoke coming from their chimneys. I waved at men on horses. I remember my stepfather opening a can of sardines and cutting onions in the train car. He was cutting up smoked bacon with bread for us. Some people gave us a funny glance and their kids would point at us. I knew we were different.

Not all of the passengers were this way. Some smiled and showed friendliness. Some tried to talk to us, but we literally didn't know a single sentence of English. But there was this one man who left an amazing impression. He gave me something of immense value. To most Americans it would simply look like a dime. But to this 10-year-old Ukrainian immigrant, this shiny, brand new 10-cent coin was the first money that I'd ever owned. I spent some hours thinking how I was going to spend it when I would eventually step off this train.

Higher and higher we went, one mountain range after another. Valleys would fall away below us. Each ridgeline was higher than the last. It was so beautiful, but my mother was anxious about heights and began to cry, trying not to look as we crested each snowy pass. The snow was so deep that they had put a special attachment on the front of the train to plow the snow.

On the third day, we arrived in Pocatello, Idaho for the night. We were met on the platform by the designated family. They took us home. We were shown to our room, and they helped us with our belongings. We washed up from the long train ride.

When it was time to come to supper, I had never seen a more beautiful table with so many different foods. Some we recognized, such as meat and potatoes. Some foods we had never seen. Our survival rule was to follow. *Watch what others do and then do what they did.*

Here are two American customs that we learned starting that night:

1. In America, families say grace before they eat.
2. At the table, families say "please" and "thank you" while passing the food around to the next person.

I was still hungry, but I had no idea in the world how to ask for seconds. That frustration subsided when dessert arrived. Wow. We wanted to learn from these Americans!

There was a blizzard outside the window, but we were warm inside. We slept in heavenly peace.

7

Wild West

1950

Only when it dawned on that idyllic, peaceful home did it dawn on me that we still had about 100 miles to go. I would have been delighted to stay in this home, but we had still another train ride before we'd get to our sponsors. After breakfast, we were ready to go. The lady of the house made sandwiches for us. The train would have no problem because the rails had been cleared since the last snow. But just in case, we had the snowplow on the front of the engine. Out here, you never knew when a mass of snow would slide down a mountainside onto the tracks.

Looking back, this might have been what it was like for so many of the earliest settlers who arrived after the railway was built. Many of them did not speak English, yet this truly was the land of opportunity. For them and us, this was the most beautiful place on earth. And they could not have imagined what they'd find at their destination.

That morning, December 1st, 1950, after more hours on the train, we eventually slowed to a stop at a tiny station in the middle of nowhere. I'm telling you it looked like the train station in the movie *High Noon*, just a building and a water tower and no one around. We did see some horses hitched to a big sleigh. The conductor told us this was our destination. By the time we got off the train, there were some people coming out of the station. Some people were getting on. The only things that got unloaded were our worldly possessions.

A man and his teenage son came up to us, smiled and shook our hands. Somehow, without even having to ask us, they guessed correctly that we were the people from Ukraine who had come to work on their ranch. Imagine that!

Image 15. The train station at Ashton, Idaho.

Yes, this is Ashton, Idaho. And yes, this family "lived in Ashton, Idaho." Their post office box and mailing address is Ashton. But it would be about a 15-mile sleigh ride to their ranch. We and all our worldly goods fit easily in the back on a bed of clean hay.

For the first few days, we lived with our hosts in a guest room. Then we were introduced to what would become our house, a one-room wooden shack covered by tar paper on the ranch. It had one window. It was no bigger than 25 feet by 30 feet. Its prior residents had clearly been turkeys or chickens. We were thankful for a place to start in this new world. We removed all the chickenshit, scrubbed every inch of that building and got it clean. The family gave us a bed, a table with chairs, a wood or coal burning stove, and some boxes to help organize our things. We had electric light. It was one ceiling bulb. We'll take it! As you might imagine, there was no running water in the house and, to my father's delight, no indoor toilet!

Thank God we still had our zinc tub and our pail. Bathing was basically once per week. Mom would heat up water we brought from the well and we would take turns bathing in the tub. After the bath, mom would use the same tub to wash the clothes. She had her washboard. But it was hell trying to dry clothes when the temperatures stayed in the teens! The clothes would freeze outside on the clothes-line, so drying had to be done in the house or in the barn, and it took forever.

Our drinking water was our ever-faithful 5-gallon pail and if we did not keep the stove burning all night the water could actually freeze sometimes.

One thing that we did miss was being able to talk to other Ukrainians. My mom read the Bible to us, and we'd pray together in the morning and every night. Our Orthodox Christian faith was very important to us.

We had to drive several miles to get to my school, and it was a true, one-room schoolhouse. One big classroom. One

teacher, a woman who lived in the back of the school building. It was a lot like the school in *Little House on the Prairie*.
Understandably, I needed to learn the first grade stuff, so I
was with the first graders initially. But I was 10 years old.
Being the biggest kid in your class, other kids are going to
laugh and make fun of you. I knew they were making fun of
me. It's probably good that I didn't understand what exactly
they were saying. I was spring-loaded to fight.

The next year, our debts had been paid, and we accepted an invitation to move to Jersey City, New Jersey.
Friends we had made in the D.P camps in Germany had
settled there and they urged us to join them. For me, setting
off from the train station was an adventure from America's
purple mountain majesties across the fruited plain. Idaho's
mountaintops had snow, but as we headed east, it felt warm-
er, with signs of new life everywhere. In Wyoming, I saw
cowboys moving their herds. The ranchers lacked for nothing. Everything was green with the rains; the prairie was
lush. Seeing them waving to us on horseback, I waved back
and wished I was a cowboy. Were these the same cowboys
that we had seen as we rode west in December? Now they
were waving goodbye. I felt sad because I loved this part
of the country.

Further east, the trees were full. The flowers, the fruit
crops, and orchards. Eventually, we passed through some
cities. Now we'd see factories, smokestacks, cars, buses,
and trucks, all in a hurry to go somewhere. My first impression was that I wouldn't like it here, but there was a feeling
of familiarity. We were back on the East Coast, where the
American chapter of our lives opened.

CHAPTER 8

Formative Years on the Waterfront

1951

Our friend, Mr. Simka, met us at the train station. He already owned a car. We didn't have much trouble fitting everything in the trunk except the zinc tub. (Yes of course we brought it!) Somehow, we got it into the car. Arriving at his house, we were treated to a wonderful Ukrainian meal with plenty of Ballantine beer and bottles of vodka. They already had a job lined up for Pop; it paid less than 75 cents per hour, but it was a job.

We also had a place to live, a basement apartment. There were only two windows, high on the wall, the half-moon type, looking up onto the street. You could see people's legs walking by. Yes, it was a little damp and musty smelling, but it was definitely livable. It had hot and cold water, it had a coal heater, it had some basic furniture, and it had an ice box. It had three rooms: kitchen, living room and bedroom. Mom scrubbed the place down and Pop put a fresh coat of paint on all the rooms.

The landlord loved us and could not do enough for us. He helped us find any furniture we decided was needed.

He was an Italian, and he owned the whole brick apartment house. He and his wife lived in it. They had 10 kids, mostly grown and married. The landlord would often have us over for supper. The mother loved me and would send me to the Italian store to do her shopping. She gave me a list written in Italian and she always gave me a big tip—50 cents! The father didn't speak English, but he and my father got along.

I always wondered what they did for a living. There were always a lot of people coming by; some were rough-looking. I remember one asked me if I shined shoes. I told him I didn't. That was a big business, shining shoes. So, I quickly went out and got a kid who did shine shoes and brought him up there. The guy looked at me like he was really impressed by my initiative. He gave the kid a dime and the kid went back out to the street. The guy then turned to me and called me "paesano" and gave me a dollar! I had never earned a dollar before. This was more than my father earned in an hour, and I made it in less than 10 minutes.

I ran down the steps to the street. I was rich. I was thinking about what I would do with it. Then I spotted the shoeshine kid. He'd gotten himself an Orange Nehi and an Italian bread and was sitting along the sidewalk. He thanked me for getting him that customer. This kid had shoe polish on his hands and his clothes, and his PF Flyers had seen better days. Tape was holding the sole on. But he had a proud look about him. Remembering the war days, I thought, *This is America, land of plenty.* I knew I couldn't keep that dollar. I handed it to the kid. He asked, "What's that for?" I told him a little lie. "Your customer thought that it was the best shoeshine he ever got, and he wanted me to give you this tip." I've never seen a happier face in my life.

This was Jersey City, right across the Hudson River from Manhattan. We were on Grove Street, just two blocks from the wharfs. Now, people called this a ghetto, but to me it was a melting pot of all ethnicities and languages: Black, Puerto Rican, Jewish, Irish, Russian, Polish, Italian, German, and Ukrainian. Rich and poor, it seemed to me that we all lived in harmony. Yes, there were teen gangs and fights, but no drive-bys or riots. The cops of the beat were friendly and knew everyone by first name. They carried billy clubs, and one day we asked one of them if he carried a gun. He lifted his coat, showing us his holstered six-shooter revolver. He said he hadn't used it except at the range.

I was assigned to the *third* grade at P.S.3 (Jersey City Public School #3). I was almost 11 years old, so here I am, two years older than the other kids!

Other Ukrainian kids my age excelled and were in their higher grades. I didn't do well in school, so I didn't care for school. And because I didn't care for school, I didn't do well in school. Hmm.

After a couple of months, the landlord asked us if we would like to move up from the basement to the first floor, an apartment behind a store front. We now had windows and a nice linoleum floor. I got my own room. The landlord gave us our choice of the furniture in the bedrooms and living room, a kitchen table and four chairs. We still have two of the chairs. They are indestructible. That was when America made the best of everything. Nothing in the world could compare to American made merchandise. Mom and Pop painted that apartment with paint provided by the landlord.

Image 16. My mother and me in Jersey City in 1952.

Mom got a job with Block Drug Company, a pharmaceutical plant several miles away. She took the bus to work every day. She made less than a dollar an hour, but it was more than Pop. She never missed work. Some mornings she hurt so badly that she would be in tears, but she'd set off in the rain or snow to work the assembly line putting pharmaceutical products in boxes. The place is still there, only about three miles from the Statue of Liberty. Mom worked there for 18 years.

Pop's job was with the US Royal Tire Company in uptown Jersey City recapping tires. He was very excited when his pay jumped up over a dollar per hour. It was hard, dirty work, a sweat shop with no benefits, no retirement, no nothing. But Pop was the happiest man in the world. Like mom, he took a bus to get to work, but I remember that a few of his coworkers, Black men, lived in our area and they eventually began to carpool to work.

Jersey City had a bar on every corner (and also in the middle of every block). Pop and some friends used to stop in at a local saloon and all were amazed at Pop's favorite drink. It was Ballantine beer and vodka. He would fill up an 8oz glass half with 100 proof vodka and top it off with the Ballantine beer.

I remember stopping by his workplace one time. It was quitting time. His coworkers were big men and always cracking jokes. They called my father 'Jake.' (His name was Jakiv.) So naturally I became 'Little Jake.' Even to-day most people call me 'Jake' instead of my real name, 'Vladimir' or 'Volodymyr.' I loved hanging out with these guys and made a point to be around the US Royal plant at quitting time.

Dad would let me come with them to the bar. They would buy me a cold Birch Beer, non-alcoholic. Back then, it seemed that in every saloon, at the end of the bar, was a big spread of food—meat, cheese, bread, eggs, sardines, all kinds of good stuff to eat. It was all free. A can of beer was a nickel. Now this was the America that we came to love!

Some of the best times of my life. America in the 50s, no other time can compare.[1]

I was struggling along in school, not flunking, but not excelling either. I could hardly wait for the end of the school year and for summer vacation. Living in the city during the hot summer days, you develop a true appreciation of any trip to the country, to a lake, or to our favorite beach.

Summer days started early, so I'd get to see all the daily activity I'd missed on school days. Everything was delivered to your doorstep. All milk was whole milk in glass bottles, cream rising to the top. You always had to shake it vigorously before you pour it. Most of us had ice boxes, so a half a block of ice was delivered every week for us to install in the top compartment.

At first light, vendors (some using horse drawn wagons) would sell vegetables and fruit. The local junkman would come by calling for rags and junk. I remember his old horse always had a hat on with its ears poking through holes.

I'd get up early and hit the saloons and streets and railroad areas looking for soda bottles and quart beer bottles to take them in for deposit. Soda bottles were two cents and beer bottles were a nickel. In a couple hours, I'd have enough to go to the matinee and see action films and

---

1   (ALL FOOTNOTES ARE PROVIDED BY CO-AUTHOR CLIFF
     WESTBROOK) Helping Jakovenko write his story, I observed that this was
     a formative image for what you will read throughout this book. Nostalgia for
     what a bar should be—this love of people who have come together for fel-
     lowship—developed Jakovenko's bar fighting and street fighting sensibilities,
     which in turn developed into combat sensibilities. You'll hear about this in the
     retrospective in the last chapter, "Soldiers."

cartoons. My heroes were cowboys like the ones I'd seen out West.

I liked Lash LaRue, Gabby Hayes, Roy Rogers, Gene Autry, and all the others. I tried to impersonate movie star Gilbert Roland, the way he would reach into his shirt at the waist and pull out a cigarette. Somehow, a match would appear, and he would light his cigarette by striking his match on his thumbnail! (I tried it and always burned my thumb trying to look cool.)

The landlord opened a clam bar and Italian lemon ice place in the store front, so we lost the use of that room, but we still had plenty of room left. I earned some money by helping squeeze lemons to make the lemon ice. I shucked clams and helped put them on plates. We had a lot of customers.

Image 17. Jersey City at Baldwin Ave and the State Highway 139 viaduct in 1950.

The young Italian guys use to hang out on the steps in front of the place and old men played some Italian board-game at the tables set up on the sidewalk. It was a scene straight out of *The Godfather*. These were a rough bunch. It was not healthy to ask any questions. I'm sure there was more than clams and Italian ice going on there. I never had a problem with any of them. The old man of the family liked me and paid good money to work in the parlor.

After a couple of years, Mom and Pop were able to afford a better home close to some of their friends. They found an apartment near Lafayette Park where, from the roof, you could see the Statue of Liberty. We moved in. It was a nice four-room apartment on the third floor. I had to change schools and ended up going to P.S. 22. This was the era of *The Blackboard Jungle*, James Dean, and Rock & Roll. Life was good, living downtown.

It was 1953 and Mom and Pop wanted to buy a home. After renting for a year, they bought a three-family building in the Lafayette area for $6,500. We moved into the second story apartment and rented the first and third floors out. Our American dream was coming true. We even bought a TV set.

As teenagers, my friends and I spent many hot summer days at Pier 5 along the Hudson River. Gene, Pauly, Bobby, Tommy, Ray, and I did a lot of swimming in the Hudson River. In those days the water was clear. Blue crabs ("Jersey Blues") are the best tasting in the world.

Image 18. The technology of our American dream.

We'd go to Black Tom Island, now part of Liberty State Park. Some of us used to brag that we could swim to the statue. We called Black Tom Island "Bare Ass Beach." It was so isolated and plenty of people didn't wear a bathing suit. In 1916, there had been a huge explosion at Black Tom Island. While the US was supplying ammunition to the allies, it was the site of a storage depot. Some say it was sabotage by German agents. This was our beach, and it was just as good as any famous beach on the Jersey coast.

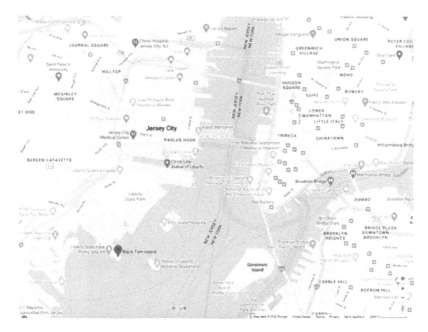

Image 19. Growing up on the beaches nearest to Ellis Island and Lady Liberty. The red marker shows Bare Ass Beach.

9

Becoming Trouble

1956

We all did our share of beer drinking and got in trouble, including one time in which we ended up in Bayonne Reform School…

We started that Friday night innocently enough watching a football game. Neither team was our high school. We were at Roosevelt Stadium, and the two schools were rivals of our P.S. 22. Lincoln High was playing Saint Peter Prep. We were sitting in the Saint Peter section, but we were cheering for Lincoln. At one point, there was a heated exchange of words between us and some Saint Peter fans. Well, someone asks the police to come over. The officer decides to escort us out and he's kinda enjoying the fact that he's impressing the fans who are now cheering him on. He's rough and calls us 'punks in leather jackets.'

As he grabs us where we we're sitting, he basically starts roughly dragging us toward the aisle one by one. My buddy Gene is irate. The policeman grabs Gene's younger brother Walter by the hair and pulls him into the aisle. Gene turns his face away from the cop and, with his teeth gritted, says to me, "If he touches me, I'm going to knock him on his ass." The cop reaches for Gene, hauling him out. It's an intensely overheated moment. Manhandling Gene, the officer looks at me and I put my hands up, telling him I'm a peace-loving man and will do whatever he wants. With a twist, Gene seizes the moment, and sucker punches him. Now the police officer is on his ass bleeding from his nose and lip. He's so damn, fighting-mad as we run past him that he pulls his pistol and hollers, "Halt or I'll shoot!"

To this day, I try to figure how he might have changed our lives that night, how close he might have been to the brink of actually pulling the trigger. This was a football stadium, and we were zigzagging among the fans.

The cop is dazed, but he's in hot pursuit after us. As we run, Gene falls down. A big man had stuck his foot out, tripping Gene to the ground. He grabs ahold of Gene, and the cop is there in a second. The policeman palms a leather slapstick which is filled with lead and starts slapping Gene on the head. Blood is flying.

I'm so angry that, now, I pull out a switchblade. Bobby stops me and says, "Leave the cop alone…"

"…let's get the guy who tripped Gene."

The police ambulance takes Gene and his brother away. Bobby and I blend into the crowd and watch the big guy who tripped Gene. Cops are taking a statement from him. When he walks away, Bobby and I follow him. We size him up. He's over 6'3" and I'm guessing he weighs about 230. He looks like a linebacker on a football team, but I knew how to take him. I tell Bobby, "I'll double him over and then you use your knee on his face."

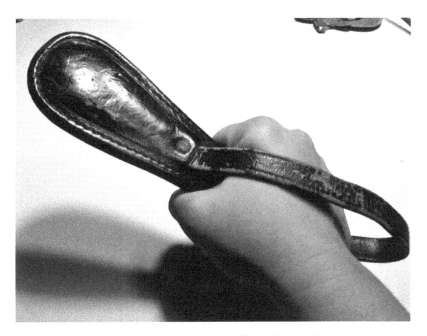

Image 20. A lead-shot-filled slapstick.

So, we walk up to the big man when he's away from the crowd and start by putting him on the spot, asking him why he tripped our friend. He immediately goes off on us, calling us animals. He says, "Decent people are taking back the streets. What are you punks going to do about it?"

[Being called "punk" twice in one day was not good for my self-image.]

Now, I had this proven technique of counting buttons on a shirt. I hit the third button as hard as I could—that's where the solar plexus is.

For a couple of seconds, he looked like it didn't bother him. Then he turned red and doubled over. On cue, Bobby worked his face over with his knee. A few yards away, people started screaming. Whistles started blowing. Cops were coming. The guy lay there on the ground bleeding, glasses broken. I added a couple of kicks to his ribs and head. "That's for Gene." I don't think he heard it; he was hurt bad.

Bobby and I started to run and some of the fans wanted to stop us so the cops could get us. We pulled our switchblades out and people backed off. If they would have grabbed us, someone would have gotten hurt. We were running scared. We were not about to get caught by the crowd or the cops.[2]

After they sewed up Gene, they took him to what they called the "Special Services Department." These were the police who handled violent teen gangs. The Gestapo had nothing over these guys. Non-violent tactics were of little interest to them. They got what they wanted by beating it out of you. I heard that a favorite of theirs was to cover you with a rubber sheet and use a rubber hose on you. The rubber sheet ensured they'd leave no marks. (It may have only been a rumor.)

Gene wouldn't talk, so they focused on Walter, Gene's little brother. Walter just happened to be in the wrong place at the wrong time. Well, he told the cops who the rest of us were. We were all picked up that same night and taken to the reformatory in Bayonne, NJ.

---

2   This was a formative moment. Set aside the fact that these were unjust actions. Jakovenko's eye for the tactical was developing. In heated moments of indignation, his mind did not panic. His eye sought—and correctly found—the big man's vulnerability. He doesn't mean to be proud of this situation. Our country needs more people like that big man. But we must acknowledge that those developing, unarmed combat fighting skills are needed in a military.

When we got there, they stripped us naked, took our clothes, and sent us to the showers. They gave us a coffee can with kerosene to pour on our hair to get rid of lice and anything else. They did warn us about getting it in your eyes, nose, or mouth. That had to be the nastiest feeling and smell. After the shower, they gave us mechanic orange coveralls to wear.

Bobby's father came first and signed for him—and beat the hell out of him right there in the front office, in front of the guards.

I was left there the longest. I guess my mom wanted me to learn a lesson. A family friend came and signed for me. His name was Rudy, and we were close friends. We knew him because he worked at Block Drug Company, where my mother worked.

[Rudy was German and in WWII and was in tanks. We're not talking Patton; we're talking Panzers. He used to show us his Nazi medals. His unit was actually part of operation Barbarossa and was in Kiev. He was like a close uncle. I came to respect him, apart from the whole Nazi thing.]

We boys all had to go to court with our parents. We would have pulled time in Allendale or Jamesburg (two rough reform schools) but some women who had witnessed the incident, said the police officer used excessive force and vulgarity and was dangerously close to killing us or innocent bystanders. We were released with a warning.

I was not doing well in school, just getting by. I could hardly wait until I was old enough to drop out. I was behind the rest of the guys. They were freshmen in high school, and I was stuck in middle school, 8th grade.

Then I met a girl. She was about my age and was an immigrant, like me. She was from England. She was sincerely interested in me and asked how I came to America. I was proud as I told her about my voyage on a military troop ship. Kindly and sincerely, she explained to me that her family had traveled to America on the *Queen Mary*. I imagined that she secretly must have considered me a pauper. And yet, she stayed interested in me. I imagined that maybe she hung around me only for protection. She knew I would defend my friends. By now, I had a reputation for "fighting dirty." [Excuse me for never having heard of any rules of street fighting. It seems pretty straight-forward. You win, or you get your ass kicked.]

[NOTE: I want to be respectful of her, so I won't use her name. There are always two sides to every story.]

In January 1957, I was finally allowed to move up to the high school. I was 16 ½. From the bottom, looking up, four years of high school would put me at 20 years old. I had no interest in that scenario. I made up my mind to quit school. Hey, Pop had a sixth-grade education. Mom had third-grade. I had eighth-grade! To me, that was good progress from one generation to the next. My parents conceded that, under the circumstances, having made it through eighth grade was pretty good. Some of my friends tried to talk me into staying in school, but my mind was already set; it was time for this wise guy to make big money.

The first job I got was at the Titman Egg Company there in Jersey City. Titman Egg Corporation was founded by a Jewish gentleman who had immigrated from Russia in 1901. They made powdered eggs and had a good reputation. With a steady full-time job, I was able to afford a 1946 Buick Roadmaster four-door sedan! I bought it for $75 from Mr. Schott, a family friend who owned a bar. Mr. Schott always looked out for us. Among my friends, who were still going to school, this gave me some status.

I was a protector. One time, my girlfriend had been working behind the counter in her stepfather's candy store. I was never allowed to hang out inside because her mother hated me, constantly telling her daughter that I wasn't good enough for her. Her mother asked the Zimmerman brothers to take her to get something to eat. There were four brothers in the Zimmerman family, but only three were there. She came out with the three and I asked her if she was ready to go get some dinner. She said that the Zimmerman brothers were taking her to their home. Well, I knew their reputation and her mother did not. A fight started up. I did well and pretty soon, it was just two-on-one. A crowd gathered. Eventually, I had only one Zimmerman yet to deal with. Then someone said the cops were coming. I said, "We'll finish this in Lafayette Park."

With a crowd following, we were walking toward the park when we passed a stoop where the fourth Zimmerman brother (he was in his late 20s) was hanging out with a certain guy who had just gotten out of jail. Everyone was afraid of the ex-con, including me.

As I passed the stoop, the ex-con sucker punched me in the face. I didn't go down, but I was bleeding from the mouth. I went into a boxer stance, hands up. I looked at him and considered my chances. I decided that this ain't worth any further investment. I went home, cleaned up, and pondered the events. That guy had sucker punched me. I'd taken a serious hit from the most feared guy. I now knew deep down beyond a shadow of a doubt that, one on one, I could kick his ass.

Some of my friends urgently came to see me. The word on the street was that the ex-con and the Zimmerman brothers were going to find me. I decided to walk down to the saloon right now and we'd go ahead and finish this. My friends all thought I'd lost my mind and tried to talk me out of it. They were more serious than normal. Nobody came with me.

As I approached the hangout, I could see the ex-con inside, sitting at a table talking to a woman. I went in and walked up to him. I told him I had no fight with him. I told him about the Zimmermans and the risk they were to my girlfriend. I told him that I was planning to marry her.

In the crowded bar, with about twenty of his friends watching, he turned and looked square at me. I turned slightly to the left. I wasn't gonna get sucker punched again. He menacingly came closer, but I could sense something. He threw a punch at my stomach, I caught it on my elbow, and I almost threw a counter punch, but something told me not to. He could have come up with an uppercut, but he didn't. Instead, he put his hand out to shake and asked, "How old are you?" Still ready for anything, I told him that I was 16. He said, "You've got guts. Stay straight. Take care of yourself. Take care of your girlfriend."

From that night on, nobody ever gave me or my girl-friend a hard time.[3]

In the summer of 1957, I got a new job near Hoboken working in a salvage warehouse. They handled all kinds of merchandise including damaged cans of food. I used to see all these ritzy restaurants that charged big money for din-ner come and load up on all these slightly damaged cans of food at cut-rate prices. Here, I was making $1.25 per hour, which was good money.

Things were looking sweet. At 17, I had a car and a steady girlfriend.

In the fall, my friends had started back into the school year. The colder months approached. Then, business seemed to be slowing down. There were rumors among my coworkers. Being one of the most recently hired, I'd be among the first to be laid off. And the word on the street was that jobs were a little bit hard to come by. After only a few months working there, the feared notice came down. I was out of a job.

---

3   Already, as a 16-year-old, Jakovenko had the rough-hewn sense of honor that prompted his Spirit to apply the Skills he'd developed. (See 'Spirit' and 'Skills' in the last chapter, "Soldiers.") He was able to calculate odds and listen to the voice of reason. He understood his limitations. He was able to hold his head high. We need to recruit young men like Jakovenko.

.

10

Spirit

1957

I started thinking about joining the military. I felt that I owed something to America. I had grown up on the waterfront, so the Navy was the first thing I had in mind. I remembered seeing a movie called *The Frogmen* that came out in 1951 with hand-to-hand combat under ships at dock as they set explosives. I can swim, and I can fight. I've jumped off the warehouse docks into the Hudson River plenty of times.

I went to the Navy recruiter and told him I wanted to apply for assignment with the Underwater Demolition Teams (UDT), the precursor to the SEALs. This was my first realization that I should have stayed in school. He said the Navy requires a high school diploma.

Well, that Navy recruiter sent me to another office to talk to the Marines. (I don't think it was because of some great admiration he had for the Marines, but I immediately liked the idea. I remembered the movie *Battle Cry*. If it was anything like the movie, count me in.)

I walked up to the Marine recruiter, and he looked sharp as he welcomed me. The Marines' dress blues are the best uniforms out of all the services. I told him I want to join the Marine Corps and he gave me an application. I just knew I was in. I was going to be a Marine. I filled out the application right there in the office and gave it back to him. I waited in anticipation as he read through it. He didn't say anything about not having a high school diploma, but he did ask me about not being a US citizen. He told me that I'd need to sign a document stating that I intended to become a US citizen. But there was a problem. I'd have to be 18 years old to sign that document. This was late summer 1957 and it would be almost a year before I'd turn 18. I hung my head and thanked him. As I was walking out, he said, "You really want to join bad, don't you?" I told him about coming to America and feeling a duty to serve in its defense. He told me to hang around a minute. He made a phone call setting me up to go see the local Army recruiter.

I hadn't given the Army much thought. I had seen a lot of 'Willie and Joe' movies and liked them. I knew that if I did go into the Army, I'd want to be in the Infantry.

Now, the Army recruiter was not as sharp as the Marine. (He looked like he could use some exercise.) He explained that the typical way to apply for the Army would require the same form stating that I intended to become a citizen, the one that could only be signed by an 18-year-old. But he told me a way to get around that problem. Strangely, the fact that I'd been in trouble with the law could work to my advantage. He told me to go talk to the judge and he may be willing to expedite my being drafted into the Army.

I went to see the judge. He was a WWII veteran and my proposal made him proud of me. He called the draft board on my behalf. My mother went with me to the draft board, and it was official. I told all my friends that I was going into the Army. My girlfriend was not happy. In early December, I received the official notice. "Greetings. You are being drafted. Report to the Newark, NJ induction center on January 16th, 1958." I was so happy.[4]

My girlfriend cried. Now, we were spending as much time together as we could. Her mother didn't care for me and made it plain that her daughter would be better off to forget about me. As the time got closer for my induction into the Army, my girlfriend and I made a vow that, someday, we would get married.

My mother and father hosted a big going-away party. They rented a hall, and the place was packed. We had good food and lots of vodka, beer, and wine. Buddy Dewilett played the accordion with his band, and we danced into the night. Polka. Hopak. American Rock & Roll. As the night and the vodka took their toll, we danced to slow tunes, 'hold each other up' tunes. One would forever bring tears to my mother's eyes, "Sail Along, Silvery Moon." She always remembered that as "the song they played when you went into the Army."

---

4   Jakovenko admired military veterans partly because of these movies, partly because of the character he'd observed in these men of honor, and partly because of the glory and praise that humans naturally shower on those who have been in combat. All of these are crucial in America's recruitment efforts.

The next day, January 16th, 1958, I reported to the Newark induction center. I made my way from table to table, filling out paperwork, standing in endless lines of recruits waiting for their physical exam. At last, we were sworn in. It was official. I was assigned to Basic Training at Fort Dix, New Jersey, and the bus was ready and waiting, engine running.

There, our whole company was draftees. Everyone moaned about getting it over with...and try to stay out of the Infantry. Not me, the Infantry was my top choice. We were taught about the various specialties in the Army. I was so sure that I was meant to be a paratrooper that at my first opportunity, I got an Airborne tattoo.

I liked the rough physical training. In the fifth week we started to shoot the M1 rifle. I qualified as a sharpshooter. I was hitting the Canadian bullseye at 500 yards from the prone position. I was proud of my talents.

In late March 1958, graduation day arrived.

Image 24. At Fort Dix, in my "Ike Jacket."

My AIT (Advanced Individual Training) was going to be Light Vehicle Drivers Course (LVDC), right there at Fort Dix. I would learn to drive every kind of vehicle up to the 2½ ton truck ('deuce-and-a-half'). I liked the LVDC. We spent 10% of our time in class (manuals, Army forms, trip tickets, and maintenance reports) and 90% was hands-on. We drove on obstacle courses. We learned security and how to drive as a convoy. We drove at night with tactical lights. We practiced proper distances in combat areas and running ambushes. We would be manning some of the Army's biggest machine guns. We had to qualify on the Browning M2 .50 caliber machine gun. The .50 cal was mounted over the cab in the "crow's nest." The assistant driver was the machine gunner and we had to fire while moving. I qualified expert on the .50 cal.

After a couple of weeks, our convoys—about 10 trucks—started training off post, driving on New Jersey highways. One task we had was to pick up loads of railroad ties and bring them back for use in field construction. I enjoyed these trips. You mixed with civilians, and they would wave at us. The kids would get excited, and everyone was friendly to soldiers. It made us feel good that they cared about us.

I was hoping that my assignment after graduation would be the 11th Airborne Division at Fort Campbell, Kentucky. It would give me an avenue to possibly go to jump school. My greatest worry was that I might never get a slot into jump school and would forever be a "Non-Airborne Personnel" (NAP). Paratroopers referred to them as "legs."

A week before graduation day I received my assignment. I was assigned to a unit in France, the 'Communication Zone.' I was dejected.

The Communication Zone was the post-war occupation of France and Germany, still lingering in 1958. Many of the French people didn't want us there any longer. Some of my classmates said they wished they could swap with me; they'd love to see France.

11

The Old Country

1958

In a glorious first for me, our aircraft lifts off. It's a beautiful blue sky as I'm leaving for France. Put yourself in my place for a moment. Climbing out over New York City, I crane to see the glorious Statue of Liberty. The first time I saw her, I was a 10-year-old D.P. (displaced person) standing on the deck of a converted troop ship. Now, I'm wearing the uniform of the United States Army, sworn to her service. How far I have come in just eight years. My heart is swelling with gratitude. I'm no longer a displaced person. I now have a country. In engine-roaring silence, my window—my assigned window on the world—parades over the scrolling blocks of humanity: skyscrapers, harbors, suspension bridges. I silently commit, "I will defend you with my life." I am settled in confident peace that my life would be a small price to pay for this country.[5]

---

5   It's clear that at this point, Jakovenko had a fully developed sense of Spirit. Though his Skills were only at a basic level, his Spirit was arguably more developed than many much older than he. Seeing the Old Country again would only strengthen this Spirit.

It was a seven-hour flight. The pilot began pointing out
the islands of Ireland and then the English Channel. The
view was spectacular. I was on top of the world. I was returning to Europe in the uniform of the US Army, the force
for Good. We received warm greetings. Along with other
soldiers on my flight, I was able to find the armed forces
detachment office in the airport terminal. They helped us
get transportation to our units.

My unit was near La Rochelle, 250 miles southwest of
Paris. It was a coastal town on the Bay of Biscay. The train
ride took us across the beautiful French countryside and
past the historical cities of Orleans, Tours, and Poitiers.
This was the area in which Joan of Arc accomplished her
heroics. Many people kindly and courteously offered some
conversation the best they could, but I knew no French. (I
committed myself to learn as much as I could.) There were
thousands of American servicemen in cemeteries there who
died liberating France. I did not feel like a stranger. This
was not a foreign land. I was European by birth. I spoke
German, Ukrainian, Russian, Polish, and English. Now it's
time for French.

Our train finally arrived at La Rochelle, a beautiful, an-
cient city. We still had 20 miles to go on a military bus to
get to the small village of Croix Chapeau to find the 28th
General Hospital, part of HQ, US Army Communication
Zone, Europe.

The buildings were fairly modern. The ward had the
patients, of course, but the building also contained the barracks for about 20 of us permanent party enlisted personnel.
It was double bunked, but it was a luxury hotel compared
to our WWII wooden buildings at Fort Dix.

I was assigned to the 64th Transportation Company. Mostly, I drove an Army deuce-and-a-half but when I had to drive VIPs, I used an Army sedan. I was on the road almost every day delivering cargo to Bordeaux, Saintes, Poitiers, Chateauroux, Nantes, Tours, Blois, Orleans, and even to Paris.

Let me tell you a grisly story. When I reported to dispatch one morning, I was told to change into my Class A uniform and pack for an overnight trip. I would drive a field ambulance (what we called a cracker box) to the hospital mortuary. At the mortuary, they explained that I was going to transport four bodies to a hospital on the outskirts of Paris. There had been a horrific murder just outside the gates of our facility. Polish nationals were providing security on the perimeter of the 28th General Hospital. I didn't know the whole story, but one Polish guard had a disagreement with several other guards. At night, he went to the guard barracks and shot three of the Polish guards while they were sleeping. He then took his own life.

I guess this was the biggest news that ever happened at the 28th and everyone was talking about it. I went into the mortuary, and they were still preparing the bodies for transport. I watched them put them in the body bags. Bloody sheets. Shoes still on one. They loaded the bodies into my ambulance. I started the seven-hour drive. Alone. It was already overcast, but about an hour after sunset...

...it's totally dark. There aren't many people on the roads tonight. And then—

What was that noise?

I hear some sort of low pitch noise back there. It sounds like a groan—what in the hell? There's a noise in the back of the ambulance! I swear I hear talking back there! Hell yeah, I'm scared. I slam on the brakes and pull over. PARK.

Forget the emergency brake, I'm out of that damned cab in about two seconds.

I'm standing on the side of the road about 25 yards from the ambulance. Just corn fields.

It takes about five minutes for my heart rate to calm a bit.

This is stupid. What am afraid of? I've got to open the back door. (I could open the access door between the cab and the back, but I figure if I see the guys in back get up to talk to me, then I'm gonna need plenty of room to start my sprint.)

There's no traffic. (I wish there was traffic.) It's cold. Distant lights of a town glow a few miles behind me. There's a gray overcast.

I walk to the rear of the truck and when my hand grabs on to the door handle, something makes me pause for a moment. Knees bent, fist clenched, poised for combat with the undead, I open the doors and can't help but step backward, prepared for the worst. Instantly, I shine my flashlight in. (Good thinking. Bright lights always blind 'em for a few seconds.) I step closer and push my hand into the shadows just far enough to turn on the interior lights.

There's no movement. Dead silence. But just when I'm closing the door, I hear something like a growl. I **_run_**. That sound of fast crunching is my spit-shined dress shoes on the gravel breaking the posted speed limit as I head toward that town back there. I'm now about 50 meters away from the truck and so I ease up. Like Olympians after they pass the finish line, my momentum carried me another 25 meters, just in the slowing down.

It takes all the 18-year-old manliness I have to walk back toward that truck. I have to look. This time, all is quiet. …and stays quiet. Another five minutes to shame myself into believing that it must have been my imagination. I close the doors and feel a little better.

I started driving again. I finally got to my destination. They were expecting me to unload them! I took a long time and went to great lengths describing the noises because I thought they'd laugh at me. They said that those noises were the bodies decomposing. The bodies had not been prepared due to the investigation of the murders. The reason for transporting them to Paris was for autopsy.

I left Paris early the next morning returning to base and did I have a story to tell. In the following days, it started being told as a legend, developing a life of its own, and I became a celebrity for a time.

I now want to tell you a wonderful thing. Please forgive me for being so brief in describing it. Out of respect for all involved, I shouldn't share more than the essential facts. On September 9th, 1958, my fiancé gave birth to my first son. For months, her mother had been pressuring her to forget me and put up the baby for adoption. I strongly wanted us to marry and raise our son as a family. As a young, enlisted troop bombarded with opinions and pressures, I was so torn about what I could do. Her letters had turned into pressure to sign the adoption papers. *I'm not responsible enough to provide for him? I've brought a life into this world, but I*

can't handle the responsibility of being a father to my son?
I said I needed time to think about it.

I was told I did not have much time.

The road of life has many intersections. Very often, there's no one to give you directions. In my case Private Maurice "Mo" Dessel was there at the crossroad. He was from New Jersey too. By November, his wife arrived and she cooked us a wonderful Thanksgiving meal. That day, Mo was very blunt: "Don't give up your son. Your girl-friend may not wait for you. Then you will have lost them both. Go get your son. He comes first. You're his father."

With Mo's help, I arranged with a chaplain that I'd go home on Morale Leave. Arriving home, I got to meet my son…John. That's the moment I first knew his name. After a beautiful, Orthodox wedding, my wife and son lived with my parents until I would come back from my overseas duty.

Before my two-year enlistment was up, I received more good news. The Army was letting me out early on what they called Operation Santa Claus. I received my discharge papers and departed on December 22nd, 1959. This was tru-ly a merry Christmas for the Jakovenkos!

I particularly loved the sound of "Honorable Discharge." I was proud. I felt I had paid a very small part of my debt to my country. I could now apply to become a citizen. I continued my military career in the National Guard and worked at a factory in Carteret, NJ.

12

The Jump

1961

In both my National Guard job and my civilian job, I was a truck driver. But deep down, I knew that I was meant for something else. What was I naturally good at— fighting. Now, if I could build an entire career on that, I could really excel. I kept hearing about "Special Forces." Nobody in the National Guard could tell me much about them. I knew you had to volunteer. They were very secretive about what they did.

I went to Camp Kilmer, about 15 miles south of our home in Westfield, to find out. Camp Kilmer was the headquarters for the US Army II Corps, which was the headquarters for all the US Army Reserve units across the Northeast. It was the home of the 11th Special Forces Group (Airborne), US Army Reserves. I was able to get an interview. They asked a few questions about my qualifications and pretty quickly they noticed my Airborne tattoo. "What Airborne Division did you serve with?"

Embarrassed that I'd let the tattoo show, I humbly told them I was not Airborne qualified. "I only have the tattoo."

They asked if I spoke any foreign languages. Happy that we'd moved on past the whole tattoo thing, I seized on this truly positive topic. I told them that I speak several languages. The conversation really brightened up at this point. Now, they were willing to circle back around to the idea of jump school.

At the end of the interview, a positive sign was that they told me to bring them my DD214, the form that serves as proof of military service indicating my honorable discharge. Within a day, I came back with the paperwork. Within a couple of weeks, I received news that I had been accepted into the US Army Reserves and was now on the list to go to jump school! I was on top once again!

In March of 1961, I had my first two-week drill with the 11th Special Forces Group. It was in upstate NY. I was in Bravo Company, and I was amazed at their professionalism. These were very experienced soldiers. Most came from the New York City metropolitan area, and many were police officers or firefighters. A lot of them were veterans of WWII and/ or Korea. Our commander, Lt Colonel Joseph M. McCrane served with the Marines at Guadalcanal and then went to West Point, playing on their championship football team which included two Heisman Trophy winners. Lt Colonel Curci was a lawyer who later became a Justice on the New York State Supreme Court. Major Galanti had been in the OSS "Jedburgh Teams" in WWII, precursors to the Special Forces.

I can't proceed without mentioning one last man that left memories of what this military profession was all about.

His name is Harry Perlmutter. In WWII, he had served with the 2nd Ranger Battalion. He was an Army-trained mule-skinner; he knew more about military mules than anyone. He showed his expertise during a two-week deployment to Fort Drum, New York, in March 1961.

This was a *very* unconventional E&E exercise (escape & evasion). We wore civilian clothes. We had to evade aggressor forces between a Start Point and an End Point that were 200 miles apart. There was a Marine reserve unit playing the role of the enemy forces trying to find and capture us. They were allowed to utilize the NY state troopers, which is a pretty great advantage for them.

But we had an even greater advantage. We were allowed to utilize Harry Perlmutter's mules. He trained us to use them in our movements across forests and rugged hills and dark valleys. Mules were our means to resupply and transport our heavy loads of food, water and ammunition so that we could stay deep in the forests far from civilization for long periods.

On this two-week journey, I learned a lot from these soldiers. What really made me feel good is that they accepted me. I felt like I really belonged. I acknowledged my lack of expertise in unconventional warfare and made up for it with my can-do attitude and my enthusiasm to learn everything they were teaching me. As I recall, no one was captured by the Marines or law enforcement. During a commander's formation at the end of this deployment, to my surprise, Lt Colonel McCrane awarded me a Green Beret. I felt the honor of what this Special Forces unit was conveying upon me. These were the very earliest years of the use of the Green Beret in the Army.

Image 25. My early 1961 Green Beret
before earning the Flash.

It was later in that year, on October 12th, 1961, that President Kennedy came to the Special Warfare Center at Fort Bragg, North Carolina, and famously announced that the Green Beret would be the official distinct headgear for the US Special Forces. He called the Green Beret "a symbol of excellence, a badge of courage, a mark of distinction in the fight for freedom."

I still had a long way to go to become fully qualified as a member of a Special Forces team, to complete my training, and to receive my SF flash, but I'd taken my first step.

But the next step was a doozy—stepping out the side of an aircraft.

Becoming a paratrooper is a requirement in Special Forces. In order to find out whether you were going to stick it out through jump school, they came up with a small test. They sent you to a skydiving club called The Swamp Fox. This club was in Montgomery, New York, about an hour north of New York City and was purely civilian skydiving. I would have to make a parachute jump there before I would get orders to jump school. I said, "No problem."

We met on an early Sunday morning in June 1961 at Camp Kilmer and started loading up the unit's jump equipment on some Army vehicles. There were a handful of us first-timers doing the jump. I was assigned a certain serious-faced young sergeant as my trainer and jumpmaster. He was a firefighter in NYC. Standing around our vehicles, he asked if I had my equipment. I said, "No," so we went to see the supply sergeant, who was known to be a real bear who growled a lot. For some reason, I could hardly sleep the night before. I don't think I was scared, just apprehensive. That supply sergeant could see that I was a little uneasy, so he gave me his best helmet, which looked a lot like a football helmet. He had done a lot of civilian jumping but, interestingly, his uniform had no jump wings. He had never gone to Army jump school. "You'll do fine. Just listen to your jumpmaster."

We mounted our vehicles and began driving north, away from the traffic of the city and suburbs. Arriving at the airport, we unloaded our equipment and started our training. We talked about the features of the parachute, exiting the aircraft, steering, and the all-important parachute landing fall. In the PLF, you transfer the energy of impact into the five points of landing. From the balls of your feet, you bend your body to a side so that the outside of your calf muscle hits next, then the side of your thigh, then the side of your butt, and finally the 'push-up muscle' (your lateralis muscle). First, we practiced the PLF by jumping from a three-foot platform. After about 20 of them, I was still having problems achieving the proper five points of contact. (Mine was more like feet, ass, head!)

We spent some time at the plane (a single engine aircraft big enough for five students) and practiced standing in the door and exiting the aircraft. Here's how it was to work. You were to be looking toward your jumpmaster for the 'Go' signal. The jumpmaster was the spotter, holding us until the best jump point. He would tell you, "Get ready!" and then connect your static line. The pilot would press the brakes so that as we stepped out, the wheels would not spin. (You could step on the wheel for some balance.) Then you'd stand up, climb out the right side, putting your foot on a step halfway down the main landing gear strut, and grab the right wing strut with both hands. At his command, you would vigorously push away, arch your back, and count four seconds, "One thousand! Two thousand! Three thousand! Four thousand!" If your parachute did not open by then, you would start emergency procedures to activate your reserve parachute.

If your main parachute deployed, then you'd begin checking your parachute for any of the following problems:

- A Mae West (One of your lines is on top of your canopy. It looks like a huge brazier.)
- A cigarette roll (Your canopy is not widening to its full diameter.)
- A blown panel/squid (There's a tear in the fabric.)

If your emergency procedures do not fix the problem, then you would perform a 'controlled opening' of your reserve, not letting your reserve get tangled up in your main parachute (which very likely would be fatal).

I was listening to all of this and hoping I could execute the procedures correctly. Yes, I was scared. We were quizzed by the instructors. I answered the questions correctly, but knowing and doing are two different things. There's only one way to find out the doing part.

"Any more questions?" "Need any more practice?" "Then let's do it!"

At this moment, everything becomes slow motion, like a dream. I pray quietly, "Right now, Lord, help me." Scared, yes, but not of dying. Scared of total embarrassment if I stupidly get injured and flunk out. The other five students are also nervous. One of them breaks the ice: "Jumping out is not what I'm worried about. It's the big bounce at the end."

We all laugh. Sort of.

The jumpmaster takes us to the parachutes, all lined up perfectly. He asks me to help the other students don their parachutes correctly. He had seen my Airborne tattoo and assumed…

Embarrassed again, but this time with my life on the line, I humbly (desperately?) tell him I'm not Airborne qualified. "I only have the tattoo."

He laughs and shakes his head. "I'm gonna put you out *first*."

We all line up for the JMPI (Jumpmaster Personnel Inspection). When the jumpmaster finishes each of us in turn, he has us sit down in a precise line on the tarmac waiting silently until he finishes with the rest of the jumpers. He runs through the procedures again and tells us to listen to everything he commands. "Do not take your eyes off me once we are in the airplane. Jakovenko will be the first one out of the plane. He has the most experience. You can tell because he has an Airborne tattoo."

The small but very loud airplane taxis to a stop and the jumpmaster leads us onboard with the engine running. It has just returned from dropping other jumpers. The jumpmaster leans in, talks with the pilot, checks the interior, and then signals us to come forward. Each jumper climbs in and hooks up to the static line. We are in order, sitting on the floor. Immediately next to my shoulder is the great open door to nowhere-ness. The jumpmaster puts a strap across the door for safety (ha!) and the door stays open the entire flight. The engine revs up a bit and we're moving. The noise and speed of the takeoff is exciting and terrifying. Wind. Bumpy. Open. Danger. Like an egg on a spatula, I feel I could easily slide across the smooth metal floor right out the opening.

Climbing to 3500 feet, it's unreal. The cars and people on the ground are so small that they seem imaginary.

We level off. Only just now do I realize that I'm afraid of heights.

The jumpmaster is acting exactly as he did on the ground—a lot of grinning and thumbs up. I look at the other jumpers and wonder if they are as scared as I am. The jumpmaster unhooks the strap from the door. He throws an orange streamer out to check the wind drift. The plane makes a big banking turn and then rolls out on jump heading. The jumpmaster loudly gets my attention, checks my static line, and gives me the signal to unhook my safety belt. He now gives me a big grin and thumbs up and I try to grin back. I can see the other jumpers' eyes are the size of dinner plates. The jumpmaster points to me and then points out the door. I'm scared but my body is moving in robotic obedience per my training. I get to the door; the wind is a hurricane. I grab the strut with one hand and put my foot on the step. Now I have both hands on the wing strut, and I touch my foot on the wheel. Man, this is daredevil barnstorming! Wing walking! My eyes are on the jumpmaster. It seems like an eternity waiting. The massive roar of the engine. My grip is super tight on the strut.

The jumpmaster points at me to go. I push off and arch my back spread eagle. The next few seconds are a blur. Did I forget to count? The next thing I know, the canopy opens with a jolt. For a second, I just hang there, limp. I look up to see the most glorious circular sight my eyes have ever beheld. My canopy is fully deployed.

Wait a minute—it looks like a panel is missing in my canopy. But hold on, don't panic. In training they showed us that the parachute is modified for steering purposes. (It's what they called a "7 Gore T.U. Modification.")

I start steering the parachute to see if those openings work correctly. I find the toggle lines with the small wooden pegs at the end. I grab them and tug right to go right. I pull left to go left. This is cool. Left to itself, it really does run with the wind. I need to turn into the wind and minimize my ground track. Where's the assembly point? (At this point, as long as I land in the state of New York, I'll be perfectly happy.)

Maybe I need to pay more attention—as I'm coming closer to the ground, I realize that I'm still running with the wind. I've got to arrest this speed. Where's the smoke? They said I'd be able to see smoke and a windsock. Dang, I must be doing about 20 knots! And I'm way off the drop zone and heading for a four-lane highway. I can't avoid it at this point. Traffic is pulling over. I crumple into the dirt close to the road.

It isn't pretty. As I'm trying to collapse my parachute fighting against the breeze, a state trooper pulls over, worried that I might get dragged onto the highway. He asks, "What kind of canopy control was that?!"

I tell him this was my first jump and I'll be going to jump school.

He says, "Good idea."

Well, there was a law against parachuting within 500 meters of a highway, but I guess he felt sorry for me and my hard landing. He had been in the 82nd Airborne Division. Some members of my company arrived in a truck. I was sore and limping. The state trooper shook my hand and wished me better luck and we headed back to the airfield.

As we loaded up the equipment for the ride home, everyone was shaking my hand. I had made my first jump from an airplane. I felt like I was part of Special Forces. I proved to myself that I could do Airborne. On the way back to post, they shared with us an old Airborne song called "Blood on the Risers." It was a tale of a young paratrooper who had a parachute malfunction and met his doom.

Back at Camp Kilmer, we unloaded the equipment and celebrated with a few beers. What a memory. I was on top of the world again. Soon, I got my orders to Fort Benning, Georgia, for jump school.

In the days leading up to my departure, everyone wished me good luck, and some of the guys said I was going to need it. They never knew *anyone* who had an Airborne tattoo to make it through. It's like an insult to the instructors and it's hard to hide. I said, "I won't let you guys down." They seemed to know the agony I was about to experience for the next four weeks.

13

Airborne

1961

I was in excellent shape. Hundreds of push-ups and tens of pull-ups came naturally for me. And I ran every day. I was physically at the top of my game. Then there was the psychological. I was told no matter what, just don't quit. I told myself that as long as I don't quit, they will not terminate me. Quitting is a matter of your own free will.

I had to report in at Fort Benning on a certain Sunday in August 1961. According to my unit, it was up to me to decide whether to wear my Green Beret. I was authorized, so I chose to wear it. Man, I looked like a soldier. My khaki uniform was tailored-fit. My brass was highly polished. My jump boots were spit shined. Everything looked in place.

Arriving at the main gate, I asked for directions to the jump school. I was told, "Just look for the red and white 250-foot-tall towers. You can see them from a mile away. There, ask people where the orderly room is. You report in there." It was true. The three massive towers were like the tallest theme park attraction you can imagine. They hoist the student up to the top using a huge ring the diameter of your fully deployed chute and then they actually release you so that you get the full experience of the final 250 feet, including your PLF.

Image 26. The 250-foot drop towers at Fort Benning.

I reported in and was assigned my barracks. I was not with the regular Army Airborne trainees. Because I was a reservist, I would be staying in a special transient barracks for officers, NCOs and the students from the Air Force, the Navy, and the Marines. There would be about 350 students in this class, with about 250 being regular Army enlisted and about 100 of us being some other classification. I drew bedding and linen and put my stuff away and changed into civilian clothes.

As we settled into our rooms, the hallways were pretty busy. Some guys were asking questions about Special Forces. I met a couple of students from the SEALs, the Underwater Demolition Teams (UDT). Some of the Air Force students asked me if I was from the Canadian Army. They'd never seen a US Army soldier wearing a Green Beret. Some of the guys were talking about going to the NCO club for a couple of beers. Apparently, these guys had not heard that Monday was always a pretty rough training day. Evenings were for resting and recuperating for the next day. Drinking during these training weeks was not advisable.

I had an ace bandage on my left forearm (any guesses why?) Some of the guys asked me about it. I said, "Well, you may as well know. I have an Airborne tattoo." They couldn't believe it. I had to show them. They asked me why in the world I got it. I said, "It was years ago and it's a long story."

"The instructors are going to smoke you over this."

I said, "They can smoke me, but they can't eat me." (How wrong I was. For the first couple of weeks, they chewed me up and spit me back out day after day.)

I read over the instructions issued to us when we signed in. It told us the training schedule, including which uniform to be in for each training event.

The P.T. (Physical Training) every morning was tough, especially the run. You had to be in pretty good shape to start Airborne training. We were warned.

Let me tell you about Corcoran jump boots. There was a tradition that, only when you graduated from jump school, you'd buy a pair of Corcoran jump boots at the local P.X. (Post Exchange). They were expensive, so you wouldn't use them for everyday training. But if you were Airborne, you wanted to have them, at least for special occasions or ceremonies.

Corcoran boots had been specially designed for paratroopers since WWII. They had extra support for your ankles, hard toes and the heels were beveled to help with the PLF and to help prevent a suspension line being caught on your boot.

One of the Navy SEALs came over and introduced himself and we got to talking. He said a lot of SEALs go to Fort Bragg, North Carolina, to train with Army Special Forces in communications, small unit ambushes, raids, and unconventional warfare. He asked about my experiences in Special Forces. I told him I was in the 11th Special Forces Group, and I've only been there a year and still had a lot of training to do to become fully qualified. Jump school is the first part of that training.

He had a Submariner's Rolex. The Navy had issued every SEAL two pairs of Corcoran boots. (They didn't have to buy them with their own money!) He asked me for advice on how to get them to look as glassy as mine. It was clear to me that SEALs were high speed. We became friends and that paid dividends later on in Airborne training.

Image 27. The brochure inside the box
of your Corcoran jump boots.

My show time was a few days later, when the black
hats turned their attention on me. The sun was just coming
up on our morning P.T. formation, 200 students in perfect

rows and columns. The dew still on the grass, we were face-down into our push-ups just prior to launching on a 3-mile run, when I noticed that a black hat was looking at me. He barked at me to do another 25, which I did while the others stood up and started forward into their formation run (making their way around me and the black hat.) He said, "Recover! Now, catch up with the rest of the formation."

When we get back from the run, we line up at the pull-up bars before we clean up and go to breakfast. When I get to the front of the line, I jump up on one of the pull-up bars and start to do my normal 15. That same black hat is talking to another black hat and looking in my direction. I have a sick feeling in my gut that my ordeal is about to begin.

"192! Drop!" (192 is my number. Our jump helmets have a number on the front and back.)

I drop to the leaning rest (the push-up position) and await the next command. The two black hats stand in front of me and say, "Knock out 25." I do the 25 push-ups. "We notice you have an ace bandage on your left arm. Why is that?"

I loudly reply, "It helps my left arm."

From my prone position, now I hear the sinister grin creak across his evil face. In a low, foreboding tone the black hat says, "You're not trying to bullshit us, are you 192? I bet you 50 push-ups that you have an Airborne tattoo under that ace bandage."

(Gulp.)

"Well do I do the push-ups or do you?"

(Pause.) (Think.) (Nothing comes to me.) I started doing the 50 push-ups.

With rodeo cheers, they call the other black hats around. "What do we have here? A 'Mr. Airborne'?"

"Recover and take that f___ing bandage off!" I stand at attention and five instructors are now surrounding me, sincerely agreeing that it was a good-looking tattoo, but not on a "leg" (a NAP). I know that "Mr. Airborne" name will haunt me for the weeks to come. After the 50, the original black hat orders me report in to each of the five black hats who would, one-at-a-time, order me to do 10 push-ups in front of him. They eventually get tired of it and tell me to get cleaned up and go to breakfast.

I cleaned up and after breakfast, I was ready for inspection at our formation. I had made extra sure to check my gig line. (This is the straight line from the front center of your chin to the buttons on your shirt, to your belt buckle to the bottom of your pants zipper.) When you get a "gig" (you fail inspection due to a gig discrepancy), you're sent straight to the gig pit, which is a mud hole where you do push-ups and sit-ups in the mud. From this day on, it seemed I always had gigs and became a regular visitor to the gig pit. If they couldn't find any gigs then the black hats would say I had a crooked, ugly face messing up the entire gig line. The black hats required me to rub my face in the mud—said it was good for an ugly face.

The black hat made sure to tell everyone my new name, "Mr. Airborne," and that I would, from now on, be the "expert demonstrator" of how to perform the various skills in Airborne training. Talking to me individually, they made it clear that I had a 99.99% probability of washing out and being sent home, forever a leg/NAP. They told me I had three strikes against me:

1.) I was from the Reserves.

2.) I was wearing a French hat (as much as I reminded them that it was a Special Forces Green Beret, they retorted that, "Only two types of people wear berets: the French and Girl Scouts. Do you speak French?!" To that, I replied in French that he is a baboon wearing a black hat.)

3.) I had that damn Airborne tattoo. "No one with an Airborne tattoo has ever made it through jump school to graduation."

We got to the phase of training in which we performed exits from a mock-up of a C-119 aircraft. For this, we wore dummy main parachutes and reserve chutes with full weight. Here we did physical conditioning called the 'squat jump.' You put both hands on your helmet and perform small 'crow jumps' bending your legs low to the ground, first with the right foot forward, jumping up to a standing position, switching to the left foot forward, and repeating until your legs were on fire. Squat jumps with full gear require everything you've got.

Over weeks two and three, the physical aspect tested my fortitude and my commitment. I would continually be singled out and pushed to perform beyond the ability of most of the class. While my platoon was doing the Airborne shuffle (a slow run, in formation), I was always one of the few guys made to run circles around the formation at twice the speed. As we marched, I would be pulled out to do push-ups and squat jumps and then catch up. The black hats were encouraging me to quit. A few times when I was dragging, a couple of SEALs dropped back, grabbed me under the arms, pulled me forward and told me not to quit. In response, the black hats would tell *them* to drop and do push-ups. At that moment, two more SEALs would drop back to grab me and pull me forward. Eventually, I'd gather my breath and fall into formation back at full pace. I would not quit.

In fact, I was only getting stronger. Each day, I was doing hundreds of push-ups. When I'd see a black hat, I would drop and do 25 just to goad them. I was able to do 200 push-ups in one set. I was becoming fanatical about push-ups.

Now, it's time for the dreaded 250-foot tower. (See the photo at the beginning of this chapter). This is the closest simulation of your actual parachute jump. You are in a real 'T-10' parachute, and you actually get released to descend on your own. The tower has four stationary arms reaching out at the top in the four cardinal directions. The instructors are constantly measuring the wind direction and velocity. Whichever arm is upwind will not be used at that moment, so a max of three students will be released on any given cycle. They drift to the ground, perform the PLF, release their risers, gather up their chute, then report to hear their grade and critique. After my chute is connected to the huge ring, a safety check is performed by a black hat. The command is then given to the motor control room at the base of that tower to take us up to 250 feet. It's a slow ascent and can be terrifying. But what a bird's eye view! You can see all of Fort Benning and far westward into the rolling forests of Alabama. It seems like we'll never get to the top. After a couple of minutes, I'm really being pushed around by the wind. Up here, everything is so amazingly quiet.

Finally arriving at the top, I wait. And wait. I feel like I'm hanging up here forever. Directions are being given from the ground through a bull horn, referring to us by our student numbers. I spot the windsock down there. The black hat with the bull horn is reminding certain ones of us, due to the wind, to perform a slip away from the tower. Then I hear snaps releasing my canopy and my first descent commences. I steer away from the tower. The black hat is still barking his comments. About 100 feet from the ground, I prepare to land per procedure. I say to myself, "Five points of contact! Five points of contact!" Curving into a banana shape, I hit and roll, and my legs come over the top of me, following through.

I must have done okay because I was congratulated on a good jump, but still had to do push-ups and squat jumps. But I didn't mind—I was grinning like an idiot!

I only made one jump. The winds were picking up, and they wanted to get the experience for as many of us as they could. We finished on Friday and were told that we were scheduled for our first jump out of an airplane on Monday morning.

On that early Army morning, buses line up taking us from our barracks formation down the hill to Fort Benning's Lawson Army Airfield. Two awe-inspiring C-119s ('The Flying Boxcar') are lined up just outside our equipment hangar. As we walk out to our plane, with the sun rising and the engines starting up, the black hat at the steps says to me in an encouraging voice, "I'll see you on the ground!" That chokes me up a little. These are the black hats who said no one makes it through jump school with Airborne tattoo. At this moment, we are all working for a common purpose.

Five minutes after takeoff, we are over the drop zone, Fryar Field in Alabama. Fryar Field is part of Fort Benning, but it's across the Chattahoochee River, which runs along the state line. In the roaring metal interior, the jumpmaster commands, "Stand up, hook up, check static line, and check equipment!" "Sound off for equipment check!" On the single-file line on each side of the aircraft, we pass the signal forward that we've checked our equipment. We pass it forward by solidly tapping the shoulder of the jumper in front of you saying "Okay!" I wait for my tap and then I point to the jumpmaster and said, "All Okay!" I am standing two feet from the open door. The jumpmaster hangs his head fully and fearlessly out the door and makes a visual safety check. He points his finger positively in my face and commands, "Stand in the door!" I assume the door position just like I've done a hundred times on the ground. The jumpmaster is watching the red light on the door. The light turns green. He taps me on the upper thigh and yells, "Go!"

Image 28. A typical static line jump from a C-119.

I spring out the door. As I'm counting to four, I'm weightless and briefly see the C-119 flying away from me. Then comes the jolt of the parachute opening. It's exhilarating, like no other feeling in the world! I check the canopy and get to work. I turn to see the other students jumping out of the aircraft. Right near me, some under canopy start to holler to me. We are each overcome with joy. With about two minutes of floating to the ground, I can see what makes paratroopers a brotherhood. This is our world. Our beautiful adventure. This technology is the fastest way to get to any spot on the surface of the earth.

My other jumps go well and then the fifth and final jump was on Friday morning. This was a 'mass tactical.' We'd be jumping out both sides of the aircraft at the same time. In war, concentration of force is key. You need to get out as fast as you can so that you are not strung out over a distance. The sooner you can form up, the more lethal your force on the battlefield. You have to empty the aircraft in seconds. I was in the door (first again, but by now it actually did feel like a reward) and I could feel the jumpers behind me raring to go. The jumpmaster says, "Go!" I jump. As my parachute deploys, I'm instantly on my game now. I go through my procedures. I look at my brothers suspended in the sky. This time, I'm totally aware of the commands the black hats with bullhorns are yelling up to us. "Make sure you check the smoke to know your winds!"

And then I was down, and jump school was complete. I'd done it.

We turned in our equipment on a truck there at Fryar Field, Alabama. We hopped on the buses back to the barracks and got ready for graduation. We cleaned up and put on our 'Class A' dress uniform (khaki) with spit-shined boots.

It was an extremely proud moment, lined up listening to guest speakers, the Colonels and a General. Blood wings were pounded on the left side of my chest. Looking back on the weeks, blood wings seemed appropriate for me. I gave my own sweat and blood to get these silver wings. And it was all worth it. During the pinning on, the black hats came over to me, shook my hand, congratulated me, and said I should come back to Active Duty and join one of the Airborne divisions.

The SEALs shook my hand and said, "Maybe we'll see you at Fort Bragg." They were attending some Special Forces schools soon. They also suggested that I go back on Active Duty but go through UDT training and try for a SEAL team.

[I later had a best friend in Special Forces who went through SEAL training. Sgt 1st Class "Dirty Shirt" Johnson earned the trident in the early 60s. He was the most knowledgeable Special Forces soldier that I ever met. He was qualified in several Special Forces Military Occupational Specialties (MOS) and was a master at unconventional warfare. After retirement, his skills were well utilized by multiple government agencies.]

Having said all of my goodbyes, I headed back to New Jersey.

14

The Cuban Missile Crisis

1962

At last, I received the wonderful notification that I was approved to become a citizen of the United States. For me, the five-mile journey from Ellis Island to this federal building in Elizabeth, NJ, had taken 11 years. I again swore to support and defend the constitution on November 27th, 1961. I was an American.

"I hereby declare, on oath, that I absolutely and entirely renounce and abjure all allegiance and fidelity to any foreign prince, potentate, state, or sovereignty, of whom or which I have heretofore been a subject or citizen; that I will support and defend the Constitution and laws of the United States of America against all enemies, foreign and domestic; that I will bear true faith and allegiance to the same; that I will bear arms on behalf of the United States when required by the law; that I will perform noncombatant service in the Armed Forces of the United States when required by the law; that I will

perform work of national importance under civilian direction when required by the law; and that I take this obligation freely, without any mental reservation or purpose of evasion; so help me God."

The naturalization paperwork allowed me to formally establish my official name in English. So there, I took the opportunity to change from "Volodymyr" to "John." Later, when my mother heard about that, she said, "Why did you change your name? I gave you the noble name of Volodymyr. As long as I'm alive, I will call you Volodymyr." (Even as an adult, my name was "Vova" if I had been good, and "Volodka" if I'd been bad!)[6]

Throughout the rest of 1961 and most of 1962, I worked for General Motors on an assembly line, and they were very accommodating of my Army Reserves obligations. The 11th Special Forces Group conducted some excellent training. Our instructors knew demolition and weapons. I took some sub-courses on unconventional warfare and made great progress toward my full SF qualification. I was on track to eventually attend SF School at Fort Bragg and earn my SF MOS which would take about a year, in total. I had now completely committed myself to earning a slot on a Special Forces A-team.

---

6   Having not been born into it but rather having to choose to become a US citizen, Jakovenko read the Constitution in order to swear allegiance with full understanding. We require immigrants to swear allegiance. We require this of our military and of our civilian officials. We all are called to recite the Pledge of Allegiance. Wouldn't it be beneficial to require all our citizens (even those born here) to take this oath at least once in their life, maybe as they first register to vote?

[The SF Operational Detachment-Alpha team (an 'A-team') is the core fighting unit in Special Forces. I'll describe this in more detail later.]

More than ever before, I knew what I was meant to do. (But world events were about to disrupt my plans.)

I'm not going to share much in this book about my marriage. My high school girlfriend and I were married now, and we had two wonderful sons, John, born in 1958, and David, born in 1960. But by this time, we'd become separated. Out of respect for everyone, let me leave it at that.

So, by the fall of 1962, I was living as a bachelor, no wife, no kids, when the attention of the entire planet was turned to focus on the Cuban Missile Crisis. President Kennedy was telling the Russians to get their missiles out of Cuba. Here was something bigger than my problems.

In October, the entire US military was mobilizing for war. …and here I was, working overtime in the spray painting area at General Motors in Linden, New Jersey. It was about 3am, and everyone had their radios listening to the news while we tried to work. The Americans and Russians were eyeball to eyeball. It truly was a situation where the next announcement on the radio might be that an intercontinental ballistic missile had been launched.

I couldn't stand it. I decided right there that this was my last night working a civilian job.

This was the real beginning of my military career.

I yelled out, "I'm going to kick some Russian's ass!" Everyone working nearby thought I'd gone crazy. When my supervisor asked if needed to see the nurse, I told him,

"No, I need to get into this war. I need to get there before they give out the last of the rifles. If we are going to war, I'm not going to miss it."

As my shift ended, a new day was dawning. I drove to Jersey City and waited for the Army recruiter to open up. After a couple of hours sitting there, I saw a guy in uniform. I walked up to him and told him I *had* to join the Regular Army.

He asked if I'd had breakfast yet and I replied, "I've had a few gallons of coffee while I waited." As we walked into the diner across the street, he said that he imagined that this might be a good day for recruiting.

As I took off my coat, he noticed my Airborne tattoo. "You're prior service?"

"I spent two years in and have an honorable discharge. I'm currently in the 11th Special Forces Reserves at Camp Kilmer." I explained that I wanted to go in as soon as possible—today if I could—Active Duty Special Forces.

He told me to bring my DD214 and other forms from the Reserves. I came back in the afternoon. He looked at all my paperwork and said it would take a little time to get into a Special Forces unit. "But if you go into the Airborne Infantry, I could have you back in the Army in a week."

I asked, "Can you assign me to the 82nd Airborne Division at Fort Bragg?"

"Yes, if you go as an E-4, prior service."

I had to drop one stripe, but I could progress. It sounded pretty good. I signed up for a 3-year enlistment.

They expedited everything about my processing into the regular Army. I will always be grateful to my brothers in Bravo Company, 11th Special Forces Group (Airborne), Reserves, Camp Kilmer, in New Jersey. My time with them put me on a fast track. My orders were to report to the 82nd Airborne Infantry Division, Fort Bragg.

I gave my notice at GM. My military status got me out of the remainder of the lease on our apartment. Everything was going so smoothly. And as I was vacating my apartment…

…my wife calls.

"John and David really miss you."

The boys really miss me. Those are some of the most heart-filling words I'd ever heard. They really sank in deep.

"Their father really misses them. Make sure to tell them that."

She realizes that she and the kids need to come back to New Jersey and live together with me as a family.

"I've joined the full time, regular Army. I've got orders to Fort Bragg."

She indicated that she understood and was okay with that. On that emotional phone call, we talked through how we could live there and build a life. It would take a little time to make arrangements with the Army for them to move to Fort Bragg. I was not making much money, but I knew we could make this work. I was happy. I was getting my family back. We'd be an Army family. I'd be a career soldier, serving my country.

It was late now, but before we hung up, I made sure to talk to each of the boys. I told them I would be seeing them soon. I reminded them that I might have to go to war and

that they needed to be good for their mother and pray that
God would keep us all safe.

I arrived at Fort Bragg on October 31st, 1962, and reported to Charlie Company, 2nd Airborne Battle Group, 501st
Infantry, 82nd Airborne Division. Over the past two weeks,
they'd been living at the air strip, parachutes issued, ready
to load aircraft to jump into Cuba for the full-scale invasion
that President Kennedy was considering. I was chomping
at the bit to join them. The 501st was 'the Apaches' (also
nicknamed 'Geronimo') and had a great reputation, the finest you'd ever hope to go with into combat. Within a couple
of days, I was in among them in full combat gear. We were
in an isolation status, ready to jump into Cuba within a few
hours. I was where I was meant to be.

Images 29 and 30. The 501st Infantry Regiment, 'The Apaches.'
Everyone has heard of yelling "Geronimo!" as you jump.
That started in 1940 at Fort Benning, the year the US
Army first started training units in parachuting.

My first three days active duty were spent at the Pope Air Force Base flight line ready to board C-119s within minutes. The scenario was that if Soviet missiles were to launch, we'd load and take off immediately. We'd have only 30 minutes to be out of range of a nuclear explosion. Regardless of whether the Soviets launched, one option that the president wanted was a full-force invasion of Cuba with an overthrow of Fidel Castro.

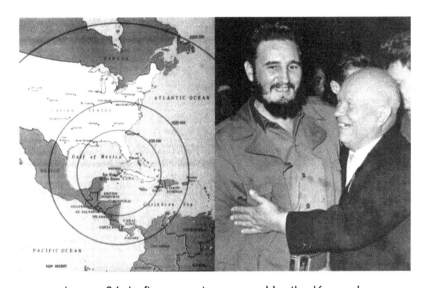

Image 31. Left, a secret map used by the Kennedy administration during the Cuban missile crisis. Right, Fidel Castro and Nikita Khrushchev at the United Nations in 1960. (AP Photo / Marty Lederhandler)

With our full gear, we had our meals brought to us in mermite cans (big serving pots in a thermos-type of container) served there in the hangar, and we slept right there too.

Image 32. Logistics wins wars. Mermite cans kept
the food hot for a serving line of soldiers.

By November 20th, 1962, the blockade and the Cuban
Missile Crisis were over, but we stayed on alert status. By
the end of November, our unit was stood down out of isolation. I was able to put my paperwork in to have my family
moved to North Carolina. In December, I found a small
house I could afford about eight miles from Fort Bragg. I
got a few days of leave and drove up to New Jersey to help
move my wife and boys. We settled in, with other young
military families as neighbors.

The 501st was the epitome of "STRAC" (skilled, tough,
ready around the clock) and our role was to be ready to
go anywhere in the world at a moment's notice. We had a
rigorous and dynamic training regimen with excellent field
training exercises.

In December of 1962, we ran the two-week 'Quick Kill' exercise which dropped us into the mountains of West Virginia to hunt down adversary units of the 7th Special Forces Group. We were successful in busting three of their guerilla teams. (Hey, it ain't braggin if it's true!) One was in a big barn, and we caught them while they slept.

In the summer of 1963, we had the three-week-long 'Swift Strike' exercise. In this exercise, we jumped in at the intersection of North Carolina, South Carolina, and Georgia, this time against the 5th Infantry Division.

Image 33. Swift Strike. The marshalling area at Camp Mackall Army Airfield about 20 miles southwest of Fort Bragg.

Image 34. Swift Strike. We jumped with full combat gear.

Our training schedule was fast-paced with a constant round of counter-insurgency training, live fire drills, range firing, and small unit tactics. Sometimes, only when the doors opened would we find out whether it was a night jump or a normal daytime jump. We were gone the better part of a year, which tends to cause strain on a family and a marriage.

I was assigned to 4th Platoon, Charlie Company, 1st Battalion, 504th Infantry Regiment and this is where Tyrone Adderly came into my life. [Later on, you'll read about how Tyrone ends up being flown to the White House to receive an award from... Well, that comes much later.] Tyrone was a "Spec 4" (Army Specialist E-4 rank) like me in 4th Platoon which was known for some reason as the "Goon Platoon." (Actually, I know the reason. It was the platoon where the commander would send the problem children. They were allowed to kick ass if the problem children acted up.) He was a super soldier with high standards. He passed all inspections. He never had to walk guard (extra hours on duty, usually some form of guard duty).

Image 35. Tyrone Adderly (photo taken in 1968)

Another super-soldier in 4th Platoon was Fred Domino. Fred had a college degree, but what was more useful was something he learned in high school. He was a competitive wrestler, and he had this wrestling hold called a 'Figure Four.' It was impossible to get out of (and very painful). I'm a big guy, yet I spent a lot of time in that Figure Four when Fred was trying to get a point across to me. I guess you can say I'm hardheaded, and sometimes had to be persuaded. Later he went to OCS (Officer Candidate School). We still keep in touch. After the Army, Fred went to law school and settled in California.

Tyrone and Fred had talked to their Platoon Sergeant, Sgt Bell, and recruited me to transfer to their platoon and I became a Fire Team Leader in my squad. Here, multiple soldiers had a professional impact on my military career. One was my company commander, 1st Lt Harrell and another was our company's First Sergeant (the commander's advisor concerning the morale of his enlisted troops), Sgt 1st Class Wemple. Sgt Wemple was both my mentor and my tormentor. He was the meanest First Sgt that ever served in the Army, but he took care of his soldiers. It was because of his persistence and leadership that I got my GED (Graduation Equivalency Diploma).

As a Fire Team Leader, I wore 'buck sergeant' stripes. We called it your 'acting jack' stripes; you got the privileges of a Sergeant (E-5, which is an NCO), but not the pay (still E-4). The company commander had that authority to make you an acting jack.

I was blessed to have a hell of a lot of excellent role models in our unit. I looked up to these men who led by example. Our unit was, at times, in the Immediate Response

Force (IRF) posture, the highest state of readiness similar to what you heard about in the Cuban Missile Crisis. During those times, we were not allowed to leave the post.

At Thanksgiving, 1963, we were on IRF status, locked down in the barracks, and they allowed wives and families to come spend the day with us. Lieutenant General William Westmoreland was the commander of our corps, XVIII Airborne Corps. He and his wife ate Thanksgiving dinner with us, and he surprised us by personally promoting some of us to E-5. Among those receiving the promotions were Tyrone Adderly and me. It was a proud moment for us.

But in my case, it was easy come and easy go. Within a month, I would be demoted to E-4 again. Here's why. I had some friends over, drinking and playing cards. We had a muster formation scheduled for the next morning and my alarm didn't go off. When I woke up and saw that I was late, I panicked. The fear of death was not as terrible as that of missing a muster formation. Trying to make it on time, I ran to my car, cranked the engine, put it in gear and screeched off. Coming through the streets of Fort Bragg, I saw a shortcut through the gas station. It wasn't a thoroughfare, but I was not going over any speed limit. Well, I must have woken up the MPs (Military Police) that were sitting there. They set it in their mind that they were going to pull me over. I tried to explain my plight of missing my muster formation, but there was a grudge between the 82nd Airborne Division guys and MPs so they were not very empathetic. (And it's possible that I called one of them, "Leg.")

They ask for my ID card. That's when I realize that, in my rush, I'd forgotten my ID. So, I give them my registration from the glove box. Leaning in the driver's side window, one of them asks me, "Have you been drinking?"

"Yeah, last night."

They walk back to check my rear license plate and then tell me, "You have a violation on your back window (pointing to the 82nd Airborne Division decal). We're gonna have to write you up for that."

I have no time for this intentional wise-ass delay. I'm getting hot under the collar. I get out of the car. The other MP doesn't like my attitude and he pokes me with his night stick.

..and then all hell breaks loose!

I'm honestly not sure who hits who first. They do their best to brain me with their night sticks. I knock one of them down and pin the other one to the car. It's known that if these MP's get you in handcuffs at this point in the fight, they will beat the hell out of you and claim you were resisting arrest. I am not going to be handcuffed. All the sudden, I hear, "Knock it off troops!"

It's two officers. I can see from their uniform that they're from the 82nd. I try to explain what happened and that I'm going to their formation. The MPs ask the officers not to interfere, but they tell them that we'll settle this after my formation.

I ride in the officers' car with the MPs following. At the parade ground, I hurry into formation. The MPs follow me out onto the parade field. The First Sergeant confronts them and tells the MPs in no uncertain terms not to interrupt his formation and to wait in his orderly room.

After getting everybody's version of what happened, the First Sergeant tells me that this is serious. The company commander will have to go to battle group headquarters to come to an agreement about what punishment he will give me.

A couple of days go by awaiting the decision. In the end, the battle group commander, a colonel, decided he would give me a battle group Article 15. That's bad, but at least they didn't go down the path of a court marital. As I stood for the punishment, I was read my rights and then I had the book thrown at me. I got demoted to E-4, reduced in pay, 30 days restricted to barracks and 14 days hard labor. I had no excuse for my actions. Still, I asked that I not be reduced in rank. That would hurt my family. The colonel stated that I should have thought of that before I fought with the MPs.

During my 30 days, I couldn't go home at night. From 6pm to 11pm, we dug ditches and spread gravel. And if they ran out of digging work, the NCO would find something else for us to do. He had us clean the battalion headquarters. I found out that the division commander's office was really nice with leather chairs and mahogany furniture. We had to clean and polish. We had to vacuum a certain way that left no lines.

I finished my punishment and got on with my life. I know that the colonel had to do what he felt was right.

When I got back from my punishment, my company commander turned my whole mindset around. He called me into his office and told me, "Sew your E-5 Sergeant stripes back on. I need you as acting jack."

This really had a profound impact on me. Here is a first lieutenant who knows his men, cares for them, and knows how to develop battlefield leaders. Sincerely appreciative, expecting nothing more, and with both of us knowing that he couldn't do anything further for me, I said, "With all due respect, sir, being an acting jack doesn't put food on the table." Still, his confidence in me meant a lot.

Only a few days later, he did something that truly changed the trajectory of my life. He offered me the one slot he had to Ranger School. He told me, "When you graduate, you'll get your E-5 back. Now, Ranger School is nine weeks and it's tough. Do you believe you can handle it?"

I said, "Yes sir. Thank you, sir. I won't let you down." As I left my commander's office, the meanest First Sergeant in the US Army growled at me, "If you don't make it through Ranger School, I am going to personally kick your ass."

15

US Army Ranger

1964

Ranger School is based at Fort Benning, and it is truly nine weeks of hell. I arrived in March 1964 and our class started with 130 students. The first three weeks consisted of map and compass land navigation, obstacle courses, reconnaissance patrolling, raids, hand to hand combat, and a long bayonet course with simulated targets (mannequins) which you attack at a full run. Each day begins with o-dark-thirty P.T. so that after you are good and tired, you hit the obstacle courses, rope climbing, and crossing logs.

You're always under the watchful, critical eyes of the instructors. They demand you give your all and still be ready to close upon and eliminate the enemy. This is the soul of a Ranger. Work as one. Never let another Ranger down. His life is your life. That spirit, that dedication, that commitment is instilled in every man who wears the Ranger tab.

We trained night and day, hour after hour. You think it will never end. You think you're always on the brink of washing out. Are my legs giving out? My feet are wrinkled like prunes. I've got to get my socks dry. Maybe get a

C-ration under a tree at whatever time of day your unit happens to pause (that's if you have a C-ration). Sleep is only
during cat naps, with never a chance to wash your clothes,
never a shower. Suddenly, they march you to the back of a
truck and you realize that the first three weeks are up and
now you're going to begin the second phase.

You get in the back of the deuce-and-a-half for a five-
hour trip to north Georgia. This next three weeks will be
in the mountains. You figure it'll be a good five hours of
rest. You're dead wrong. It's April, and with only a canvass
roof, it's like you're inside a refrigerator. You bump and
rattle for hours. But to be honest, these five hours are about
the best rest you've gotten over the past three weeks.

The truck stops. The forests, dramatic terrain, and river
gorges are beautiful. You are at the Ranger School mountain camp near Dahlonega, Georgia.

Your first expedition launches off, up into the woods. A
few hours hiking deep in the forest along a military crest
(tactically you don't want to be moving along a crest and
you don't want to be moving along a stream, so you move
along a line approximately one third the way down from
the crest of a ridge), you resign yourself to the fact that
you are chilled to the bone. It's colder than a well digger's
ass. Although you are moving, and the sun is out, you are
constantly in the shadows, never actually getting any sun
to warm you.

Every now and then you spot an old tar paper covered
shack across the valley, probably someone's hunting cabin.
You imagine there must be a potbelly stove (you see a pipe
sticking out) and probably some cots. There's probably a
nice dry wood floor in there and a table with chairs, warm

and dry. But you're hours from your destination. There are no other humans within miles. Oh, how you long for those old World War II barracks back at Fort Benning.

Here, you learn cold weather survival and mountain climbing with knot tying (which has life-or-death importance). You practice crossing obstacles, tactical operations in mountainous terrain, patrolling, day and night raids and ambushes.

You're thinking you're in good physical shape after the three weeks at Fort Benning. Then the mountains change your thinking. You have muscle aches in places you didn't know you had muscles. Three mountainous weeks. Cold, wet, sleepless, grueling…and you're being graded. I was obsessed. "Lord, please don't let me fail." I could not go back to my unit humiliated.

You have to reach deep down inside of you to pull it off. You're somewhere in the back of a 25-man combat patrol along an uncharted mountain slope. Your heavy eye lids are burning from sweat and dirt. You can't wipe them—your hands and arms are smeared with sweat and dirt and grass and sand. It's o-dark-thirty and you've been moving for hours. Up, up. It's foggy. (It's actually the haze of low-lying clouds.) Your mind is foggy but you're functional. You're doing your job and trusting that your leader is headed in the right direction. Then you hear a whisper. They're signaling you to come up front. As you pass, each guy is securing his zone of responsibility. The patrol grader tells you, "The patrol leader is dead from a moccasin bite. You're now the team leader." (A moment of panic hits you. 24 other guys are relying on you to lead them excellently, with life and limb on the line.)

Image 36. A class at Ranger School's mountain
phase at Dahlonega, Georgia

In the Rangers, how to assume leadership is a big
thing, and maybe the biggest thing. There must always be
a smooth transition to the next man in line to take charge
right down to the last man. When you're among Rangers,

you're among leaders. They know how to lead a unit and every one of them are watching you to see if you know how to lead a unit. The Ranger patrol grader was now going to be grading my every move, my every word, my every decision, and my every thought.

The famous line is, "What are you going to do now, Ranger?"

After a moment, you conquer your anxiety, and you start to function. You check security, you get a headcount, you locate your position on the map, and you pick your assistant leaders who will execute your orders. Sometimes, you don't get many hours—sometimes you get only a few minutes—before the moccasin bites you and the grader picks another leader. If that happens to you, most likely he's decided your grade for that portion of the patrol. When there's a pause, the Ranger patrol grader will come over to you to critique your performance and give you a pass or fail.

To this day, I remember how delicious the food tasted when we got back to the mountain Ranger camp. Seven days on patrol, we ate a couple of 'C-Rats' (Field Ration, Type C, good old C-Rations of World War II fame) and mostly stayed hungry.

The third and final phase was in Florida at Eglin AFB. Freezing in the mountains, we so looked forward to a warm May in Florida. After six hours on the road, the truck pulled to a stop on an old, abandoned bombing range. We were laid back absorbing as many rays of the sun as we possibly could.

Suddenly, the quiet of the mid-day is cracked by a jet fighter screaming down on our convoy. To us, it feels like he broke the sound barrier. At that same moment, we are surrounded by explosions and automatic fire. We scramble off the trucks. We've been ambushed by a well-positioned unit of 20 to 30. We take immediate action to counter the ambush. Hunkered down the best we can, we quickly establish leadership. The decision is made to charge a certain emplacement, running through chest-deep, ice-cold water to get to it.

From the moment we start, it's *not* going well. It is obvious to everyone that if this had been real, most of us would be dead or wounded.

Then we hear loud whistles. All firing stops. Someone on a Bullhorn says, "You are now at Auxiliary Field #7, Epler Field. Welcome to Amphibious and Jungle Training, Florida Ranger Camp." What a realistic simulation! We form up and, after head count, get back on the trucks. We arrive at our camp area and receive our orientation to Phase 3—'Swamp World' phase.

Here's how we received our orientation. Coming off the truck, we walked down into a pond in single file, walking on a two-foot wide 'bridge' of PSP. [Pierced Steel Planking is a material used by Construction Battalions to quickly build a military runway. They are metal planks with holes stamped ('pierced') into them every few feet so that they easily lock together.] But you can't see this bridge. It's submerged in the pond so that the water is up to your knees as you walk on it. "Do not step too far to the left or right. The water would be over your head." You must follow precisely behind the man in front of you.

We get to some rows of bleachers. Guess what? The bleachers also are submerged. "Take your seats, gentlemen." It's up to our chests. The sun is warm, but the swamp water is ice cold. The instructor, too, is chest deep in water with his laminated notes on a life preserver in front of him. The cold doesn't seem to bother him at all.

He barks out our scenario, "The Yellow River in the Far East has overflowed its banks by 1500 meters on both sides during a time when we will be conducting tactical operations in theater! You will learn to survive and operate tactically in its swamps and jungle terrain with little to no support from others. You will learn how to come ashore from the ocean aboard an LCU (Landing Craft, Utility). You will conduct small boat operations in the ocean, including capsizing boat drills. You will actually overturn your boat and all members will get back in and continue the mission." (If we'd thought hitting the beach was for Marines, think again.) "You will learn to cross water obstacles. And you will learn river navigation in small boats."

We were introduced to the Ranger camp mascot, a 14-foot alligator named 'One Eye.' "He's friendly as long as he's not hungry."

"Here, snakes are referred to as 'Mr. No Shoulders.' Moccasins/cottonmouths are plentiful. They thrive in the swamp water. They feed on fish, frogs, and Ranger students. But on dry land, the rattle snakes and copperheads thrive, and the deadliest one of all, the very colorful coral snake."

"Scorpions try to get up next to you to keep warm. They will sting you if you press against them." (In your mind you hear, "Is this worth it?" It's the voice of reason.)

We start our training in waterborne/riverine operations, jungle movement, and patrolling at night. For swamp crossings, we walk in, deeper and deeper. Your feet are always muddy, but now that cold, cold water immediately steals all warmth from your thighs. Knowing what's next, you press forward and receive that icy shock to your genitals. Deeper you go. When the surface scum and bugs are at chest level on the shortest Ranger in your team, safety rules require that you make a 'wet bridge.' A wet bridge is created with up to 120 feet of nylon rope. Two strong swimmers tie off the ends on trees and you hold on as you move through. Keep in mind, I'm not talking about crossing from one side of a river to the other. We're walking through a tree-filled swamp. There is no shore. You keep up this process until you get where the water level is safe again. And we're doing this at night, so after each 120-foot stretch, a head count is taken. (That first night, we did over 20 wet bridges before we got to shallow water.)

The water is inexplicably cold. This is crazy. We're in Florida in May and we're faced with hypothermia! Once out of the water, we tend to move at a fast pace. That warms us back up.

We are weeks on the rivers, on the Gulf waters, on the swamps, on the mush, walking jungle rope bridges. It seems like we're never simply on dry land in the sun. We are never able to dry out. We're never able to get clean, never able to eat a meal in any form of civilization.

We have to be mentally sharp though we're spending days getting sleep and food only sporadically at whatever time of day we happen to pause. We are constantly being sent on back-to-back patrols and being graded and brutally critiqued in the bug-infested, moss-covered jungle.

On one day, as we arrive at our objective, we are ambushed. As always, we have to mount the appropriate counterattack, and we end up hand-to-hand with the aggressors. In the melee, I hear my name being yelled. One of my Ranger buddies was being dragged off by the aggressors. I'm irate. I roar, "Let him go!" and charge at them like a wild man, and they (wisely) drop him. At that moment, my mind cleared as I heard numerous trucks blowing their horns loudly for a long time. It was the only time we heard that, and we all knew what it meant. The end of our time in Swamp World. It was over.

Hours later, as we arrived back at Fort Benning, cleaned up, and formed up for our graduation ceremony, it was such a proud day in my career. Only 65 had made it to the end.

I received orders indicating my Ranger tab and specifying that I was to be promoted to E-5/Sergeant.

16

Skills

1964

When I got back to my unit at Fort Bragg in late May 1964, our name had changed. We were now the 3rd Battalion of the 325th Infantry Regiment. I was assigned as the Squad Leader for 2nd Squad. A Squad Leader's job is never done. Our 44-man platoon was kept together in one barracks building. We had cleaning responsibilities and if your areas didn't pass inspection, then a G.I. party was held in your honor, which meant you cleaned again. A Squad Leader worked long hours. Sometimes you didn't get home until 9pm, so it made family life hard throughout the rest of 1964 and most of 1965. I admit that.

The squad is the basic element in the Infantry. Your leadership has a direct impact on the soldiers and the mission. It's the leadership position that has eyeball contact. In a close quarters combat situation, these men's lives depend on each other. No short cuts can be taken. There will be no excuses. Mistakes and deficiencies must be revealed in training. We must hone our skills and capabilities for that day when we find ourselves on the battlefield.

Let me tell you a story that had a tragic ending. This is my version, and I offer it with a personal perspective. In October of 1964, the 82nd Airborne Division was tasked to provide the opposing forces to test and evaluate a new approach to land warfare called the "Air Mobile" concept. When bringing a warfighting body into a theater, the quicker you can rally and organize, the sooner you can concentrate your firepower and control the area. In air mobile, rather than inserting a large unit by parachute, they would be inserted by a convoy of helicopters. The unit was the 11th Air Assault Division (Test) and it had been activated only a year and a half prior to this test.

The exercise was called "Air Assault II" and it was conducted in an area sprawling across North Carolina and South Carolina. We made a mass tactical parachute drop into South Carolina. We assembled and moved to our staging area within 24 hours. All units, friendly and aggressor, had field grade officers and senior noncommissioned officers attached as graders and umpires. Anytime contact was made, the graders would observe the simulated battle and decide the outcome of that battle, documenting and reporting up the chain. The battlefield techniques were assessed. Casualties were estimated. This had the potential to change the modern battlefield. This was light, lethal infantry, a cavalry that uses helicopters instead of horses. It would also be very expensive, using hundreds of helicopters in battle to outfit a 10,000-man division.

Many in the Pentagon were backing this approach, so there was an unhealthy pressure to validate the concept. The leadership in the 11th Air Assault Division was good, but it appeared that they needed more training and more time to work together. We saw some tactical problems, and they needed to modify their combat techniques.

My unit was occupying high ground, dug in well, with good fields of fire. Knowing that helicopters couldn't land properly on rocks, we had all the open fields covered. We heard them coming and it was an awesome site. As a matter of fact, it was frightening. They were on us within seconds of us hearing them. First, their gunships were overhead at tree top level. Then came the mass formations of helicopters. The troops kept coming. As they dismounted to the LZ (Landing Zone), immediately our company engaged them. We were brutal. We had cover and concealment, and they were now on foot, in the open, trying to maneuver toward us. We fired M60 and M16 machine guns and 40mm M79 grenade launchers. We started firing mortars (simulated) and called in artillery on the LZ. Over the next few hours, we completely decimated them.

All this was being documented by the umpires attached to us. The Air Cavalry (the 11th Air Assault Division) continued its assault, so we executed our FPF (Final Protective Fire). Finally, the umpires stopped the battle. The mountains quickly became peaceful again. The leadership of both units received their critique and provided their reports. Most of us watched the umpires and field commanders, imagining what was being said. It had been a long day.

Our company commander came back. He was really upset. He briefed his Platoon leaders who, in turn, briefed us. The umpires declared that the Air Cav won this battle. That was absurd. They had landed in our kill zone and we annihilated them. Everyone was upset. There was no time to complain, and no one to complain to. It was time to move to our objective. It took half the night to get there. We knew the deck was stacked in favor of the Air Cav. The exercise was called 'Air Assault II,' not 'Airborne Infantry II.' It was nothing but whitewash. The Pentagon wanted this unit validated for combat. Apparently, even some of the umpires disagreed. But the approval was sent up the chain.

[Now here's the tragedy. One year later, this same unit was rushed into its first real combat, and they lost 237 Americans. The place was the Ia Drang valley in South Vietnam, November 14th -20th, 1965. It's chronicled in the sad movie *We Were Soldiers*. I always wondered how those high-ranking leaders felt about the false validation that led to these unacceptable losses in a single battle.][7]

The 82nd Airborne Division continued to conduct normal training, including a blue-chip demonstration conducted yearly to show its combat capabilities to high-ranking officials and foreign dignitaries. Sometimes it would be a mass tactical drop of troops and heavy equipment at Fort Bragg's Sicily drop zone. This always seemed like we were spending millions of dollars trying to impress someone who didn't have a clue whether this would really mean anything

---

7   Jakovenko used this lesson to teach other soldiers over the years. An honest assessment, acknowledging poor performance and not sugar-coating the results is a Skill that falls under the category of Science. The facts and the data are what they are. In the last chapter, "Soldiers," we summarize the degree to which 'Skills' is an Art and the degree to which it is a Science. We must acknowledge the data and not explain away cold hard facts.

in actual combat. Most of us called it a dog and pony show, wasting the time and money that should have been spent on real training or on new equipment and weapons we could really use.

In fact, our Latin American neighbor, the Dominican Republic, was in real turmoil, at risk of becoming a communist state. We could see that we really needed to be preparing for that.

17

Combat Experience

1965

On April 26ᵗʰ, 1965, we were once again placed on alert, Defense Condition 3. Two battalions of our division were to live at the hangars at Pope AFB, IRF status. They were the 1/505ᵗʰ (1ˢᵗ Battalion of the 505ᵗʰ Regiment) and 1/508ᵗʰ. (The way to say this is "The 1ˢᵗ of the 505ᵗʰ" and "The 1ˢᵗ of the 508ᵗʰ.") Full combat gear and parachutes. Sleep on the floor with your kit bag for a pillow. Meals from mermite cans. C-130s were the new aircraft for Parachute Infantry Regiments. There was a plan named Operation Power Pack for evacuating Americans from the Dominican Republic and ending the civil war. On April 25ᵗʰ, President Johnson had given the authorization for the commanders to proceed with executing the plan.

One version had us flying to a forward staging airfield on nearby Puerto Rico and then parachuting, mass tactical, into San Isidro Airfield, eight miles east of Santo Domingo. But it was decided that parachuting in might seem too aggressive, inflaming the local populace, who were already on pins and needles. General Earle Wheeler, Chairman of the Joint Chiefs of Staff, instructed the commanders to go direct, landing us in our C-130s at San Isidro Airfield. Just after sundown on April 29th, the C-130s departed Pope AFB and flew directly to San Isidro Airfield. They landed just after midnight on Friday morning, April 30th, 1965. It took a lot of C-130s to take these first 2,200 soldiers into the Dominican Republic. Per the plan's timing, a battalion of Marines were helicoptered into Haina (a coastal town 10 miles southwest of Santo Domingo) the day prior from the USS *Boxer*.

Image 37. The Dominican Republic

Our four battalions of the 325th Infantry of the 2nd Brigade, 82nd Airborne, each with about 1,000 men, were told to be on alert at home, equipment ready for deployment. When the phone rang on Sunday morning, May 2nd, my Platoon leader told me "Power Pack," which was the code word to report for deployment. You had to be at the airfield within 30 minutes, so you can only briefly say your goodbyes. Your family knows you are going to war. They see the news. It's hard to describe how you can leave your family, not knowing when or if you would be coming back. But this is what you've trained for. This is what your country requires. This is the Immediate Response Force ops tempo of a Parachute Infantry Regiment. We lived by 'STRAC.' When America thunders, the 82nd Airborne is its fateful lighting. We are the terrible swift sword and we have been loosed.

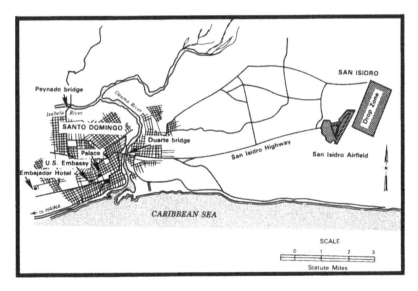

Image 38. Santo Domingo, the capital of the Dominican Republic.

Image 39. Honduran soldiers of the Inter-American Peace Force
arrive at San Isidro Airport in the Dominican Republic, 1965.

When our C-130 landed at San Isidro Airfield that
Sunday, we were briefed on our first mission tasks. We
were to secure and defend the eastern bank of the Ozama
River, north of Duarte Bridge (#1 in Image 40). Within the
day, we were in place, but snipers and infiltrators on both
sides of the river engaged us immediately. Throughout the
following days, there was no way to identify who was of
which faction. They could be of…

A.) The democratically elected President Bosch [elect-
ed in 1963 and overthrown in 1963] who didn't
want the US military there,

B.) The military-installed President Reid [an anti-
communist installed in 1963 by General Wessin y
Wessin] who welcomed the US presence,

C.) The communist DRP Dominican Revolutionary Party, or

D.) Other smaller factions of armed civilians.

The force directly hostile to us numbered approximately 1,500 regular army (which had been orchestrated to stage a coup to re-instate Bosch) and 5,000 armed civilians (armed by the military defectors supporting Bosch and the communist party DRP). Among the hostile forces were also many of the Dominican Navy's frogmen and large numbers of police officers.

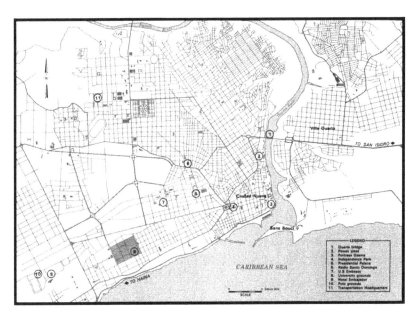

Image 40. Santo Domingo (See the expanded Legend below.)

Legend for Image 40:
1. Duarte Bridge
2. Power Plant
3. Fortress Ozama

4. Independence Park
5. The Presidential Palace
6. Radio Santo Domingo
7. US Embassy
8. University Grounds
9. The Hotel Embajador
10. The Polo Grounds
11. Transportation Headquarters

No matter who you were with, it became very unhealthy for anyone to use boats to fire on Americans. We would immediately introduce them to our M40 106mm Recoilless Rifle. This weapon is powerful enough to destroy tanks. Here's how it works. There are perforations in the massive shell casing (see the photo below) and chambers that direct much of the blast backward. As the gunpowder detonates, about half of the blast goes backwards and the other half forward to push the huge 22-lb projectile down the rifled barrel. Sir Isaac Newton would be proud, but the real advantage of using these equal-and-opposite forces is the weight. Because of the way the barrel manages the pressures, the walls of the barrel can be much thinner. So, instead of weighing 2,000 lbs, this weapon weighs only 500 lbs, which means that four guys with a jeep can set this gun up anywhere in just a few minutes.

As a courtesy to our victims, this weapon provides the customer a preliminary sound that would be an indication that they should immediately abandon ship. For the M40, the Army developed a 'spotting shot' to show you exactly where your projectile is going to hit. You see, the M40 is loud, and with all the back blast, the M40 puts out a clear visual of your location, which means that you need to hit your target on the first shot. That spotting shot is a .50 cal round fired from a .50 cal spotting gun mounted, precisely aligned, along the top of your M40 (you can see it in the photo below). You'd aim using a specially mounted optical sight and when you fire the .50 cal, you'd see the distinctive explosion of the .50 cal round's spotter charge (like a tracer round). You use that to adjust your aim for the M40.

The next sound is the main gun. If the spotting round indicates that your current aimpoint is good, the enemy will be hearing the main gun fire only two or three seconds later. That main gun round will be breaking the enemy river boat in half.

Image 41. An M40 106mm Recoilless Rifle. See the holes that direct much of the blast backward to reduce the recoil. Note that one soldier is aiming the .50 caliber 'aiming round' rifle mounted on top of the barrel.

Small arms fire was constantly in the air. This was urban warfare.

[By the end of this, 13 of our brothers in the 82nd Airborne are killed in action, 44 Americans die in the fighting, overall, and 283 are wounded.]

We were briefed on identifying friendly soldiers versus enemy soldiers. One characteristic was the way they wore their hats. The friendlies would typically wear their hats with the bill to the rear; the enemy bill would more likely be toward the front. (But honestly, we couldn't depend on how anyone wore their hat!)

Our next mission was to secure a power plant that was on the river's west bank (#2 in the diagram above). We quickly took it and then my squad (2nd Squad) was assigned to defend the side facing the river. Our main threat was enemy frogmen coming up out of the river. There were plenty of Dominican Navy (who had joined forces with the revolutionaries) that had been taught by American SEALs over the years. If we saw bubbles in the river, we wouldn't waste much time thinking about it. We would just toss a couple of grenades in the water and see who floats up.

Sgt Tyrone Adderly's squad (1st Squad) had a very dangerous job. They were on the roof of the power plant. In the daytime they couldn't move without being shot at by snipers; only at night could they sit up.

Many times, I grabbed a couple of cases of C-Rations and took them to the roof. Tyrone was a great Squad Leader; his men came first. As he would cycle guys up to the roof for the following watch, I saw that he personally stayed up there. He wouldn't bring a replacement for himself. In his mind, he knew the enemy better than anyone else in his squad. Someone might get killed up there. Our friendship was sealed under fire. My respect for him was immense even at that early date (and there is more to come about Adderly).

Image 42. I'm proudly pointing to my Combat Infantryman Badge with my squad in the Dominican Republic, 1965.

My squad received a combat patrol mission to destroy a boat that intel suspected of carrying arms and ammunition. My squad included my RTO (Radio Telephone Operator), two fire team leaders (fire team Alpha and fire team Bravo) carrying M16s, two M79s (one for each team), four other men with M16s (two on each team), and an M60 (attached). We proceeded up the west bank of the Ozama River about a

¼ mile. At this point, we departed the Friendly Front Lines (FFL). We patrolled about a ½ mile further upriver at which point we got to the suspicious boat. It was a traditional boat for hauling medium-sized loads along the river and it was half-sunk. We boarded it and looked in the hold. It was empty. After less than five minutes surveying and verifying that this was the suspected boat, we turned and headed back. We had walked about 500 hundred yards when…

…the area explodes with gunfire!

It's an ambush. (This is where Ranger School pays for itself. *"So what are you gonna do now, Ranger?"*) We work like one body. We suppress the enemy's fire, even in ambush. The enemy fire is coming from the windows of the buildings along the river. So, we are caught between those buildings and the river. The riverbank is not steep, and there's nothing to hide behind, so all of us immediately return fire. A squad has a helluva lot of firepower, and especially having our M79s and M60, we are able to keep a lot of heads down. The enemy seems to be firing semi-automatic from just about every building and every window and every rooftop. We're spread out and I'm yelling to the point man, "Go, Go, Go!" We're moving fast along the dirt road that runs along the bank. From concealed positions, every building sent fire our way, including the historic "Columbus House." As we move, we are surprised to suddenly see a guy opening a door and it is only one second later that we've put him down. We only have 300 yards to go before we reach the sandbags of the FFL. We communicate our presence on the radio as we approached the FFL but the 82nd Airborne guys at the FFL were already quite aware of which ones were us and were supporting us from their positions. We were blessed that our nation saw fit to provide us with superior firepower. One lesson for me was the benefit of the M60 attached.

Over the next few days, we were assigned to man checkpoints between the loyalist and rebel zones. Basically, the term 'loyalist' means "loyal to President Reid," who had been the president since the military installed him in 1963. The term 'rebel' really just means "any of the other groups" (all of the political groups that wanted Reid removed.)

The barbed wire and checkpoints were set up to control who goes into the downtown, the seat of business and government. A curfew of 6pm was declared. Once we closed the "Free Zone," the checkpoint would not open again until 6am. I hated this, because often it kept families apart for the night. But I followed orders.

Image 43. American troops of the 82nd Airborne Division issue food and water to civilians, on May 5, 1965, in Santo Domingo during the civil war.

Tyrone and his squad were very strict on this. One time, I was visiting him and there were only a few minutes remaining before 6pm. We heard this pitiful voice yelling his heart out. It was an old man, just now arriving, way back in the line. He was on a bicycle with a cart attached, full of bananas. He could see that he wouldn't make it before the 6pm closure. As Tyrone started to close the barb wire, he pleaded, saying he worked hard all day. Strict Sgt Tyrone Adderly turned his back. The old man started to cry. There was a crowd gathered there who also wanted to cross. This was a heart-breaking dilemma. Suddenly, to my surprise, Tyrone opened the wire just enough to let the old man in. The others would have to wait until morning. (I would sometimes let people in after curfew, especially women, children, and old people. I knew I could get in trouble, but something in me really connected with the plight of these people at the checkpoint. I, too, had lived behind barbed wire, as a child. I closely considered each case and would never put any of our soldiers in danger by my decisions.)

By May 5th, a deal was brokered to cease hostilities. The Organization of American States would gradually assume all peacekeeping duties. But this did not stop all sniper fire and there were some small-scale firefights yet to come. [Note: later, on June 15th, the rebels would mount one more offensive. Five American servicemen were killed in that fighting.]

We expanded the free zone. We were now deep into what had recently been held by our enemies. We in 2nd Squad occupied the roof of a two-story house as an overwatch. You never knew who among the civilians might be a sniper. Tyrone's squad occupied its street level. We regularly received sniper fire. Hit-and-runs by the rebels were common. They were so brief that we only responded to more substantial enemy assaults. Per the rules of engagement, most sniper fire wasn't justification enough for us to go root them out. From our rooftop vantage, one of our roles was to give supporting fire to Tyrone's squad with our .50 cal machine gun. We had our area under control.

Our building started to become a tourist attraction for visiting, high-ranking government officials. Tyrone started having to give briefings to these dignitaries. His soldiers were breaking starch (putting on clean uniforms) sometimes three times a day. 2nd Squad, in contrast, was breaking sweat!

We were notified that we would be making the final push outward to occupy the remaining portions of the city. Since we, Charlie Company, were the attacking company, we were required to brief some high-ranking officers, including a general. First, Tyrone and his squad put on an outstanding briefing. It was about 30 minutes long, which was perfect. They used a sand table to create a terrain model showing the sequences of fire and movement. It was the best briefing I had ever seen. He even had match sticks in the sand to bring attention to important events in the sequence. For instance, at the point where his squad was to blow a hole in the wall for the rest of us, he lit the matches, resulting in a lot of oohs and ahhs. The general was very impressed.

Then it was my turn.

I had no notes, no model, no charts. Just a map. I used my hand and pointed to our location and said, "We are here." Then I took my palm and moved it in the direction of the attack. I said, "2nd Squad will sweep along this street, clearing the buildings of enemy resistance and setting up our defensive position. We'll coordinate our defense with other squads and be prepared for counter attacks."

The awkward silence was broken by the general asking me to show him my axis of attack. I again employed my riveting, expert, hand gesturing. My whole briefing was about 10 minutes. I could sense that, inside his mind, Tyrone was shaking his head and chuckling.

"That'll probably work," said the general.

(From then on, I used Tyrone's briefing techniques.)

[A note for military professionals. The planning is important, deadly serious. Throughout my career, I used Tyrone's briefing techniques and always gave Tyrone the credit for showing me just how well a briefing should be given. In universities (training Army ROTC cadets), in large training exercises (ramping up for deployments), and in actual combat zones, we need to set this standard of professionalism. I emphasize that the mission is to get everyone back safe. You know that the first contact with the enemy can change your situation dramatically, therefore you empower dynamic decision-making and ensure that your team knows they can adapt the plan as needed. Well-trained, well-briefed, disciplined soldiers using good movement techniques, operational security, and cover and concealment will accomplish the mission.]

It was time to prepare for the battle. I went back and talked to my squad. It was evening, and we'd launch our mission the next morning. I hoped to assure them that we're all ready for this. I could sense that as a team, we were feeling some nerves. Troops don't like to show it. We keep it inside, but we all had the same thoughts, and we knew each other well, and trusted each other. After my talk, my guys were saying, "It's ass-kicking time." In the morning, we reported at 0400, ready to move out. In our final brief, Charlie Company commander's intel staff emphasized the ROE (rules of engagement). We were not to shoot unless we received fire. These city blocks included residences. These civilians were caught in the middle of a civil war. We did not want to harm anyone except those who would be foolish enough to engage us with hostile fire. This is not a free fire zone. Caution and judgment are required. There were women and children.

We moved out silently to our Line of Departure (LOD) and crossed the final FFL. It was 0415 as we launched. This was pretty much the last square mile held by the rebels. We moved cautiously, scanning all buildings and alleys, always expecting a booby trap or an ambush. The darkness held the coolness of the morning, but the humidity promised a muggy day when the sun would rise.

After a few blocks, maybe a ¼ mile, the sky is still black. In the humid, slightly foggy, pre-dawn, noises seem to carry further with more clarity. Still, we encounter no enemy resistance. Our 16 men (Tyrone's eight and my squad's eight) are moving in, around, and among each building as we've progressed about four blocks so far. So quiet. Dogs barking now and then. There is the quiet hum of the motor of our 'mules' (a four-wheeled utility vehicle, narrower than a jeep). We are using our mules to carry our extra ammo, water, and the equipment we'll need to set up a new checkpoint once we secure the blocks within our objective.

Image 44. A 'Mule' used by marines.

For this mission, our mule has a 106mm Recoilless Rifle mounted on it. Each of us is watching each window on each floor on each building. Then, we think we hear a heavier noise like armored tanks, tracking along a street nearby. We move more cautiously now, never knowing what we might see around the next street corner.

As dark turns to dawn, we reach our objective and set up our defensive positions with strong firing lanes looking down each street of the intersection. The Recoilless Rifle covers all main streets. We have advanced the "Free Zone" about one mile. We communicate our situation and, within a half-hour of us arriving, we are reinforced with American tanks on streets parallel to ours. They set up to cover the intersections to our left and right. We use the equipment we've brought on our mules (barbed wire, etc.) to establish our check point. The tank units do likewise on their streets nearby. This rebel zone is now under American control. When the citizens of Santo Domingo awake, they are surprised to see American troops in control of the entire city. I have not heard one shot fired, and many civilians are spared being hurt by a firefight in their neighborhoods.

Dead bodies were lying in the streets. For the coming days, we pacified the area with a methodical slate of missions assigned to us searching for snipers and weapons. The Red Cross begins the long process of safely picking up those bodies, at times being fired upon.

In the remaining weeks of May, our battalion carried out an energetic civic action program. We distributed food to thousands of civilians. We provided medical assistance in the neighborhoods.

Problems would sometimes arise during the food distribution. In our civic action food mission, we only had enough to feed 500 people. But thousands would line up, some starting to queue up the day before. When family members are going hungry, people will do just about anything. (I experienced that in the Displaced Persons camps.) We had to line up an infantry platoon and make it clear that we would not tolerate a riot. There was just about no way to win the hearts and minds of the people. Some troops would add to the problem by letting young pretty women go to the front of the line, while others had waited there all night. When I saw this, I would move those girls back to the end of the line and discipline the troops.

Some nights you could hear gunfire. We had the Dominican Army MPs patrolling the streets with US Army MPs in support. Morale among us infantrymen was actually pretty high, and we were ready to engage, but our rules were that when there was a problem, we had to report it to higher headquarters, and they would task the civilian police to respond first. We were there to help the civilian authorities only if problems escalated.

And then came the long, slow process of clean up. Garbage was being dumped in the streets. Sanitation seemed non-existent. Rats and flies were everywhere. Even though we were helping the civilians, hate and "Yankee go home" was everywhere. To us, it felt like the locals wouldn't help clean up the tons of garbage in their own streets. They just kept dumping more. The infantry was detailed to clean up the area, so we were issued shovels and brooms. This was the gratitude bestowed upon the American soldiers for bringing an end to a conflict that had been costing so many lives. We dutifully cleaned up the blocks in our area and put 55-gallon drums along the streets for the locals to put their garbage in and we began a daily pick up of those 55-gallon drums. There was a kind of arrogant resistance. Very often, we would find that some civilians would not put the garbage in the drums and would instead dump it in the streets to cause more work for us.

Anger among the troops was rising and many complaints were filed up the chain of command. The troops' complaints fell on deaf ears. In fact, the high-level briefings were stating that the civilians were complying with cleanup activities, a total lie.

One morning, as we were standing there, a woman came out and dumped garbage on the street around the drum. My soldiers were disgusted and angry. They yelled curse words down the street at the Dominicans. One soldier came over to me and said, "This is bullshit!" I was their leader. My first responsibility was to take care of them. I called two of my men over. "Scoop up a shovel full of garbage and follow me." I went up to the door where the woman disappeared and banged on the door with my M16. The door opened slightly. She saw me standing there and tried to slam it shut. I jammed my foot in, holding the door open. I told the two soldiers to pour the garbage inside the house. They hesitated. I repeated the order. I then told them to go get two more shovels of garbage and add to this pile inside the front door. I left a couple of my squad members there to make sure they didn't throw the garbage onto the street again. We then went to the next house. Still irate, but now with a practical method, I asked if anyone spoke English. The man indicated that he spoke some English. I explained in no uncertain terms that the people of this neighborhood will help clean up their street. I told them, "People's garbage will go in the 55-gal drums, or I will put it in their house. This will be the last day Americans are going to shovel garbage."

From that time on, we only had a couple of times that we had to perform this demonstration again. Soon, the garbage was consistently put in the drums.

It was now mid-June. There were still Dominicans who hated Americans no matter what we did for them, but many really appreciated us. In our sector, we had some gunfire at night, but no casualties.

One night around 0200, Sgt Adderly and I were patrolling our neighborhoods. We were talking about plans for returning to the US. All of a sudden, there was machine gun fire right nearby. We leapt over a nearby four-foot stone wall, took cover, and prepared to return fire.

But everything immediately became deadly quiet.

We could see smoke and smell cordite. There was no further sound.

Sgt Adderly had taken about six inches of skin down to the bone on his shin from diving over that wall. We called in the incident. We searched the area but could not find anything or anyone. We never did find out who fired. But it's the kind of thing you don't forget. That was life in Santo Domingo in 1965.

One of the biggest problems we had was on Sunday nights. The Dominicans in our sector would sit on their porches and listen to music, drinking, and dancing. It was a block party atmosphere. Young men would try and impress the ladies. Fights would break out. Add into the mix American patrols who would try and break up the fights and soon you'd have a riot—against the Americans! "Yankee go home!" So, what Adderly and I did was to stop the fight before it ever happened. He and I would carry these nice, light, 4-foot broom handles made of pine. When a couple of guys would start to scuffle, we'd go ahead and crack them with the broom handle to get their attention. It wouldn't cause physical harm. It would just sting. We'd tell them, "Have a good time, but don't fight." Then, we would always make them shake hands. Most of the time, it worked.

We looked forward to going home to America. A little bit of America came to us. It was the USO show with Bob Hope and the beautiful ladies. As a young recruit in 1958, there was a saying. "If you stay in for a 20-year career, you're guaranteed a CIB (Combat Infantryman Badge) and a Bob Hope show." To Bob Hope, I say, "Thanks for the Memories." It was definitely a morale boost.

We had a good commander for the 82nd Airborne, Major General Robert York, from Birmingham, Alabama. He was an outstanding leader, but he was reassigned before the end of our tour. We thought the reason must be political and that the American ambassador must have had a hand in it. General York cared about his paratroopers and told the rebels, "If you fire on my troops, you will suffer the consequences." We were by now a peacekeeping force, a buffer of blocks between the sector of the city that had the government buildings and the sector of the city in which the rebel organizations could hold their meetings while negotiations took place. In late June, the rebel sector—the southeast part of town called 'Ciudad Nueva'—was packed with people celebrating political rallies. Gunmen in the crowd were spoiling for a fight after being stirred up by Castro's communists. Gunfire started being directed toward us. The paratroopers obeyed their orders and held their fire.

After plenty of patience, the command was given that we could return fire. Both sides poured a heavy volume of small arms fire. Then the rebels tried to penetrate our lines with a tank. As it opened fire, we engaged it mercilessly with our 106mm Recoilless Rifles. The tank attack was short lived, leaving a tangled, burning hulk. The word was passed to advance. Chomping at the bit, our attack was quick and decisive. The paratroopers moved through the back yards and between buildings, avoiding main streets. Over this short time, some paratroopers had moved over 30 blocks and were even occupying a rebel headquarters building. This is where the political negotiators objected. They made the paratroopers withdraw all the way back to the original assigned defensive positions in the buffer zone.

We heard that General York had told the ambassador not to give back the blocks in the rebel area that had been taken. So, we assumed that General York was reassigned because of his authorizing the advance. It was a sad day for the 82nd Airborne Division to say farewell to its commander. We later found that his new assignment was to command the Infantry School at Fort Benning as of July 1965. Two years later, he received his third star and was given command of the XVIII Airborne Corps at Fort Bragg.

In October 1965, we were told that we were deploying back to Fort Bragg. Another battalion of the 504th Infantry would be replacing us in a few days. Happy to be going home, we soon had our equipment packed. Now came the point at which they required us to lock our M16s in rifle racks. The Squad Leaders protested. It felt too soon. We'd be sitting ducks if some die-hard rebel wanted to hit us in the couple of days remaining. Against our protests, they made us turn in our ammo. The only people who would keep their ammo were the guards. They were posted around our barracks. On the last night, most of us were dreaming about going home in the morning. Some were up late playing cards. All of a sudden, automatic gunfire broke out **_inside_** our building. We hit the floor. We tried to get to our weapons, to no avail. One of the young troops in our brigade had gotten drunk and was not ready for his assigned shift on guard duty. His Squad Leader verbally reprimanded him. The young soldier got his M16 and ammo, loaded a 20-round magazine, and put the weapon on automatic. He then confronted the Squad Leader.

The Squad Leader was packing his bags to deploy back to Fort Bragg. He would soon see his wife and children after being gone for almost seven months. The Squad Leader lunged across his bunk in an effort to disarm to the soldier but was hit with automatic fire at point blank range. He died instantly.

It was such a sad ending for the men of "Charging Charlie." We were Charlie Company, 3rd Battalion (3/325th Infantry), 2nd Brigade, 82nd Airborne Division. 1st Platoon, 2nd Squad was my team. Here we went through some of the heaviest fighting and never lost a man, and then, on the night before going home, a man is killed by one of our own.

Among Tyrone's squad and my squad, none were wounded or killed in the Dominican Republic. I would always say to Tyrone, "I'll watch your back. You watch mine." We were such good buddies that everyone used to say we were twins. Sgt 1st Class Wemple, our First Sergeant, was the one who started calling us "the salt and pepper twins."

The next morning, we loaded onto a C-130. That afternoon we landed at the 'Green Ramp' at Pope AFB, the same place we deployed from six months earlier. Buses took us back to our division area and we started to unpack, securing our weapons and equipment. We Squad Leaders accounted for all sensitive and high dollar equipment and turned them into the arms room and the supply room. We were then briefed about safety. ("Be careful and take it easy as you acclimate back into stateside society and home life.") We were given a few days off.

Before being dismissed, we were told there would be an inspection when we came back. Higher headquarters wanted us all to sew the 82nd Airborne Division patch on our right shoulder. They explained that this represented being in combat with the 82nd. Normally, we wore the 82nd Airborne Division patch on our left shoulder. We'd wear two 82nd Airborne Division patches, one on each shoulder.

The only person I ever saw with an 82nd Airborne Division patch on each shoulder was a Master Sergeant Sylvis. He had served with the 82nd in a weapons platoon in WWII. He had three or four combat jumps with them, which is *extremely* rare. (Today, there is basically no one in the US Army with multiple combat jumps.)

Beyond this, we were told to sew on our Combat Infantryman Badge (CIB). The message was clear. The commanders wanted to show that we had combat experience. Now, a lot of us had a little frustration about these CIBs. We saw that some soldiers were awarded it even though they were not actually there. Even though they never left Fort Bragg, they were still carried on the company roster, which had not been updated to show the accurate list.

Let me pause here to tell you about a truly exemplary soldier in our unit. Staff Sgt Bernie Newman had an Expert Infantryman Badge (EIB). It's about the most prestigious award an infantryman can achieve in peacetime.

[The first time I had tried for it was in 1963 with the 501st. I failed. Out of our battle group (which was around 1,500 men), only twelve were awarded. I failed only one station, NBC (Nuclear, Biological, & Chemical Warfare). When the instructor yelled, "Gas!" you had to mask up and give yourself an epinephrine injection for nerve gas. (For training, it's simply sugar water.) You stick it in your thigh, fully depress the syringe's plunger, and then give it to the instructor so that he can judge whether the tube is empty. I had about one drop still in it, and he failed me.]

We had a ceremony to award the CIBs. Well, we all knew who was on the orders to receive the CIB and Staff Sgt Newman wasn't thrilled to be awarded a CIB that was cheapened by giving it to those who never deployed and had never seen any combat. I couldn't see it from where I was, but I heard that when they were pinning on, Sgt Newman did an about face and told them to pin it on his back. Sgt Newman was a walking encyclopedia, a mentor for me, and one of the best noncommissioned officers I ever met. Some died earning that CIB. Others just got it for being listed on a sheet of paper. Feelings were strong, but nobody felt there was any use in arguing about it. Everyone wanted to start their well-deserved time off after a job well done in the Dominican Republic.[8]

---

8   In the final chapter, "Soldiers," we propose an objective definition of what constitutes "Combat Experience."

18

Who Will Go

1965

Now it was November 1965. We were back at Fort Bragg, doing post support. Vietnam was heating up. Consider this comparison. By May 17th of 1965, we had 23,000 troops in the Dominican Republic. That's the number of troops we had in Vietnam in 1964. But now, in November of 1965, Vietnam had ballooned to 184,000 US troops. A country unknown to average Americans had now become the center of the news. There were daily casualty reports from Vietnam. Among the many political and military factions, the communists were making the largest gains. It seemed like every day everyone was on the offensive. Developments in Southeast Asia were moving fast.

On Thursday morning, November 18th, most of us in 1st Platoon (about 30 of us) were on detail at the rigger shed, shaking our parachutes and untangling suspension lines. Someone passing through said that they'd just heard on the news that the 1st Air Cavalry Division just suffered a loss of a couple hundred KIA at a place in Vietnam called Ia Drang. We were shocked. It was America's largest loss of soldiers since the Korean War. We all knew the 1st Air Cav very well. That's the unit that we had aggressed against last year when their designation was the 11th Air Assault Division (Test).

There in the rigger shed, we got to talking, re-analyzing that exercise (Air Assault II). "They should have taken the time to refine those air mobile techniques and train more before being sent off into combat." We knew field training exercises, and we were confident at the time that the performance should not have been validated by the Pentagon. They were good troops. But many of them were only just beginning to get experience in this new approach to land warfare.

Their sacrifice brought most of us closer to deploying to Vietnam, but it would not be as a unit.

It would be as 'replacements.'

Over the next few hours, as we were shaking the parachutes and prepping them for re-packing, it seemed like our detail got smaller and smaller. Every few minutes there would be a call for another individual to report back to the company area. And none of them were coming back to help us shake parachutes. Eventually, less than a dozen of us were left in the rigger shed, with still hundreds of chutes to go.

It became obvious that shaking parachutes had no priority that day. I said, "I'm gonna find out what's going on."

I got to our Charlie Company building and hardly anyone was there. I asked a clerk where everyone was.

"Most of the company came down on a levy for Vietnam. They're at personnel to begin out-processing."

I asked if he knew whether I was on the levy.

"I don't see your name."

I went to personnel and got in one of the shorter lines to see if I could find out if my name was on whatever list that table was processing.

[I believe this 'replacement' policy (calling up individuals; breaking up units who trained together and worked as a unit) caused problems in Vietnam. Our unit's men knew each other's strengths and weaknesses. This policy took away the leadership, followership, and cohesion developed among the men. Trust is crucial in a combat situation. This was a formula for disaster. All told, we had a 1500-man levy that came down for replacements to multiple units in Vietnam. Many of ours went to the 1st Air Cav. We preferred to be with other paratroopers like the 101st Airborne Division ('The Screaming Eagles') and the 173rd Airborne Brigade ('The Sky Soldiers,' also known as 'The Herd'). But we had no choice. The pencil-pushers decided where we would be assigned.]

Some guys were applying for an exemption to get out of this levy, for family situations coming up during the holidays. Almost all requests were denied. I thought I heard a clerk say to one of the men who had family problems, "Get me someone to go in your place, and we'll see what we can do." Our unit had just come back from the six-month deployment to the Dominican Republic only a month ago. As I stood in line waiting my turn, I heard a young sergeant from Alpha Company tell the clerk, "My wife is close to giving birth. I want to be there for the birth and to help my wife. She has no one that can help her here in North Carolina."

So, I leaned in and asked the clerk, "Look on the levy and see if I'm on it."

The clerk rudely said, "Wait your turn!"

I almost snatched that young soldier from behind his desk. I said, "Again, please look. If I'm not on it, I'll take the sergeant's place."

We were both sergeants, E-5, infantry, and Squad Leaders. Calming down, I said, "Give the guy a break. He's been gone for over six months to the Dominican Republic. He needs to be here when his wife has the baby."

The clerk looked at me. "Give me your name and social security number and get out your ID card."

My name was not on this levy. He then checked with his admin supervisor and came back. "You two, go see that staff sergeant. He's the one who can make it happen."

We did some paperwork. It was official. That was one thankful sergeant from Alpha Company. "May God bless you and protect you."

And that was it. I was now on orders to depart for Vietnam in less than a week.

19

Vietnam

1966

Without going into all the details, I just want
to simply say that my marriage was falling apart. Out of
respect for all involved, I won't explain more. My friend
Rick Conaway and his wife Elouise drove me to the airport. Elouise was in the passenger seat. As I got in the back
seat with my duffle, she scanned the front of the house for
my wife. She saw that the house was dark. "Is everything
okay?"

"Yes."

Elouise sat close to Rick. They were talking softly, and
I didn't say anything. I really didn't want to disturb them.
Rick was going to be gone for a year, going to war. It's possible that they may not see each other again. As we drove
down deserted streets toward the airport, I thought how
blessed Rick was to be with his wife.

We pulled up in front of the terminal. I told Rick, "Let
me take your bag inside and I'll wait for you in there." I
figured they may want to spend a few more minutes alone.
Inside, there were quite a few guys with their wives, and

some had their children. The early morning, middle-of-the-night grogginess made it seem even sadder. We had to travel in uniform. I could see that many of the soldiers were paratroopers from the 82nd Airborne, but I didn't know any of them. Rick's familiar face came through the crowd. We processed in and got our boarding passes.

At that time, you had to go outdoors to board the plane. Piedmont Airlines had mostly prop-driven planes. Rick and Elouise stood holding hands and talking. The call was announced to board the aircraft. They said their final good-byes with Elouise in tears. We boarded, and through the window we could still see Elouise standing there. She had a long coat and her hair held up in a lovely white kerchief. It was a cold December morning. And she was standing out there.

The plane taxied out, revved its engines, and started off. The glow of the blue lights of the taxiways gave enough illumination near the old terminal building that both Rick and I were sure we could see Elouise standing there, waving to us. I will never forget that sight of her and the white kerchief. My heart was breaking for both of them. Rick stared for a long time out the window. Briefly, I could see Rick's face had tears.

I reached into my 'AWOL bag' and took out a pint of Cutty Sark and took a long drag on it and offered it to Rick. He had a drink. "She'll wait for you. A year will go by fast."

I took another swig.

When we arrived at Atlanta, we flew in a jet airliner to San Francisco and then buses transported us to Oakland Army Depot. In a briefing there, they explained that we would be on our way in less than three days. We were free to explore Oakland and enjoy the night life but had to be back by midnight each night. The policy was that we had to wear our uniforms, even in downtown Oakland.

It was late December 1965, and the sun set very early. We started bar hopping. Apparently, most of the 1,500-man levy was right here in Oakland! I saw some friends from Fort Bragg, and we decided to hang out together.

Well after dark, Rick and I came (stumbled?) upon a bar called 'the Black Saddle.' It had a country band playing. We'd noticed motorcycles outside but didn't give it a second thought. As we walked inside, we made it through to the bar. The bartender said loudly, "The first one is on the house. I ain't seen this many paratroopers in town since the Korean War."

Soon, we started to feel the presence of the owners of the motorcycles. There were about a dozen that we could see. I felt a little uneasy and said to the rest, "Let's finish our beer and head out. We don't want any problems. But keep your empty beer bottles. We may need them to exit."

As we were trying to leave, a couple of bikers came over and blocked off our path to the exit, "Hey! Where do you think you're going?"

I said, "We have a short night and a lot of bars to visit."

One of them, a giant much taller than us and maybe about 250 lbs with a dark beard and long bushy hair was wearing his black leather Hell's Angels Oakland Chapter jacket. '1%' was embroidered on the front. "Some of your friends were here last night."

(My instinct is to count buttons. But he's wearing a T-shirt.)

"So, when are you shipping out?"

"It could be tomorrow."

The big guy says, "Well, your money's no good here. Come on over and meet the rest of my guys."

We ended up having a hell of a time. These guys knew how to enjoy themselves. Their women wore leather jackets with no sleeves and had tattoos on their arms. Some were pretty good looking, but all of them could hold their own if the bar broke out into fighting. Our time was spent at the bar, not at tables. We ended up missing the last bus back to the Army terminal and it was close to the midnight curfew. I thanked them and said we had to call a taxi. The big guy said, "Nah, we will give you a ride back."

We got on the motorcycles, and you can imagine the impressed look on the MPs' faces at the gate when about 20 Harley-Davidsons roared toward them. There, we said goodbyes. They hugged us and said, "Be careful and come home soon."

We got back to the barracks and found out that we were shipping out in the morning. There were instructions on the bulletin board about what clothing items we'd be taking to Vietnam and what things we would not be needing. You were to put the things you don't need (like most of the Class A dress uniform items I brought) in these certain boxes they provided and address them to be shipped home. I don't quite remember what dress uniforms we took to Vietnam. I want to say that we used short sleeve khakis.

We were bused to Travis AFB and boarded a big yellow Braniff Airlines jumbo jet. What a hell of a way to go to war! All Braniff airplanes were painted in bright colors. The stewardesses wore silk outfits with vibrant patterns. If they were apprehensive about flying us to Vietnam, they sure didn't show it. These lovely women were smiling and seemed like they touched every soldier that boarded the aircraft. Most of the flight crew personally welcomed us on board. As troops would sit down, drinks were served right away by the stewardesses. They were a class act. They couldn't do enough for us. We flew to war in style, with outstanding meals and plenty to drink.

The stewardesses seemed to spend extra time with some of the more apprehensive soldiers. We all understood that this was not a vacation trip. We knew deep down that some of us would not be coming back passenger style. Instead, it would be quartermaster style, in a box. But that old mechanism kicks in. It's always the other guy. "I'll make it back." We ate, drank, and laughed. It was a good flight. We knew we were appreciated.[9]

Most of us were dozing when the pilot announced that we were beginning our descent. He said we'd be descending steeply into Saigon for tactical security reasons. We landed at Tan Son Nhut Air Base and were met by O.D. (Olive Drab) buses with steel mesh over the windows. We were taken to a part of the base called "Camp Alpha," a tent city where we could rest over the next couple of days as we in-processed.

---

9   Honest conversations in times like these are crucial. The people with Combat Experience need to speak to the soldiers with none. It's a duty to share your Combat Experience. It's not bragging. It's not about a hero story. It's serving the future generations.

They broke us down into "controlled mobs." Seriously, they assigned you temporarily to a certain numbered "mob" and you were expected to follow the schedule for processing, meals, etc. After the initial briefing, you'd get your instructions from the P.A. system. They would call your mob number and tell you to get into formation. We were guided to our designated tents and were told to change into fatigues. There would be a formation in an hour to give us further information. We all looked forward to that formation because most of us were totally confused. We started to wonder, *How the hell are they fighting a war? No one seems to be in charge!*

Eventually, our mob was formed up in front of some big wooden unit patches on poles. They went down the line of poles, calling the unit name, (i.e. "1st Air Cav") and then calling out each person assigned to that unit. You lined up under the unit patch and that's when you knew where you were going.

As you might guess, a lot of soldiers got called for the 1st Air Cav. Most of us from Fort Bragg hoped we wouldn't be put in non-Airborne units. Most of us were hoping for the 101st Airborne Division or something similar. "For the following names, fall in under the 173rd Airborne Brigade unit sign!" That's when I heard my name. I smiled.

I was proud to join the Sky Soldiers. 'Tien Bing' ('Sky Soldiers') was a nickname recently given to them by the people of Taiwan. Based at Torii Station, the US Army garrison on Okinawa, the 173rd was the region's Immediate Response Force, training extensively with mass parachute jumps onto numerous Pacific Islands. They were the first brigade to arrive in South Vietnam. I could really respect these guys.

I distinctly remember how amazingly hot and humid it was. Most of us were soaked from perspiration but it didn't faze me. I guess the six months I spent in the Dominican Republic acclimatized me. Some troops who came from Alaska were really hurting. As a matter of fact, our first casualties came not from combat, but from the heat.

We boarded some deuce-and-a-halfs and were taken to the US air base at the town of Bien Hoa, eighteen miles northeast of Saigon. Bien Hoa was a city of 60,000 and the name Bien Hoa translates as 'land of peaceful frontiers.' The air base was originally a key French airfield and was now a strategic base for both the Vietnamese and the American air forces. The 173rd occupied the northern and eastern flanks of the air base.

Image 45. Bien Hoa Air Base. An American U-2 reconnaissance aircraft parked beside South Vietnam Air Force A-1 Skyraiders.

This was another tent city, but not as big as the one we just left. We unloaded our duffle bags and hung around, uncertain when someone would ever take charge and tell us what, when, and where. Eventually, a young E-5 called roll. "You won't be here more than one night. Those tents over there are for you. Over there are your latrines and that large tent is your mess hall. Find an empty cot and then go to chow. After that, hang loose in the tent area."

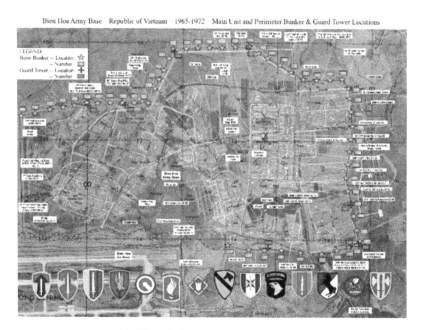

Image 46. The 173rd Airborne Brigade had the
area in the lower central part of this map.

We lined up at the mess hall. Some of the guys advised me that maybe I should hide my Ranger tab. The word was that some Sergeant 1st Class had been looking for Ranger-qualified men to volunteer for some kind of long-range patrol unit. I'd considered taking off the Ranger tab because it might come across as bragging in Vietnam. I had taken off the sewed-on Combat Infantryman Badge and the 82nd Airborne combat patch on my right sleeve. I'm kinda glad I did. Those still wearing them were catching all kinds of smartass remarks from the recently-seasoned combat veterans of the 173rd Airborne Brigade passing by us. Some of these guys making the smartass remarks had only been in Vietnam a couple of months, so they had less actual combat experience than we had in the Dominican Republic earlier in the year. As I'm passing through the crowded mess hall, one guy in a laughing group was yappin' his mouth at a young paratrooper from his old unit, the 82nd Airborne, 1/508th, saying things like, "These guys found their Combat Infantryman Badges in a Cracker Jack box." It just happened that 1/508th took most of the KIAs in the Dominican Republic and one of those killed in action was a close friend of the young paratrooper. With one punch, the young paratrooper put that mouth on the floor.

I thought, *This mess hall serves breakfast, lunch, and justice.*

I was satisfied with what I'd seen. I went back to eating. The food wasn't bad. I remember the ice-cold Kool-Aid. It never tasted so good. (I could never get enough cold beverages or ice during my whole time in Vietnam. It really stands out in my memory.)

While I was still eating, I heard a kindly voice behind me. "When did you go through Ranger School?" It was an old Sgt 1st Class who introduced himself as "Doc." He had a small monkey on his shoulder. "After you finish eating, I want to talk to you about your assignment. It'll be Ranger-related work."

After I finished, I went to see the old sarge with the monkey. He informs me, "You've been assigned to the Long-Range Patrol (LRP) unit of the 173rd. This is in Echo Troop of the 17th Cavalry Regiment, 173rd Airborne Brigade. It's the ground reconnaissance element of the 173rd. It's attached under the 172nd Military Intel Detachment."

My LRP platoon had a young lieutenant as commander and was comprised of about five six-man teams. I was assigned to one of the teams as a member for on-the-job training with the potential to become a team leader.

This sounded reasonable to me. The sarge said typical patrols would be in hostile territory with a specified period of time to return and report findings. This I understood. Ranger School had prepared us to execute reconnaissance patrols that we did in major exercises in the 82nd. But this was real-world, live-fire. We wouldn't have all the predetermined zones or safety measures. Here is where you get your Ranger School final exam. You hoped your grade wouldn't be awarded with full military honors at a cemetery or a memorial wall.

You hoped you wouldn't die because of your stupidity, taking a few of your soldiers along on your trip to heaven. My greatest concern as a noncommissioned officer was not to get anyone else killed because of my stupidity. In a firefight, some may die because that's the nature of war. But to have any of your soldiers killed because of your blunder…

"Doc" sent me over to Echo Troop, 17th Cav. I was processed in and met the calvary troop commander, a captain in a slot authorized for a major, which gave the captain tactical control as well as administrative support. After just a few minutes of listening to the Air Cav troop commander, I knew our lieutenant's LRP platoon had a hard row to hoe. The commander didn't think highly of the group I was going to. This LRP platoon was low on the totem pole. It sounded like we would mostly be used for trash detail and KP.

After that briefing, I was picked up by a member of my LRP platoon and taken to our LRP area consisting of 'GP Medium' (General Purpose, Medium) tents. I met the team leaders, a few staff sergeants and some buck sergeants. I also met some of the members of the teams. They seemed to be motivated and of high caliber. This seems to always be the case in high-risk volunteer units. I was assigned to Staff Sgt Williams' team.

I was given a folding cot and not much more. I was issued an M16 rifle that looked like it had seen its day. I got seven 20-round magazines and some field gear. This is when I got my first-ever couple of sets of camouflage fatigues. It's the first time I'd ever seen that uniform. They were constructed similar to the jungle fatigues I'd had. I was told we'd wear camies (camouflage uniform) only in the field, when conducting LRP missions. Another surprise was to be issued a .45 cal pistol. That was a plus. You can never have too much armament. A '45' was insurance (especially considering the shape my M16 was in.)

It was early January 1966, and over the coming weeks, I did not see much of our LRP platoon commander, the lieutenant. He did not have a chance with that captain. From my perspective, it seemed the only thing the captain cared about was making major. I was not impressed with him or his leadership style. And I'd only just gotten there. I knew I would not last long under his command.

In weeks to come, we did very little training. We pulled lots of ash and trash details, KP, and guard duty. We had a large perimeter to guard. In Image 46 (of Bien Hoa) above, you can see the blue stars around the perimeter. There were small guard towers at a few of the star locations but most of them were just small bunkers. We faced rice paddies, small hamlets, the Song Dong Nai River, and the infamous War Zone D, which I would get to know well. It was considered hostile territory, sanctuary for large units of our enemy, the Viet Cong (VC). (Remember that the VC is not the North Vietnam Army. The VC are a communist militia operating within South Vietnam).

Early on, when we did go on LRP missions, they consisted of short walks after dark. We set up ambushes close to the hamlets on used trails. To my recollection, I don't think we made even a single enemy contact on any of these nighttime ambush patrols.

Over the following weeks, Echo Troop deployed in support of 173rd Airborne Brigade combat operations. We would ride in our jeeps, sometimes rigged with a Browning M2 .50 caliber machine gun (kept in place with sandbags). We didn't conduct any LRP missions. We didn't have any helicopter support needed to insert teams behind enemy lines. Our team sometimes conducted a stay-behind in conjunction with road clearing operations by Echo Troop. This was dangerous for our teams since there was no emergency extraction helicopter capability for us. If you become engaged in a firefight with a superior enemy force, the normal procedure would be to call for extraction by chopper.

I made up my mind to transfer out of this outfit. It was dysfunctional and unprofessional. They had suffered some

KIAs and WIAs. The troops, NCOs, and lower ranked officers did well under fire. They should be appreciated for their combat performance. But it felt like the commander got all the credit and awards and the troops had little to show for their performance.

The icing on the cake was when the commander of Echo Troop returned from War Zone D with a dead enemy soldier spread eagle on the hood of his jeep while he was driving through town. I guess he thought he could show off his trophy like it was deer season. I knew the further I get from this idiot, the better.

By early March of 1966, I was happy to get transferred to 2nd Battalion, 503rd Airborne Infantry Regiment. Both the 1st and 2nd Battalions of the 503rd were attached to the 173rd in Vietnam. I was assigned to Charlie Company, commanded by a Captain Leahy. I would be the Squad Leader of one of the three squads in 1st Platoon, which is led by a first lieutenant. My company's First Sergeant had the nickname "Hammer Head," and he told me I'd be the Squad Leader of 2nd Squad. I'd be briefed by the Platoon Leader on all company SOPs.

A Spec 4 St Clair was currently the Acting Squad Leader and the First Sergeant explained that St Clair was known to be good at the job. So, I asked why he would not keep St Clair as Squad Leader. That did not go over well with the First Sergeant. "You are a Ranger-qualified E-5 and hopefully want to make E-6. You're in the zone for promotion. If you think you can't handle the responsibility of a Squad Leader, then I can arrange for you to become an E-4 and make St Clair the E-5."

I liked that First Sergeant. He was straight-forward and didn't pretend. He told you like it was.

"You'll meet St Clair and the rest of your squad later. They are in town celebrating after a two-week operation. They're scheduled to go on another one in a few days. Go to supply and draw your weapon and equipment."

I went to company supply. The supply sergeant got word I was coming and had all my equipment and weapons ready before I arrived. I lucked out. He had just received a new shipment. He issued me all new stuff including new jungle fatigues, and new boots. He gave me a good looking, almost new, M16 (said it had belonged to the previous platoon sergeant for 1st Platoon.) He gave me fourteen 20-round magazines. (He said, "You can't have enough magazines on an operation. Most soldiers carry about 25 loaded magazines and another 500 rounds in their rucksacks.") I also received a bayonet, an LBE (Load Bearing Equipment), and two 2-quart canteens, a good ol' steel pot (helmet), and an entrenching tool.

"As soon as you get your ammo, load all your magazines."

He showed me which tent was 2nd Squad. Inside, was a young soldier cleaning his M16. They had a dozen or more cots on each side of the aisle. "Are you the Squad Leader that we heard was coming?"

"Yes."

"That one right there should be your cot. But for now, the Acting Squad Leader has it. He and the rest of the squad are in town."

I asked, "Why didn't you go?"

"I don't drink much." (I could tell he wasn't telling the truth.)

"How old are you?"

He'd just turned 19 and had been in Vietnam almost two months.

I picked out an empty cot and decided, *That will do for me*. Rucksacks were at the end of each cot. The floor was dirt but was in the process of having wooden floors put in. By each cot was an M16 and an LBE with ammo pouches full and ready to go.

I put my gear together the way I always carried my equipment, but I had to modify my load some to accommodate as much of that extra ammo as I could. I spent the afternoon packing my rucksack and got to know the young private. He was from the Midwest. I said, "The First Sergeant thinks highly of 1st Platoon. He said you guys are hell on wheels in a firefight."

The private said, "The First Sergeant is the best in our battalion. On one of our operations, he was shot in the leg. The company was taking heavy fire and it was close-quarters combat. They were MEDEVACing our wounded and resupplying the company with ammo. The First Sergeant refused to get MEDEVACed. He would grab a couple of cases of ammo and take it over to the troops in contact. Or he'd take them a couple of 5-gallon cans of water. The troops were low on everything. The company commander was yelling over to him to get on the MEDEVAC chopper. He would act like he couldn't understand what the commander was saying. The First Sergeant won't carry an M16. He has an older M14 and carries 20 magazines."

We talked about the problems with the newer rifle. He said, "A lot of troops are having problems with the M16 and it's not because they don't clean it. It'll jam and fail to feed and extract. Sometimes it'll rip off the rim of the cartridge. All of us made our own rifle cleaning rods about 24 inches long to knock out the jammed cartridge top and bottom." (I made a mental note to make one of those the first chance I get.)

I asked if the M16 problems had been brought up to the chain of command. "Yes. Supposedly they are giving everyone a new bolt assembly. Mine is still the old aluminum bolt."

I asked him if we had a full squad and he said, "Yes, now that you're here. The squad is all Black guys except for me."

I asked him if there is any problem for him being the only White soldier. "No, they treat me like any other squad member. About half the platoon is Black and half is White. Some squads are all White; some are all Black. It doesn't seem to present any problems among us. Everyone works as a team in the field. The First Sergeant tells people that we are the best you could ask for."

At some point in my unpacking, I stepped outside to look around outside the tent. Not far away was the perimeter berm. I could see the trenches and small bunkers. They looked out onto good, clear fields of fire and then, at about 300 meters, began a rubber tree plantation. The perimeter bunkers had three or four soldiers manning M60 machine guns. One I could see had a Browning M2 .50 cal heavy machine gun.

As I was walking around, I have to admit I did have some apprehension about meeting 2nd Squad for the first time. But, as always, I did not believe in reading from notes or rehearsing what I was going to say to my new squad. I always believed it had to come from the heart.

Later that afternoon as people from 1st Platoon started to drift back in from town, I was back in our quarters working on my equipment. A couple of the other Squad Leaders came over and introduced themselves. They asked where I was coming from and who I was with back in the states. When I told them I was with the 82nd for the last four years, they asked if I had been sent to the Dominican Republic. They asked, "How come you don't wear a Combat Infantryman Badge?"

I said, "I wear that on my Class A uniform."

If I remember correctly, I was the only one in my Platoon, besides the lieutenant who had a Ranger tab. They asked when I went to Ranger School. A couple of them said they are hoping to go, but that allocations were hard to come by.

To a man, they told me 2nd Squad was sharp and that St Clair was good at what he did. And at that, I finally got to meet St Clair. He and a few other squad members were just coming back. One of the Squad Leaders brought him over and told him, "Meet your new Squad Leader." (Not as smooth an introduction as I'd hoped for, but the ice was broke!)

St Clair was very gracious and understanding. He joked, "It's about time you showed up. I'm tired of doing Squad Leader work without the pay." He shook my hand and said, "We'll get the squad together." Some were still not back, so I suggested that we wait until we have everyone before we have any kind of meeting. So, St Clair introduced me to some of the squad members individually as we came across them.

"Do you want me to move my cot out and put yours in?"

"No, it doesn't matter where I sleep."

Later that evening I met the platoon's lieutenant. He briefed me on how he likes to run things. "Squad Leaders are responsible for their squads, and I'll be responsible for the Squad Leaders."

Sounded like a good plan to me.

I asked for some time in the morning where I could meet with my squad. He said he'd give us some time right after the company formation. I asked St Clair to handle the squad report in the morning.

The next morning, following the company formation, everyone was in the GP Medium tent for the meeting. As St Clair introduced me, he stumbled over my last name. There was no reaction from the squad members, no smiles, basically blank stares in an awkward silence. (I actually would rather they would have laughed. It might have lightened things up and revealed a little about their personalities. As it was, if there was a welcome mat at the foot of 2nd Squad, I sure didn't see it.)

I pronounced my last name and followed it up with, "Just call me Jake."

St Clair is now the Alpha Fire Team leader. Bravo Fire Team stays the same.

I decided to address the Black and White topic. "I, a White Squad Leader, am replacing an Acting Squad Leader who is Black. We've got eight Black squad members and one White guy, who was the only one who, for whatever reason, stayed behind while everyone else went to town.

"This is the only time I will mention this issue. It's on my mind. I figure it's on your minds. All I can say is that we have something in common. I don't want to die and neither do you. I don't care what's happening in the world or what's happening where you come from. This is 2nd Squad of 1st Platoon. That's the only thing that matters. If I get hit and you get hit, the blood is still red. I will give my total loyalty and dedication to 2nd Squad and will never ask you to do anything I'll not do. I'm a career soldier. I volunteered to be here. And my aim is to get you home to your loved ones. Your safety will always come first before mine.

"We must work as a team. This is a two-way street. I expect the same from you, no more, no less. Do we have a problem with this?"

One soldier spoke up (maybe for all the other squad members). He said, "The only problem we have is you. We don't know how you're going to act under pressure."

"That's a good question. I don't know either. Time will tell. And it won't be long." (We would be going on an operation in a few days.)

They asked about my accent, "Where are you from?"

I told them about Ukraine and the Soviet Union and Poland and Germany and coming to America 15 years ago. When I mentioned Jersey City, a few of the squad members smiled. I had guys from Jersey, Philly and New York City.

Coming away from that first meeting, I felt we'd started to connect.

20

Emotion: Vietnam

1966

In March 1966, Charlie Company assumed the designation of being the Eagle Flight company for the 503rd. This meant we had to be on alert, standing by to depart on choppers to reinforce a unit within 30 minutes of being called. Eagle Flights were missions directly to units engaged with an enemy.

The call came about mid-morning. We scrambled onto deuce-and-a-half trucks and were on the air strip at the helicopters within a few minutes. Alpha Company of the 82nd Aviation Battalion was attached to 173rd Airborne Brigade to take us to hell. They were called 'the Cowboys' and it fit. They were the best damn helicopter pilots in the world. In formation with them were the Falcons, gunship UH-1Bs whose role was to provide fire support to keep the enemy away from our LZ and our ground troops.

'Eagle Flights' prey on fleeing Viet Cong
• May 1, 1967

Image 47. An example of a *Stars and Stripes* newspaper article about Eagle Flights.

1st Platoon loaded first. We were briefed that some Viet Cong had just attacked a group of civilian contractors. The company was RMK-BRJ. They did a lot of construction work for the government. It was about 15 miles away, so it only took a few minutes to get there. This RMK-BRJ compound was near Saigon.

Someone on the ground threw smoke for us as we approached. We came in hot, landed, and secured the immediate area for the rest of the company coming behind us. The Falcon gunships were circling above. As we established a perimeter, 2nd Platoon and 3rd Platoon went looking for the bad guys. They came back a little later having made no contact.

Image 48. The US Army needed a lot of rock and gravel to construct roads in the soft mud of the Mekong Delta. There were only two large sources for crushed rock in the area and RMK-BRJ's University Quarry outside Saigon was one of them.

In the meantime, we'd secured the area and found the contractors. It was clear what had taken place. A heavily armed force of around 30 Viet Cong came into the area. The three or four American contractors who were working with some civilian Vietnamese were unarmed. (They'd never had any problems with the Viet Cong before.) Everyone had been herded into a gravel pit. The Viet Cong had held a mock trial accusing the American contractors of invading Vietnam and sentenced them to death. They shot the American civilian contractors in cold blood. They must have enjoyed it, as evidenced by the amount of AK-47 brass casings around the bodies.

The Vietnamese living nearby, who surely saw the executions, would not tell us who, what, or when. They were of no help to us. The VC could be anybody.

Image 49. University Quarry-Saigon, opened in 1965. Its name derived from the fact that it was near the future Saigon University. "Saigon University Mining Products Company", or SUMPCO, for short.

It was decided that a platoon comprised of four rifle squads would stay on the site to provide protection for the RMK-BRJ contractors as they reorganized. Included in that platoon was 2nd Squad of 1st Platoon. The perimeter to secure was about 600 meters; that's 150 meters per squad. That's kinda spread out. The platoon's lieutenant agreed, but said we'd have to do the best we can. I asked for some augmentation:

• An M60 machine gun team to be attached to my squad

- At least two more M79 grenade launchers
- Some more M72 LAWs (Light Anti-tank Weapons)
- Some more frag grenades
- Plenty of trip flares
- A couple of cases of Claymore mines
- An express commitment of illumination and artillery support and
- 24-hour commo support

If worse comes to worst, there are always the Eagle Flights standing by.

I may not have gotten all I needed if it wasn't for a little help I received from the old man from my days in XVIII Airborne Corps, who had promoted me at a Thanksgiving dinner for the Immediate Response Force on 30-minute standby. When General William Westmoreland, now commander of US Forces in Vietnam, heard about the execution of the American contractors, he personally got involved. He instituted a policy of issuing contractors M16 rifles. He promised more direct military protection and, as a result, I got everything I'd asked for. And what's more, my squad was given the starlight scopes, which would give us some night vision. This was the first time I'd ever laid eyes on a starlight scope.

Image 50. A Starlight Scope.

It was such a change from our normal world. In this tasking, we knew what we were going to do for many days to come. We didn't have to do the menial ash and trash details. (Back at the company area, it had felt like we were getting put on that every day.) We were away from the flagpole, on our own. The lieutenant gave us general instructions to protect, defend, safeguard, and assist the RMK-BRJ personnel and their compound against the Viet Cong.

I had an 11-man squad with an M60 crew attached (three soldiers) for a total of 14. Time to get to work. I put the M60 position in the middle of our perimeter with an M16 defensive position 50 meters to his left and another 50 meters to his right. The M60's fan of fire would cover our 150-meter front.

The defensive positions were three-man strong points. All fields of fire were assigned and interlocking. Trip flares and Claymore mines would be put out and would stay active night and day. The perimeter would be manned 24 hours a day. I instituted daylight five-man patrols to recon our forward areas around the RMK-BRJ area. We set up our patrol roster with each man's schedule.

The management was so glad to have us. They could not do enough for us. They were very vocal offering whatever we needed.

I explained that our first priority would always be our perimeter. I told them about the strong points and how we could use some help digging them and designing them with overhead cover. Entrenching tools would take forever and these RMK-BRJ guys were all about digging. They immediately got to work with equipment and materials and their civilian labor building the bunkers just to our specifications.

Taking St Clair with me, we established a daily meeting to go over any problem areas and the day's plan of operations. It was important to coordinate our scheduled movements, especially at night. Deadly force was authorized.

The managers built a mess facility large enough to provide us with meals and, often, with entertainment. There, they provided movies at night. They built us a laundry facility and showers (hot at last!) They built a small cantina that sold comfort items like snacks, cigarettes, and soda (cold at last!) I established a daily truck run back to Charlie Company at Bien Hoa. This resupplied us with more radios and batteries and mail runs. Outgoing mail we did through RMK-BRJ. We scheduled daily commo checks with our unit at Bien Hoa, sending in our daily SITREPs (Situation Reports).

We coordinated a schedule for breakfast, lunch, and supper. The food was great, like eating in a restaurant. We had laundry service. We made a movie roster with multiple showings so that everyone could go when they weren't on duty. After a while I authorized a special treat. Each soldier could have two cold beers during the movie. During this tasking, my squad would not be allowed offsite, so this was the only alcohol our guys would have. I took full responsibility for this decision, not asking permission from my Platoon Leader. This was starting to feel like being the palace guard.

After several weeks, our squad was cycled out of this special duty. Another unit would relieve us, and we'd return to Charlie Company. It was time to say goodbye to our civilian friends. They really appreciated us. We thanked them for taking care of us like we were family. One of the managers said if I ever get out of the Army to think about working for RMK-BRJ. I did give it a thought. In 1966, my annual earnings were $5,996. But you've got to love what you're doing.

You can't put a price on the value of being a soldier.

Search & Destroy: Vietnam

1966

Returning from that assignment in late March 1966, the squad now tended to have a lot of smiles. As we'd see each other around Charlie Company, there were a lot of, "How you doin', Sarge?" My men now referred to me by a new name, "Sergeant Jake." I appreciated the healthy balance of respect and friendship from my squad members. However, in the back of mind I still remembered those words from one squad member, "We don't know how you're going to act under fire." I had to earn their respect when that time came. I thought back to the feelings that I had as a child in the middle of WWII and my feelings during my first fire fight in the Dominican Republic.

I knew I had the ability to lead a squad. I knew I had the best training. Every firefight is different, but one fact remains constant. Some will live, and some will die. I asked the good Lord for the wisdom that I would need leading these men in my first contact with the enemy.[10]

It would not be long. In April 1966, our unit, the 2nd Battalion of the 503rd was tasked to conduct a heliborne assault into an area called Song Be and to conduct a search and destroy mission. (History records that from April 10th to 25th, we carried out Operation Denver to locate and capture or destroy Viet Cong and North Vietnamese Army personnel, supplies, and equipment.) Intelligence reported heavy enemy concentrations in our AO (Area of Operations).

Song Be is in the Phuoc Long province due north of Bien Hoa. (On Image 51, I've indicated it with a blue star. The province's capital is Phuoc Binh, which is co-located with Song Be.) **Sông** is the Vietnamese word for 'river,' so Song Be means "the Be River." The entire province around the river is referred to as "Song Be." The battles took place around the town of Phuoc Binh.

As I prepped my gear, I applied the good advice I'd received, "Carry lots of ammo and grenades." I started with twenty 20-round magazines. In my rucksack I carried an extra 15 boxes (which had 20 rounds each). I had eight frag grenades, three WP ('Willy Pete') white phosphorus grenades and a few smoke grenades. Some of the guys laughed, "Don't forget to leave room for water and chow. If we get into heavy contact, we may have a problem with re-supply."

---

10   Notice that, in his prayers, he doesn't make the primary focus, "Please bring me home safe." Instead, make wisdom the priority in your requests. Combat Experience can teach you to accept that God is sovereign over the events in our lives. We don't get to control much about when we die. But we do control how we conduct ourselves during the time we are given.

Image 51. The blue star indicates the Song Be region.

My men taught me a new term, "the Blood Squad." "We hit the jackpot. Charlie Company is the Blood Company, 1st Platoon is the Blood Platoon, and 2nd Squad is the Blood Squad." It means Charlie Company will be the first company on the ground at the hot landing zone

(LZ) and we will be the first squad. We are to move immediately into the jungle and take up defensive positions around the LZ. As the choppers return bringing in the rest of the battalion, we will be the base squad with the other squads building left and right along the line to form the perimeter. We will be laying down fire upon the wood line immediately. If we encounter bunkers on the LZ, we are to assault them immediately, taking the bunker under fire, throwing grenades inside, and keeping moving.

Our (1st Platoon's) first mission priority is to set up a perimeter and secure the wood line. 2nd Platoon would clear bunkers and other obstacles at the LZ and then reinforce our perimeter at the wood line. So together, the mission of Charlie Company is to secure the LZ for the rest of the battalion coming immediately on our heels. Alpha Company and Bravo Company have objectives around the LZ and can provide reinforcements to Charlie Company if we are in heavy contact. They will set up mortars on the LZ to provide supporting fire as the LZ becomes secure. Some men have the role of carrying mortar rounds, and as they jump off the choppers, they'll run immediately to the mortars to drop the rounds off for the mortar crew, then run to their assigned position.

This will be as hot an LZ as we'd ever have, so there is immediate artillery support standing ready. There are three batteries of the 3rd Battalion, 319th Artillery Regiment. There are the 161st Field Battery of the Royal New Zealand Army. And we have a 105mm Howitzer battery of the Royal Australian Army. All five batteries fire the 35lb 105mm projectile at ranges up to 11,000 meters (six miles). Their mission is to provide swift, accurate, and continuous fire support for the maneuver elements.

We also have tactical air support, F-100s from Bien Hoa Air Base with bombs and napalm.

Even with all this support, I still feel apprehensive, this being my first hot heliborne assault. I keep thinking about the Ia Drang valley where the 1st Air Cav lost over 200 soldiers using helicopter assault.

I'm standing with my 100-man company on the grass beside the airfield at Bien Hoa, about to board our choppers with their engines smoothly chomping at noisy idle, blades slicing the air. Mine is the base squad for the battalion, the trigger, the Blood Squad, and Alpha Company of the 82nd Aviation Battalion ('the Cowboys') is our ride. They are lined up before us, ready to take us on a one-way ticket with their 18 helicopters (two troopship platoons and one gunship platoon).

The order of battle has us broken down into a series of "lifts." Everything starts with a calculation of how many helicopters can fit into the footprint of the objective's LZ. In this case, six helicopters will fit into the LZ and 1st Platoon will be on those first six. The aviation unit inserting 1st Platoon is 1st Aviation Platoon, 'the Ramrods' of Alpha Company, 82nd Aviation Battalion. The Ramrods' other helicopters will be carrying 2nd Squad and others from 1st Platoon. As soon as our six helicopters will lift off from the LZ, the second group of six helicopters will immediately land, inserting 2nd Platoon. This aviation unit is 2nd Aviation Platoon, 'the Mustangs.' The 3rd Aviation Platoon is 'the Falcons,' eight UH-1B gunships providing supporting fire on that hot LZ from beginning to end.

Image 52. An unofficial patch of the 82nd
Aviation Battalion, made in-country.

Image 53. An unofficial patch of the 3rd Aviation Platoon of
Alpha Company, 82nd Aviation Battalion, made in-country.

[Note: Later in my tour, I got to know the helicopter crews on a very personal basis, when I ran a six-man LRRP (Long-Range Reconnaissance Patrol.) Their mission was to do the inserting and extracting of teams far beyond enemy lines. Sometimes, those extractions would be under emergency conditions in heavy contact with the enemy. They, as we, lived by the creed "Never leave a man behind," living or dead. You could be sure of it. Those extraction and gunship helicopters would come to get you no matter the danger. How can you explain the dedication of those helicopter crews? Simply stated, if you're in a firefight, those helicopter crews would fly through the gates of hell, doused in gasoline, to come and get you out.]

It's time to launch, so now we move forward from the grass, onto the tarmac and climb aboard our choppers. We are in the lead chopper. The other half of our squad loads up in the second chopper. Within seconds, we are airborne and humming at tree-top level. At 80 knots, it only takes 10 minutes to get to hell, so we just leave the doors open, slid to the rear. I'm on the left, at the wall-less opening. The left door gunner sits to my left, facing outward. It's too loud to actually talk to him. His tinted visor is down. He's deadly serious, there to protect us all. There's another door gunner on the opposite side. Both have M60s with endless ammo belts. I have a moment of envy. But honestly, I don't think I could carry any more than I already have. And our buddies in 1st Squad are bringing an M60 crew to the party, so we're just fine.

So, with the two pilots up front, that's a crew of four plus the five of us (half of our squad.) On each infantryman, we've made a careful decision about every pound that we carry on our person. If we had room for a few more rounds of ammo, we'd pack it into our LBE. We are bulked up, finding a perfect balance of equipment and body, weight and strength, capability and maneuverability. There's no question. We've got everything we can handle.

As we approached the LZ, the eight gunships of the 3rd Aviation Platoon (the Falcons) fan out, slightly ahead of us. They encircle the LZ and lay down suppressing fire upon the wood line. You can hear groundfire. A couple of the helicopters are hit but are not fazed.

Six of the Falcons' choppers have two miniguns (7.62mm rounds at 4,000 rounds/minute), two pods with 2.75-inch rockets (14 rounds), and two door-mounted M60 machine guns. They also brought their two "heavy ships," which they named 'Frog' and 'Hog.' Frog's specialty is a nose-mounted M5 grenade launcher (with 150 rounds of 40mm grenades). Hog's specialty is rockets. In addition to its door guns, it has larger rocket pods with a total of 48 rockets.

With gunships firing in all directions over our head, we drop into a clearing with long green grass whipped by our chopper blades, a meadow of chaos. Before the skids are completely settled, we spring out of the Hueys and quickly form one line as base squad, just off the left of the nose of the chopper, firing in the direction of the ground-fire, which is coming from a wood line. There is no doubt when someone is firing in your direction. It sounds like the snap of a bullwhip. The closer the round is to you the louder the crack.

Image 54. Near Ben Cat, South Vietnam.

1st Squad is immediately with us to our left, in a 40-foot line. Their M60 crew is firing. The M79 grenadiers are putting 40mm H.E. (high explosive) rounds into the trees. One of our grenadiers hits an enemy soldier directly! He's about 200 yards from us and it looks like he must have been looking for better cover. His upper body is instantly blackened in dark smoke. He continues his run for a couple of staggering steps before crumpling to the ground.

Our six choppers deafeningly rise (man they must feel like sitting ducks at this moment), slowly gaining altitude and airspeed. We are protecting them as well as ourselves. Their door gunners are protecting us as well as themselves. Every one of us accepts the fact that each of us will have tense seconds of vulnerability in this assault plan. Each of us is entrusting our lives to the others for cover during those tense seconds.

In this early minute of the assault, it's all I can do to keep people on line and firing. Now 3rd Squad is on line to my right within a moment. All are firing in line, and we are covering about 180 degrees of the LZ. The smell of gunpowder is strong, acrid on the back of our throats. The heat from the firing of our barrels combines with the heat of the day to create a mirage-like distortion of the tree line through our sights.

Our gunships are still firing heavily into the wood line in 'keep their damned heads down' mode. Every few seconds a rocket zips off one of their pods. You can tell the difference in the smell of phosphorous versus gunpowder. Phosphorous has a little more 'heat' and not as much acid on your palette.

"Let's go! Go! Go!" We're not digging in here. We move and cover. Forward is life, on the attack, on the assault. We don't encounter any bunkers out in the open. All three squads are able to move forward at the same pace. Everything is in the woods. Get to the trees. It seems like an eternity before we reach the tree line, but in reality, we are at the trees within about two minutes.

The second set of six helicopters is now landing, with their 30 infantrymen. They immediately assess the situation in all 360 degrees, covering any potential vulnerabilities. They move toward us while at the same time establishing security in all directions of the LZ.

As those lift helicopters depart, the gunships are holding their fire, seeing that we are now engaging at the enemy line.

Image 55. The front line of a battle near Ben Cat, South Vietnam.

As we arrive at the trees, we have a close call. Someone on the ground fires a couple of M72 LAWs, one to our right and one to our left. The LAW is mainly used for anti-tank or bunkers, not for shooting snipers. Firing into a forest, if the LAW's 67mm round hits a tree before it reaches its target, it will detonate—and it puts out shrapnel.

Now in the woods, we find ropes hanging from trees. The gunfire has died down and is distant. The enemy had been up in the trees for sniper positions. A little further forward, we found fires with rice still cooking. We found a lot of equipment and some weapons. They'd established fighting positions at a perimeter. The interior of their camp has a few bunkers. The enemy left in a hurry. Blood trails were everywhere.

Image 56. A paratrooper giving a "last chance" call
before clearing a Viet Cong Army bunker.

We assess the status of our men. In our entire platoon
(three squads of 10 men each), no one has been hit. Charlie
Company (our three platoons) now secure the LZ and the
immediate area.

Within 20 minutes, Bravo Company arrived on the second lift, the second roundtrip by the twelve helicopters.
They were immediately sent forward by the battalion commander to pursue the enemy. When your enemy is limping
with casualties, that's the time to rout them.

More lifts followed with more reinforcements. We provided security for the LZ. Eventually, the lifts bring resupply, and we get a distribution of ammo. I was surprised to
realize that I had fired ten magazines (20 rounds each). I

had thrown two grenades and I also had thrown a couple of smoke grenades to mark friendly locations so that the gunships could adjust with our advance.

Image 57. UH-1D Hueys insert paratroopers of the 173rd Airborne Brigade, into an area northeast of Ben Cat, 30 miles north of Saigon, one of the strongest Viet Cong centers in the country.

It was getting toward late afternoon and the lifts were complete. We now began our move toward some high ground nearby. That's where we'd set up for the night, securing a larger area than just the LZ. We dug in and set up a perimeter. We set our listening posts and set up an ambush on a small trail that crossed another higher traffic trail. Our ambush design had Claymore mines and trip flares.

We maintained a '50 percent alert' through the night, with half of each unit manning the perimeter watch. Then at BMNT (Beginning of Morning Nautical Twilight, the thirty minutes leading up to sunrise), we went to "Stand-To" (100 percent of our personnel on watch, at arms). Sometimes the enemy would attack at this time of the morning, so for those 30 minutes, everyone would man the perimeter.

It turned out to be a quiet night. After dawn, we ate C-rations and got ourselves ready to move out. 1st Platoon would lead the company with 2nd Squad on point. I asked for my favorite M60 machine gun crew to be with me on point; if we run into anything, I always believed in a machine gun in the assault.

We moved through the forest (it was more forest than jungle in this area), toward a link-up with a Vietnamese Ranger Battalion out of Bien Hoa. By late morning, Charlie Company had successfully effected the link-up and they were now on our right flank, securing a vast amount of ground quickly. We moved most of the day without making any contact.

Late in the afternoon, we heard that Bravo Company, on our left flank, had caught up with the enemy. We could hear gunfire in the distance. It sounded like they may have hit a good-sized ambush. Like a tornado scale from 1 to 5, this sounded like a 'number three' firefight. Suddenly on our right flank, closer to us, the Vietnamese Rangers got into something. A firefight was building up there too. They said they were pinned down by sniper fire. Our Battalion Commander was where most Battalion Commanders spend their time (about 3,000 feet above us) and kept asking, "What's the hold up? Why are we not moving?" The answer came back from Bravo Company, "We are maneuvering, but slowly. We are under heavy fire. We need some TACAIR or artillery support." (But I seriously doubted that they were within the artillery's area of coverage.)

To our right, the Vietnamese Rangers had American advisors with them. I guess they were having a tactical problem moving the Rangers forward. Stuck between Bravo and the Vietnamese Rangers, feeling like we were just sitting there, our Charlie Company commander, Captain Leahy, got tired of the Battalion commander's haranguing. He asked our 1st Platoon Leader, "Lieutenant, do you have contact with the Vietnamese Ranger advisors? If so, tell them to move their ass forward!"

Word came back to our 1st Platoon leader who relayed to our Captain Leahy, "The Rangers are still pinned down."

"Well, Lieutenant, unpin them! We're all gonna move forward!" Our 2nd Squad was the closest to the Rangers and had radio contact with the American advisors. Our 1st Platoon lieutenant told the advisors to pass the word among the Vietnamese Rangers, "There will be friendly troops to the left front, moving forward to engage the enemy. There will be lots of firing. Smoke will mark our location. You must ID any target before shooting."

Our 2nd Squad got on line with 1st Squad's M60 machine gun being base and we did what Captain Leahy, always used to preach, "Never send a man where you can send a bullet." We made full use of 'recon-by-fire' up into the 'sniper level' of the trees, and at waist height, and at low-crawling cockroach level. We fired and we moved. After advancing about 200 meters, we got down and established a perimeter.

It took about half an hour for the rest of Charlie Company (the rest of 1st, 2nd, and 3rd Platoons) to move up to our location. I don't know what happened to the Vietnamese Rangers at this point, but Bravo Company was still in heavy contact with no relief in sight. The Vietnamese Rangers had clearly resolved their problems and we were now in a position to help Bravo Company by flanking their enemy.

Captain Leahy had a quick meeting with his platoon leaders and coordinated a plan with Bravo Company's commander, again full of cautions about friendly fire. To get to Bravo Company, we had to cross an open area and would end up on the flank of the enemy. It would be crucial that we not go too far and end up being fired upon by Bravo Company. At a certain point, we would mark friendly locations with smoke. We would link up after the initial attack and before entering the enemy position.

We move out in unison as a company. Pretty soon, we reach an open area and all three Platoons held at the tree line. Word is passed to 'fix bayonets.' We all look at each other and you can hear a couple of guys quietly exclaim, "Say what?!" Within seconds, we are on line, faces toward the open, green and yellow, grassy meadow.

"Move! Move! Move!" is quietly shouted by many along our line. We come out of the tree line, now yelling and shooting and running. We can hear some return fire, but it isn't coming at us. I believe we've routed the enemy, completely scaring them and surprising them from their soft flank. They seem to have panicked, fired a few shots at Bravo Company, and run for their lives in retreat. We link up with Bravo Company.

There's no interest in celebration. Our problems are not over. Bravo Company has casualties. They (and we) are low on ammo and water, and this is not a good place to spend the night. The battalion commander wants us to be on high ground for overnight and to get us a re-supply before sunset. We establish a small LZ in that open meadow.

Image 58. Paratroopers at the edge of a
clearing 13 miles north of Ben Cat.

We do get the wounded out over a couple of chopper lifts,
but it ends up feeling too dangerous to bring in all the re-
supplies that we want. We have to get to the high ground. If
the enemy decides to reinforce and jump us again, we'll be
at a tactical disadvantage. We have to move now.

Our destination is about 5 clicks (kilometers) away
(more than three miles). Most of the land is flat, but our
path will be an uphill climb at the end. Along the way, on
the radios we are informed that an engineering unit is going
to rappel in and cut the LZ needed for re-supply. Captain
Leahy, contacts our 2nd Battalion commander to let him
know that the enemy situation is still bad. They need to
wait until the infantry gets there to secure the perimeter.
"When it's safe, we'll let the engineers rappel in."

The reply was, "It's too late in the day The engineers are already on their way."

After we've progressed about 3km, we hear gunfire coming from the direction of the LZ. The engineers are already there and in contact. The firefight is on. We are paralleling a highway, Highway 13, I think. The battalion commander tells Captain Leahy to reinforce the engineers and fast. Well, the fast way to get there is the highway but that's very dangerous. There's going to be an ambush waiting for us along the highway. Captain Leahy decides that, in this case, speed will have to be our tactical advantage. Our daylight is burning away. We move onto the highway and spread out, moving as quickly as we can.

Image 59. 173rd Airborne Brigade deals with
Viet Cong sniper fire near Ben Cat.

My 2nd Squad is on point again and the old man reminds us to feel free to apply 'recon by fire' as we move. There'll be plenty of ammo resupplied when we get that

LZ secure. Again, my M60 machine gun crew is right up front, followed by our two grenadiers. We move fast down this road with recon-by-fire, grenades launching forward to about 200 meters ahead of us. We're "hell without wheels." We're spraying any hiding place with machine gun fire. Anyone within a mile knows we're coming.

Within 10 minutes, we're getting close to the firefight, which is now intensifying. Radio messages are sounding desperate: "We need help now!"

Only a few hundred meters more. The sky is not as bright as it was. The trees are casting longer shadows.

From the engineers: "Mark your location with star clusters and smoke!"

We reply, "OK, we're on the side of the highway, so don't shoot in that direction!"

We successfully link up with the engineers and get to work securing the LZ perimeter. Within five minutes of us calling the 82nd Aviation Battalion, we can hear the distant sound of the re-supply Hueys approaching. They're now circling, awaiting our word to come in hot to drop off water, chow, and ammo. The engineers are working like beavers, knocking down trees, creating the LZ. Looking up every now and then from our perimeter, we can see those white plastic 5-gallon jugs of water strapped inside the open doors of the Hueys. There's no shooting now. They accomplish one landing into the LZ before the sun goes down.

It was now time for us to dig in for the night. We were thankful for the plain old luke-warm water, having been out of water for hours since our double-time race down the highway. We were told we'd get more water at first light and maybe later in the day a 'Class A' supper (hot food).

It was quiet now. I checked on my squad. They were tired. *Thank you, Lord, that we all are safe.* We had a hell of a day. I took inventory. Who needed what: torn uniforms, cut boots, jammed weapons, how much ammo. I carefully walked over to my company commander and turned in the list. On long operations (sometimes three weeks or more), the uniform can just rot right off of you. Other times, the jungle can rip it up in short order. At dawn, we'd be resupplied, hopefully in one lift, if we got our list correct.

Resting on the hillside, there was time to think. I thought about the great respect I had for these soldiers. They are magnificent fighters. It is awesome power that we invest in these men, lethal, disciplined, efficient, and noble. Some are too young to vote or drink. They are fighting and dying for people who'll never know them or appreciate them (and some who'll never give them any measure of respect). I knew I didn't matter. My mission is to bring as many of them back home as I can, even if it costs me my life. These men are on loan to me from their mothers and fathers, wives, sons, and daughters. I have to do everything in my power to reunite them with their loved ones.[11]

After a successful resupply in the morning, we established security in the area. We hit some empty base camps and found some caches, but as far as contact with the enemy, we had none. So, later that day, we were helicoptered back to Bien Hoa.

---

11 Commit yourself to the welfare of those who serve. Let that be the reason for you to continually improve your Skills. It's a worthy purpose for your life.

22

A Grenade Right in Front of You: Vietnam

1966

Over the coming week or so, we came back out to Song Be and did some local operations around the area. It was platoon-sized work, securing a few grid squares around our base camp.

Image 60. Paratroopers of the 2nd Battalion, 173rd Airborne Brigade, on day 12 of a patrol in the region of Song Be.

In one of these walk-out operations, we were coming back after three days. We had not made contact with the enemy. We were only about 300 meters from our (2nd Battalion's) perimeter. We were still tactical, spread out in a platoon column. We were in a fairly open area, not deep in the forest. Our Platoon Leader was in the middle of the formation when he suddenly yelled, "Grenade!"

The whole platoon hit the dirt, expecting automatic fire and an ambush. But there was nothing. After a few moments, I looked where the lieutenant was lying. As 2nd Squad leader, I was the closest to him. I said, "You, ok?"

(Calmly): "Yes."

I ask the obvious question, "Was there a grenade?"

(Calmly): "Yeah. I'm lying on it."

I quietly say, "That's not a healthy thing to do."

I crawled closer to make sure the lieutenant could hear what I was going to say next. "Listen to me. You can get out of this. You're not going to get up. The thing to do is to just start rolling away from the grenade and then just keep rolling and keep rolling until it goes off."

I could see him shaking.

"You're gonna be alright. When it goes off, the blast will spread upward and outward. You stay low and it won't kill you." After a while with nothing said, I told the lieutenant, "Listen, you're going to be just fine. We'll count to three and on three you start rolling. Ok?"

"Ok."

I counted, "One, two, three!" He started rolling like hell. I'd scooted back about 15 feet from the lieutenant. I got down even closer to the earth and…

…nothing happened.

20 seconds have passed. Now 30 seconds have passed.
I looked up for a peek. The lieutenant was still rolling.

I stood up. I walked over. The grenade didn't have a
fuze on it (the entire gray metal assembly in the photo below). It was an M26, our American grenade. I picked it up
and told everybody that all was well, "All clear."

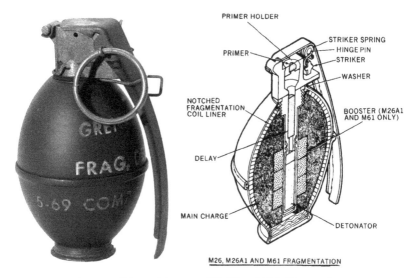

Image 61 and Image 62. The M26 Grenade.

It was obvious that it came off one of our guys' LBE
(load bearing equipment). The lieutenant came over. The
fuze (an M204A2) is the whole top section, including the
primer/striker assembly, and now I could see the fuze hanging on his ammo pouch on the right side of his gear. His
grenade had unscrewed and fell in front of him. He heard
the thud, looked down, and thought it was an enemy grenade thrown from some undetected spider hole.

Think about this for a second. If it had been an enemy grenade, the explosion would have killed him and me
and one or two others in our formation. It also would have

maimed several. The split-second action this young lieutenant took would have saved the lives of his men. He was
ready to sacrifice his life for us. We knew him very well.
We'd watched his every move, every decision, every word,
for months. Today, though, we had a deeper view. We could
see his thoughts. It was clear to us that he had prepared his
mind and heart long before this moment of decision came.[12]

When we arrived at our base camp and then returned
to Bien Hoa, we turned in equipment at 2nd Battalion and
sacked out on our cots. I spent some time thinking about
the significance of what the lieutenant did. I talked to the
other two Squad Leaders. We all believed he should be put
in for something. I wrote it up and gave it to the Charlie
Company commander, Captain Leahy. I believe it was beyond the call of duty. I don't know what Captain Leahy and
his staff did with my recommendation, but I do know that I
had the highest respect for this young lieutenant.

By June 1966, I was halfway through my Vietnam tour. By
this time, I had been on operations in the following areas:

- War Zone D (you can see it on the first map below,
  Image 63)
- The Iron Triangle (see Image 63)
- Phuoc Vinh (see Image 63)
- Phuoc Tuy (see Image 63)

---

12   Listen to veterans. We hope you'll learn how best to listen to a veteran telling
     stories. No one is a perfect storyteller. Don't expect perfect stories. Simply ap-
     preciate them.

- Ben Cat (see Image 64)
- Ho Bo Woods (read the caption on the second map showing the tunnel camps, Image 64) and
- The Plain of Reeds (see Image 65)

There were numerous Eagle Flights which I can't possibly recall at this point. Since Eagle Flights were alert responses, short-notice (or no-notice) with no pre-planning, they are harder to keep track of.

Image 63. The area we operated in, just north of Saigon. You can see War Zone D, The Iron Triangle, Phuoc Vinh, and Phuoc Tuy.

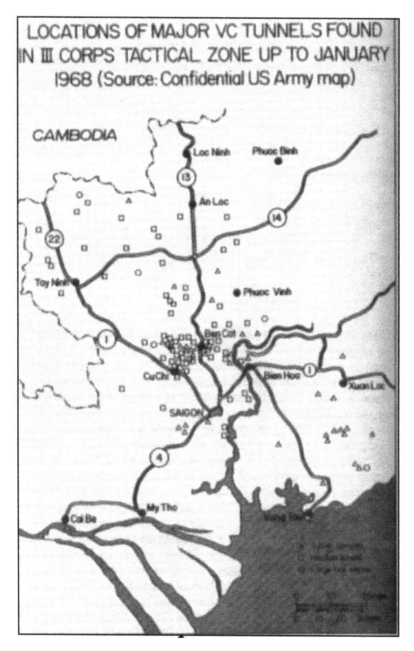

Image 64. Each square and triangle is a major underground
camp built by the Viet Cong. The huge concentration
between Cu Chi and Ben Cat is the Ho Bo Woods.

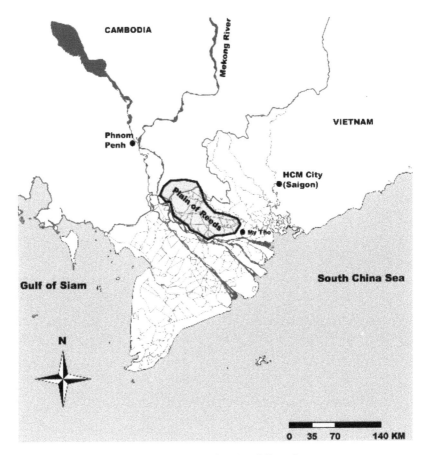

Image 65. The Plain of Reeds.

To this day, I regularly thank the Lord that we didn't lose any squad members. That's right. Under the command of Captain Leahy, we didn't have any KIAs in the company.

23

LRRP 6-Man Team, Vietnam

One day in June 1966, I was asked to come to a meeting with a Captain Palmer. Strangely, the meeting was scheduled to be held at Echo Troop, 17th Air Cav. I found the office, knocked, and Captain Palmer told me to enter. I reported in and he returned my salute. "Please, sit down, Sgt Jakovenko."

"Do you know why I called you?"

(I had not a clue.) "No sir."

He sat and looked at me for a few moments, almost making me feel awkward and judged. Captain Palmer told me he was directed by the general (Brigadier General Paul F. Smith, Commanding General of the 173rd Airborne Brigade) to officially stand up a Long-Range Reconnaissance Patrol (LRRP) unit which would be attached to Echo Troop, 17th Cavalry Regiment. (We'd heard about this new concept with organization and reporting structures different from LRPs.)

I said, "Excuse me, Captain, but that's a strike against your idea. I've been in Echo Troop before. That commander was a loose cannon who treated us like trash."

He explained that there's a new commander of Echo Troop, a Major Sutton.

I paused my negativity. "I knew a Captain Sutton when I was in 2nd Battle Group, 501st Infantry at the 82nd Airborne. He was a company commander and an outstanding leader."

"That's him. He's been promoted. My LRRP needs Ranger-qualified leaders. It's an all-new unit. It will consist of six-man teams. We'll be given very dangerous missions, including area, point, and terrain reconnaissance, scouting for enemy unit locations, reconnaissance for LZs and DZs, enemy trail watching, Battle Damage Assessment (BDA) in remote areas, raids, ambushes and (the most dangerous) prisoner snatches."

The longer he pushed his sales pitch, the more I realized that his wording turned into telling me that I was kind of 'being volunteered.' "Does that sound pretty good?"

I said, "Not really."

To this, his face was confident, but puzzled. "Why not?" Now, he sincerely paused to let me explain what I thought were some good reasons.

"First of all, I really have a confidence in my infantry squad. I have 11 men armed to the teeth and, whenever I ask for it, I get a 2- or 4-man M60 machine gun crew attached. That's 15 men that could deal with just about any situation that comes up in a war zone. We are part of a proven infantry company with over 160 men. You want me to go where _battalions_ don't like to go—and I'm supposed to go there with only six men—and find enemy units that, for all we know, may turn out to be full regiments.

"Second, I'm an E-5 as a Squad Leader. My Squad Leader slot calls for an E-6 and I'm ready to make E-6.

As I understand it, LRRP team leaders are typically E-5s. There's no chance of making E-6 as an LRRP team leader. In LRRPs, the only slot for an E-6 is the Platoon Sergeant."

The captain saw my point. "I'm working on that issue."

Then he re-approached with, "Keep in mind that General Smith is behind this."

I said, "Sir, you're creating an 'all-volunteer' unit and right now, I can't seem to find my volunteering spirit."

Captain Palmer never changed his demeanor. His voice was steady and consistent. But as he was looking at me, I saw in his eyes a mortar round burst: "When you were in Ranger School, did they teach you that it would be easy after you got the tab? I think I'm going to need you to write a 500-word essay documenting why you, as a Ranger School graduate, would not want this assignment."

[Let me pause to tell you something about leadership. In this first meeting, I was able to crystalize my opinion of this man. Up to now, there was nothing that just jumped up and said that this man is a great leader. In many ways, he was just a plain average captain, looking like a hundred others with those silver bars. But this captain had his own way of commanding. He had a certain quality that you wish all commanders had. He truly had internal fortitude, and you could tell that he cared more for his troops than for his career. His eyes were a very pale blue and they seemed to have no expression. You felt like you were looking into infinity. I realized that there was a super-salesman quality about him. The product he was selling, I really didn't want to buy. But then I realized his personal strength. It's the way he talked. It's the way he maintained eye contact. I learned a lot by observing his style of leadership, and I put it to good use in my Army career.]

After the explosion in his eyes subsided, he said something that came from the heart and hit me like a 2x4. "In our vocabulary, Rangers have no command for 'stack hands, now!' It has to be your own decision."

The Ranger motto is, 'Rangers <u>lead</u> the way.' A Ranger unit is going to be built with people who are leaders.

Sitting in front of his desk, there was no need for any rebuttal. The salesman had won. I decided to join the LRRP.

I left Charlie Company, 2/503rd with a heavy heart. That squad was my family. I felt responsible for them. I promised myself I would see them return home to their loved ones. It's hard to explain the connection you have with others during war, especially in the Infantry. When it's your team's job to close with and destroy the enemy, there is no closer bond.

Speaking of the enemy, let me make a comment about them. You would be wise to have respect for the enemy soldiers. We had something in common. We were soldiers. We were the ones to fight and to die and did not have the time to discuss who was right and who was wrong. This was combat, and someone was going to win, and someone was going to lose. 2nd Squad had my commitment that my guys were going to make it home.

I said goodbye to my squad, shaking hands, walking around in our tent from one man to the next. I had great respect for these young American men who in most cases had only recently graduated from high school. We had two sayings: "It don't matter" and "Until that time." The meaning would vary from man to man, handshake to handshake.

I reported before the end of June 1966 to Echo Troop, 17th Cavalry, 173rd Airborne Brigade, and in-processed to the LRRP Platoon. Although I'd already been assigned here from December 1965 and through the early months of 1966, I hardly knew anyone. I guess most of those guys had deployed from their home base in Okinawa in May 1965, so most had rotated back home by now.

Immediately, I was amazed how organized everything was. Captain Palmer had picked seven Ranger NCOs, including me. Six of us were E-5s and there was one E-6 who was the Platoon Sergeant. These men were all volunteers and wanted to do more than sit in the rear area in support units. They wanted to get in the fight.

Image 66. We were the "Long-Range Reconnaissance Patrol Detachment" of the 173rd Airborne Brigade. Today's 75th Ranger Regiment traces this as part of their lineage. By July of 1966, all divisions and brigades in Vietnam were authorized to form LRRP units.

As far as our men, most of the young troops had to be trained to do reconnaissance combat skills the way we wanted it done. For this, Captain Palmer coordinated with 5th Special Forces Group in Nha Trang. We flew as many of our men there as we could to be trained with a Special Forces unit called 'Project Delta' (no relation to Delta Force) which ran an LRRP school. (Later that year, on September 15th, 1966, Project Delta was re-formed with a broader mission as the 'MACV Recondo School.') Our LRRP teams were being modeled after Project Delta Special Forces teams. We benefitted greatly from the expertise of the Special Forces.

Image 67. Combat support facilities, the Nha Trang Air Base, and a portion of Nha Trang City. Looking North Northeast.

Image 68. 5th Special Forces Group Main
Gate at Nha Trang Air Base.

Arriving at the school, the candidates would go on 'The Run' to wear everyone down and get your attention. It's seven miles carrying a 35lb sandbag. Then, as you catch your breath, you'd get an orientation from the Commandant of the School, explaining what you were going to be doing and what was expected of you, including the strict physical and academic standards. Those who could not keep up would be quietly returned to their parent unit. Project Delta would not be wasting any time on candidates who were falling behind. There was a lot to teach. P.T. every morning. 18-hour days. This was not for a badge. No one wanted you to quit. They wanted you to learn, return to your unit, and apply this in combat immediately. The Cadre was introduced, and your studies began.

Image 69. Entrance to the Project Delta
compound in Nha Trang in 1966.

The first week was nearly all classroom work, learning the concepts of the Long-Range Reconnaissance Patrol. This was not merely academic. This was real-world. Land navigation using the actual charts you'd be using in combat. Medical training in a combat zone, starting an IV and using Blood Expander Kits, putting in stitches. Identifying the equipment and weapons of the enemy that currently surrounds your unit in the field.

The second week was nearly all hands on, using the explosives your unit is using against the enemy this week. Firing the weapons your enemy is currently using against your unit. Rappelling from UH-1s and CH-47s with current equipment and techniques. Guiding a helicopter with the radio, smoke, and hand signals currently being used for identification and authentication.

The third week, you prepared for and executed your 'final test,' an actual combat patrol. This is the only school to have a live combat patrol as part of the curriculum! If you passed, there was a graduation ceremony, and you were returned to your parent unit after a couple of days of R&R at the Nha Trang beach.

Image 70. Entrance to the Recondo School, Nha Trang. The word Recondo comes from reconnaissance commando.

Prior to this school opening up, many of the early LRRP volunteers never had the chance to attend any formal training because the 173rd Airborne Brigade was constantly out on operations and would constantly be pulling their personnel back to their normal units. Spec 4 Larry Cole, a member of my team, said it was the finest Army school he ever attended. The instructors were subject matter experts, professional and personable. (You'll hear a story about how Larry helped in saving my life.)

But some of us NCOs did *not* get the opportunity to go to Nha Trang, including me, since I'd been to Ranger School and had been a part of Special Forces already. We had to have LRRP teams constantly running operations for our brigade in War Zone D. So, back home at Bien Hoa, I did the on-the-job training in War Zone D, standardizing on the current SOPs taught at Nha Trang. We trained on SOPs for infiltration and extraction, locating and approaching an enemy force, surveillance, ambush, and prisoner snatch. But I greatly admire what the Army did through Project Delta, the 5th Special Forces Group, and the Recondo School.

Units like the LRRP have always attracted soldiers that understand high risk and don't mind being called upon to do hard things. Here are a few more of those good men.

LRRP Team 5's leader was Sgt Guill. He made two combat jumps in WWII (with the 11th Airborne Division) and two jumps in Korea (with the 187th Regimental Combat Team). Let's put that in perspective. The only jumps that qualify as combat jumps are those where a sizeable unit is jumping into territory that is controlled by the enemy. They are *very* rare. In the entire Vietnam War, there was only *one* combat jump. And in all the combat operations in the decades since then, there have been only three more. Sgt Guill had earned the Combat Infantryman Badge (CIB), three times over. It was an honor to be in his company.

Guill didn't talk much of the past. Some guys were telling me that he had, at one point, attained the rank of Master Sergeant (E-8) back when he was in Special Forces, but here he is, one of us E-5s. It was a mystery. Whatever the cause, he was truly an asset for our LRRP. For me it was Special Forces' loss and our gain. Though Guill didn't tell us anything about his past verbally, you could read all about it whenever he took his shirt off. There were scars, including multiple bullet holes on his body. Guill was a natural recon patrol leader. He knew how to operate in the jungle with only six men on his team.

Sergeant Roger Brown was the leader for Team 7. He was outstanding. Everyone called him 'Ranger.' 'Ranger Brown' was born to be a Ranger. When the doctor slapped him on the ass, that baby yelled, "**Ranger**!" Roger was a meticulous planner. Ahead of a patrol, he rehearsed all the actions the team could encounter. His team completed the only (to my knowledge) successful prisoner snatch in War Zone D. He volunteered for several tours in Vietnam. He eventually became a commissioned officer and was assigned to the original 75th Ranger Regiment when it was created in January 1969. The 75th combined all the LRRPs into one unit. He served as a Ranger Platoon Leader and later as a Ranger Company Commander in the 1st Ranger Battalion. He was always there for the young soldiers. (It was my great privilege to see Roger Brown inducted into the Ranger Hall of Fame in July 2004.)

Sergeant 'Snuffy' Smith was the leader for Team 1. He came from the 82nd Airborne and I had first met him in Ranger School in 1964. He would come up to me after they gave us our mission briefs grinning and say, "You know,

Ranger buddy, if I didn't know better, I might think they're trying to get us killed."

The leader of Team 2 was a big Texan, "Bronco" Williams. He was known for always being able to make contact. It seemed like his team would always be (helicopter) extracted hot. He was a good team leader. He always cared for his team. The men were always his top priority.

Sgt Gary Hamilton led Team 6. He came from the 82nd Aviation Battalion. He had been a door gunner on one of the UH-1B gunships. There, he'd been doing a lot of infils and exfils and he said he was tired of being a spectator. I guess he was like, "I wish I could hop out and take a walk around." I became good friends with Gary. He wasn't a very talkative guy, but sharing a drink one day, he explained to me that he was asked to leave 82nd Aviation Battalion. They were in support of an infantry unit in heavy contact with the enemy. The Falcons were providing supporting fire. Gary was leaning way out of the gunship, attached by a monkey strap, firing his M60 machine gun. The M60 was a free gun on a lanyard cord (it was not connected to a tripod or anything metal). Well, the gunship started receiving hits from the ground and the pilot made a sudden, evasive maneuver. It threw Gary off balance, he fell forward, he and the M60 spun around, and he shot the tail rotor of his own gunship. He was politely asked to find a better home. Perhaps he would fit well in the Infantry. Gary joined the LRRP. His wish had come true.

Mine was Team 4. My Assistant Team Leader was Corporal Mike Howard. He later got a team of his own. Mike used to be with the Golden Knights, US Army parachute team. He had thousands of parachute jumps. What he did best was a demonstration called 'the cut-away.' If your main parachute malfunctions, the cut-away is the procedure for getting rid of the main canopy before activating your reserve parachute. Mike used to tell us how he thrilled the audience with the cut-away. He'd jump from 10,000 feet, freefall to around 7000 feet, and then activate the main canopy. He'd create a malfunction called a streamer, falling at high speed to about 2000 feet. At that point, he'd cut away from the streaming main, then fall to around 1000 feet and activate his reserve. 1000 feet is a safe altitude. But Mike was confident and would push it. Many times, after the cut-away, he would fall to 500 feet before pulling his reserve. The word was that he got fired and then re-hired (which was unheard of). He said that sometimes his foot would touch the ground immediately after the reserve chute would reach full inflation. I guess that would drive the safety people crazy. [Last time I saw Mike was in 1974 at Fort Bragg, NC, where he was an instructor at the Military Freefall School for HALO (High Altitude, Low Opening) jumps.]

Spec 4 Chris 'Turtle' Christensen was one that I knew when I was in Echo Troop in 1965. He had extended his tour for an extra year. I never saw him get excited. No matter what the situation was in combat, he was calm and cool-headed. He was once in a P.T. exercise called 'the mud pit' where a group of soldiers have to wrestle/push every other guy out of the pit. He was immovable and victorious and won the title, 'the Mississippi Mud Turtle.' That and his cool temperament established his nickname. His outstanding recon abilities always enhanced any team. He was an excellent field soldier. He carried an M1 carbine instead of a machine gun and he was one of our M79 grenade launchers. Turtle spent more time "in the hole" (on combat patrols) than anyone else. He was assigned to my team but would also volunteer to go out with other teams if they were short a man in the time in between our patrols. He had multiple tours in Vietnam, also serving with the LRRP detachment of the 101st Airborne Division.

There was Spec 4 Ricca, who was a great Assistant Team Leader for me. Corporal Kiser (we called him 'Corp') also was an excellent ATL. He came from an artillery unit in the 173rd.

Image 71. One iteration of Team 4.
Back Row (l-r): Bo Bolen, Gary Wolfgang 'Wolf' Loetz, 'Corp' Kiser.
Front Row: Collins, Vern Ward, Jake

I owe a debt of gratitude to the soldiers I served with. I'm an old man and can't remember all the men's names, but here are a few others I don't mention elsewhere in this book: Lang, Boen, Butch Brune, Lotz, Thomas, Fraley, Baker, Porter, Potter, Larry 'Sweetpea' Jones, Williams, and Jack Lewis.

I want to tell you a theme I instilled in my team. Here's the way I'd teach it.

"Years before he met my mother, my stepfather had fought the Nazis as part of the resistance in our homeland Ukraine. He shared with me lessons he'd learned about fighting an unconventional war. You have the hunter and the hunted. Be the hunter. You chose the time of engagement. When you hunt Siberian tigers, the advantage lies in being the first one to see your opponent. If you see the tiger first, you have the advantage of your long rifle to kill the tiger from a distance. But if the tiger sees you, the tiger has the advantage of stalking. He has studied every inch of this terrain for years and will pick a time and place for a close-quarters attack. The tiger will use surprise, speed and violent action to defeat you. The tiger will always leap on its prey and his underbelly will be exposed. In that moment, do not waste a moment fumbling for the rifle. The only option is to drop to one knee and draw the knife which you must always be carrying in your waist band. The last chance you have is to rip the belly of the tiger. You will be seriously hurt, but never give up, even if you are certain that you are going to die. Do something before dying. It may not be the day for you to die."

I told that story throughout my military career. Most guys would stand there, looking at me. They'd wait for the moral of the story. But I wanted them to decide their own moral. I always thought it was a good picture of individual struggle. It's really up to them to determine in their own heart who will perish and who will win. You think you have the technology that might give you the decisive advantage. But I tried to draw on the intangible strengths of each man in our six-man team, something far more important than technology. We would have to act as one in each difficult situation, in the worst moment of their lives. Together in that moment, we had to choose to be the hunter.[13]

Captain Palmer kept records of the teams inserted into the hole. Our team, Team 4, had 14 insertions into enemy-controlled areas in a four-month period from June through September 1966. The typical mission lasted three days. One insertion was more than enough for a lifetime.

In September, the LRRP unit got a new Commanding Officer. We hated to lose Captain Palmer. We considered him the godfather of 173rd's LRRP detachment. But you couldn't find a better replacement than Captain Robert Carroll. Their style of commanding was different, but they had one thing in common. The individual soldier came first. When a team called for extraction, that had priority over all else. They never questioned the Team Leader's decision for extraction. The time for questions would come after the team was safely extracted. And, as you'll see, Captain Carroll would soon earn our great respect in this regard.

[In September, the recordkeeping system changed, and I did not keep track of how many insertions we had after that.]

---

13 Share your story. Don't worry about making it a perfect story. People with Combat Experience need to tell their stories to the younger generations.

24

LRRP Prisoner Snatch, Vietnam

1966

Out of all the missions and insertions, there are two that I will remember for the rest of my life and they both came near the end of that tour. I'm not sure whether I passed through the gates of heaven or of hell.

The first is a firefight on September 21st, 1966. I apologize if this comes across as bragging, but it might help you to know ahead of time that for this action I received a Bronze Star and my only Purple Heart. A lot of guys have experiences like this and my hope is that this will help them tell their stories.

Mike Howard was my ATL, and we were in War Zone D, about 40 miles northeast of Saigon. The mission was to snatch a prisoner from the Viet Cong. Prisoner snatch is pretty much the most delicate and dangerous mission. When a mission called for a prisoner snatch, it would be performed on the last day of the mission. This was deep in VC-controlled territory. Our last patrol was recon-only. For this patrol, our focus changes from recon to combat. Set an ambush, kill most, but capture at least one alive. I have yet to see a VC soldier volunteer to be captured. Changing your team's mindset from recon to prisoner snatch is like jumping from one boat to another mid-stream.

On this mission, we (Team 4) have eight guys. We inserted on 20 September 1966 at last light and then we travelled until it was pitch-dark and set up our RON (a camp in which you will Remain Over Night) location. At first light we moved out and found an active, freshly used trail within a few hours. We decided on a location for the snatch, and then set up left and right security.

Mike and I are going to do the snatch. We're deep in the jungle, and I'm coding the SITREP to our higher command. I'm carrying an M3A1 .45 cal 'Grease Gun.' It has an optional silencer. I think you see the logic. If only two or three soldiers come down the trail, we quietly dispatch the ones we don't want, and the prisoner can be subdued without alerting others that may be within earshot. The M3A1 Grease Gun is an excellent submachinegun for close quarters battle. It's a little heavy, since I'm using a 30-round magazine, but its knock-down power is good.

Sitting here, I have the sub machinegun in front of my chest and a map in my left hand. My radio is in my lap, and in a low voice, I give the coded location and situation with the handset. It's a very quiet task. Mike and I are less than 10 feet from the trail.

Suddenly from the left, there are three Viet Cong: one in front, and two others about 15 meters behind him. Left side security sees them first and gets our attention. Mike hears them at about that same time. He's to my left, and he reaches over and pokes me in the ribs with his right hand. I look up. They're moving at a fast walk from my left to my

Image 72. United States Submachine Gun, Cal. .45,
M3 was called the 'Grease Gun' or 'Greaser' because
it looks like the mechanics' tool. Because it's not rifled,
it would not be in the category of a machine gun.
Hence, it is in the 'submachine gun' category.

right. Now the lead one (about 40 feet in front of the other two) is passing in front of my position.

I drop my map, making a little noise and at that same time, left side security opens up on the two guys in the back, dropping them immediately. I believe these three guys are alone, so I quickly raise my Grease Gun and yell "Dung Lai!" ("Stop!") at the lead man. He turns around, seeing what has happened to his comrades and starts running away off the path into the jungle.

Mike takes a semi-automatic shot and succeeds in wounding his target. I fire a burst with my submachinegun. The Grease Gun actually shoots relatively slow, compared to a normal machine gun, so I have a little more aiming control. I'm standing behind him and only about three feet off to the side. I don't think Mike appreciated me shooting over his shoulder like that. He turns and yells, "God dammit, Jake!"

It's over in about one minute. We have two VC dead and one wounded, lying near the trail. We patch him up as best we can to make sure he doesn't die on us. We have our prisoner!

I call in the situation and ask for immediate chopper extraction. We put our wounded VC prisoner on a stretcher. (On patrol, we always have at least one guy bring a collapsible one in his pack.) This only takes a few minutes and—

…all of a sudden, left security opens up *full-auto*!

Get out! Get OUT! Evidently, the three VC we've hit are a point security element for a larger unit! I know the helicopters are on the way. We're in a hurried retrograde (a fighting withdrawal toward our LZ), with two of us lugging a VC on a stretcher! We're moving away from the trail, but the two bodies will indicate to them exactly where to start off into the jungle to begin looking for us.

After a few hundred yards of lugging the stretcher with the deadweight of this VC through the hilly jungle, we hear that our LRRP Company commander, Captain Carroll, is in the air. I tell him loud and clear on the radio, "This is an Amber!" which means, 'Get us out quick.' Captain Carroll knows this is an emergency extraction of the highest priority. Our lives are in danger, and we are in heavy contact with a much larger enemy unit in hot pursuit.

We are organized. We're doing our SOP break-contact tactics. The man furthest ahead, pauses along the path and sets up protective fire to the rear to let all the other guys pass him. Then the next guy furthest ahead would stop and set up the same thing.

After about 400 meters, I can hear the enemy catching up with us, a lot of loud voices and sporadic gunfire. They're spread out in search of us. We can't make it out of here carrying a wounded VC! Realistically, it's slowing down two guys to handle the litter through the jungle, so only six of us are actually able to perform the break-contact and fight. This VC is an enemy soldier. Our lives are in danger. We are going to be overrun by our pursuers. I can hear our helicopters coming. They're within a couple of miles of our LZ now.

After slipping and running and stumbling in the shadows under the jungle canopy through the sharp, broken bamboo and all the undergrowth, we can now see the sunlight of the LZ. It's the most beautiful sight! But it's 200 meters away from us. And we're exhausted. We have to stop to let the porters catch their breath. Mike Howard and Larry 'Red' Cole are with me. We're almost going to make it out of here.

We've got a minute while we're waiting, so we're checking on the prisoner. He's unconscious by this time. We try to patch up wherever he's bleeding from. This guy looks dead. "Is he breathing?" Dammit, no pulse. What? He's dead. Goddammit, our prisoner's dead! Dammit, this guy was the reason for this patrol.

We all immediately spring toward the LZ, freed from the ball-and-chain. It's like we have rockets on our feet. We're going to make it. This is the fastest 100-yard dash that any of us thought we could ever run.

Hot extraction! Our chopper is now overhead, rapidly descending the last 100 feet. The enemy now knows exactly where we're going by the sound of the helicopters. They're no longer spreading out; they're concentrating straight toward us. They're driven by max adrenaline, just like us. They're at max heartbeats per second, just like us. But they have a biological advantage over us—a concoction of vengeance and righteous indignation coursing through their veins. They are the hunter now. We are the prey. They are unified, focused and driven to kill us and down those helicopters. Our eight guys are now shooting at all comers. First there are two or three VC running toward us, diving, firing. Single rounds, full-auto, an explosion of one of our grenades. Now there are about ten of them firing at us. As the chopper settles, the door gunner on this side is firing his M60 over our heads. We're sprinting from the trees to the chopper, 40 feet away. A couple of gunships are firing their rockets and 40mm grenades to good effect.

Image 73. This stock photo from Vietnam
captures elements of this story.

What a sight! Captain Carroll is on our extraction bird! I could hug him! In seconds, we are crammed into the chopper. We're grabbing on to canvas straps and metal handholds. We're lifting away. Away from the enemy unit, blasting their muzzle flashes from the darker jungle apron around the LZ. Lifting away from the lifeless body bleeding on the stretcher there under that banana tree with gauze and an open canteen lying a foot away. Ascending away from the popped blue smoke and scarred tree trunks and long, yellow-green grass blown flat under the wash of the chopper blast. Moving south, away from the LZ, away from the open field, handing off the danger to the Huey gunships.

Less than 20 minutes later, we landed at the helicopter parking area on Bien Hoa Air Base where a deuce-and-a-half truck then took us back to our unit. In our intel debrief, we reported "Prisoner captured, but he died of his wounds. The body was left for his unit to find." I sincerely hope his unit gives it proper respect.

We feel great because we didn't lose anyone. We made contact and came back without any casualties. I was the only one who had to go to the dispensary. I had wounds on my right hand on my index finger and thumb. And when the medics at the dispensary first saw me, they were scared as hell, because I was covered in blood. But actually, most of the blood was that of the VC prisoner.

I showed them that the blood was coming from my hand. It took about eight stitches. They treated me and sent

me on my way. I was considered a "Casualty as a result
of hostile fire." My name came down on a casualty feeder
report and orders were generated for a Purple Heart.

Image 74. Tiger stripes. Here in 1966, we're just about
to launch from our base camp on the prisoner-snatch
mission. Mike Howard is in the background.

25

LRRP Hot Extraction, Vietnam

1966

On October 3ʳᵈ, 1966, I was promoted to E-6 Staff Sergeant. As we neared the end of 1966, we were also nearing the end of my 12-month tour of duty in Vietnam.

My last ATL was Spec 5 (Specialist 5, an E-5 rank) Reed Cundiff. Believe it or not, he came from a finance detachment. To be frank, he didn't go out of his way to impress the other team leaders. He wore Coke-bottle-thick glasses. To them, he seemed just a quiet ordinary soldier from the rear area. I picked him because he had a certain calm about him. He never tried to get your attention. But sometimes you kick some dirt and up comes a ten-carat diamond. That's how I see the day that I picked Reed for my team.

Reed was on my last patrol of this tour, December 8ᵗʰ, 1966, where I got my second Bronze Star. That mission turned really sour and we had to fight our way out. We were still fighting at the LZ for a late evening emergency extraction. Late evening is cutting it close. The window for extraction closes at sunset.

In November 1966, we'd gotten news that Captain Carroll was leaving. Our new commander was a West Point graduate. Right from the git-go, we knew he wasn't like Captain Palmer or Captain Carroll.

I don't like to slander (and this is just my side of the story), so I will just call him "Captain." We just never clicked with him. Morale began to drop.

The only salvation was that we still had Lieutenant Vencill. Lt Carlton Vencill had been our XO (Executive Officer) all the way since Captain Palmer's time. We had a strong bond among the six team leaders and we had been hoping that Lt Vencill would become the commander. He was an outstanding officer and leader, always there for you. (I always considered him worthy of being a sergeant!) The troops respected him. But it was not to be.

We were deployed forward and working out of a base camp. One day, Ranger Brown, the team leader for Team 7, got alerted for a mission and went to the captain's hooch to receive the mission brief. Ranger came to me immediately afterward, "The (%$#@) just gave me my mission lying on his ass in a hammock!" Preparing a team for insertion is the most important thing in the world. If you think otherwise, then you are not fit to command them.

My opinion was, by now, cemented. I said, "That son of a bitch is going to wax a team with that attitude."

My worries were almost realized, and it was with my team.

Operation Canary (December 4th – 14th, 1966) was a covering operation in which the role of the 173rd Airborne Brigade was to help secure Route 15, a highway running 40 miles southeast from Saigon to the coast.

[NOTE: This was all in coordination with other large units including some from the Australian Army and was in support of the 9th Infantry Division coming ashore at the port city of Vung Tau (you can see it at the southernmost point on the map below). The 9th Infantry Division was from Fort Riley KS and would come ashore on Dec 16th.]

Image 75. Our launch point is shown with the blue marker. The north-south road nearby is Route 15. Helicopters took us south from there to our infiltration LZ.

On the evening of December 8th, we (Team 4) launched from our base camp east of Saigon [Landing Zone Stump (Army map reference YS364865) near Xuan Loc] and infiltrated by helicopter at last light to a small LZ about one mile to the east [Map reference YS385875]. We immediately moved south, away from the LZ with Corporal Manuel Moya on point, then Larry Cole, followed by my RTO, then me, then Reed Cundiff (ATL), and Roger Bumgardner at the rear.

Image 76. Spec 4 Larry 'Red' Cole at Bien Hoa in November 1966. Red had come to us after graduating from Project Delta LRRP School at Nha Trang on September 3rd.

Image 77. Manuel Moya and Reed Cundiff departing on an LRRP mission aboard a UH-1 Huey. Tiger Stripes uniform. Photo credit: Co Reentmeister, a photographer with LIFE Magazine.

We kept a quick pace, pushing 400 meters through some thick jungle, making sure we were not followed. At that point, we stopped for a security halt and to make contact with our air relay, callsign 'Cigar,' an Air Force O-1 Bird Dog observation plane.

Image 78. Cessna O-1 Bird Dog armed with
white phosphorus 'Willie Pete' rockets.

We confirmed radio contact and told him we were safe.
The messages were quick, concise, out. The sun had set.
The jungle was dark, no moonlight. Sounds of birds and,
every now and then, a land animal. (This area was a tiger
preserve during French colonial times.) Now we'd go radio silent. We were on our own until our next pre-arranged
radio contact time at dawn.

We spotted a large grove of thick, tall brush and set
up our RON (Remain Over Night) in there. We needed
to become invisible. Making contact tonight would likely
mean death for us. Extractions or rescue attempts would
never realistically be attempted prior to dawn. We all took
turns pulling guard. As much as anything, the guard is
needed to stop us from snoring—that could compromise
our position.

Before first light, we are all ready, Stand-To, for that critical half-hour. Then we move out. This is Recondo life. On the move, finding enemy units, relaying to Intel the size and location. Try *not* to engage. We are 30 kilometers from our organic 173rd artillery support.

Several hours into the morning, Moya stops us. He sees an east-west trail about 50 meters ahead of us. It's more than a trail; it's a substantial dirt road. This is our objective, trail watching for enemy troop movements.

Trail watching is dangerous because if you can see the enemy, they can also stumble upon you. We set up on the south side of the road. About 50 meters to our right (east), there's an old base camp with some defensive positions. There's a partially concealed observation position that gives us a good view to the road. We decide that it's maybe worth considering as an RON for later tonight, but we'll set up a good distance away from it for now and observe whether anyone uses it today.

Moya and Roger Bumgardner (trained as our squad's 'senior scout'), become left security, observing the road westward. Reed Cundiff, my ATL, and Larry "Red" Cole (for this patrol he's our 'junior scout'), set up as right security looking to the east (including the old abandoned base camp). I set up in the middle about 10 meters south of the trail. For this mission, my RTO (Radio Telephone Operator) also has the role of medic for our team.

We are a primary observation team and, as such, we make our aerial relay report at our specified time, a little after noon. I report that we are at our objective, I give our location and status. Quick, concise, out.

Less than an hour after we are in position, we hear foot-steps and talking coming from the west on the trail. It's two males and a female, all armed with carbines. They are re-laxed, with weapons strapped to their backpacks, not even on their shoulders. It becomes quiet again, with only the sound of an animal, now and then. Only a few minutes lat-er, a young male in a light blue jacket comes down the road armed with a carbine. He's moving slowly and looking all around. Now we see that there are two more Viet Cong males close behind him. They have rifles but are more at ease walking. Quiet jungle again.

About an hour goes by. An older male with a rifle strapped to his pack is leading seven females walking alongside bi-cycles they were using to carry very large packs.

A long, boring hour of warm humid air. Soft sounds of birds and jungle animals. Then...

All of a sudden, in the distance, to the east, we hear a gunshot. The jungle gets quiet. That gets us all listening closely. A few short minutes later, we hear an argument. It's two guys with AK-47s coming into view from the east. They're annoyed about something. Reed doesn't think it's the normal Vietnamese dialect that we're used to hearing. Looking at them, they are much larger and taller than the typ-ical Vietnamese we're used to seeing. We also see some pith helmets. All this makes us think that these are not Viet Cong (the communist militia operating within South Vietnam) but are regular North Vietnam Army (NVA) or advisors from China that our intel folks tell us are working in the area.

At our prescribed mid-afternoon reporting time, I turn on the radio and make contact with the O-1 air observa-tion relay. This report takes a little bit of time. Reed has recorded all the data in his notebook and gives us the full report. My RTO reports the numbers of enemy, the type of activity, and times.

Now, it's getting into late afternoon, and we've been seeing more and more Viet Cong and NVA traffic walking by. We eventually have to (non-verbally) acknowledge to each other that we are in the middle of a large enemy movement. The shadows are long and I'm considering where we're going to spend the night. It's around 4pm and the sun sets at 5:30pm. With so much road activity, there's no opportunity for me to walk about to choose a great RON.

Dammit, now a true, platoon-size force (looks like a weapons platoon) is coming from the west. They're wearing the typical VC black uniforms and they move down the trail in tactical silence and discipline. Reed Cundiff recorded that the count was 17. As they pass, it looks like they have two Browning M1919 .30 cal machine guns, a .50 cal heavy machine gun, and an 82mm mortar. The .50 cal is slung from a pole carried on the shoulders of two VC. The mortar is carried in a similar way.

Image 79. A Browning M1919A6 .30 caliber machine gun.

Military-Today.com

Image 80. A Browning M2 .50 caliber machine gun.

Image 81. A Russian WWII M1941 82mm mortar.

Their sound does not march away into the distance. Instead, they sound like they're going to occupy the old abandoned base camp and maybe spend the night, same as we were considering. We still have an hour of daylight. We'll see what happens.

Great. Now 16 more enemy soldiers pass before us from left to right. They stop just a little bit down the road to our right, near the base camp. They're talking. The sounds of packs being dropped. This is only about 40 meters from us. They start unpacking. They're sending out security. Two guys with one of the M1919 .30 cal machine guns march back up the trail from our right to our left and set up about 10 meters up the trail beyond Moya and Bumgardner, who are dead silent, heads down. At this point, we're practically surrounded.

Now, my thoughts are that we have an open area about 200 meters south of us that we are hoping to use for our extraction LZ. But I'm obligated to consider the likelihood that it could be occupied or within observation of enemy forces. The VC/NVA have learned to keep all open areas under observation. They know how Americans and Australians and South Vietnamese are using helicopter assault for both large operations and for quick reaction force insertions that could be on them in minutes.

We hear someone playing a tune on a harmonica in the camp to our right. With the sun going down, I decide that I can't just let our situation deteriorate. I break squelch on my radio three times, steadily (pressing the TALK button). That means urgent info to follow and that I am not able to talk at full voice volume. I turn my radio volume down so that only I can hear. "Cigar" gives me a "Roger" and asks me a few basic questions that will be answered *yes* or *no*. Breaking squelch once means *yes*, twice means *no*.

Cigar: "Are you ok?" (I break squelch twice for "No.")

Cigar: "Are you close to the enemy?" (I break squelch once for "Yes.")

Cigar: "Do you need emergency extraction immediately?" (Break twice.)

Cigar: "Will you need emergency extraction?" (Break once.)

Our extraction LZ was to the south of us and would require us to push through 200 meters of jungle/forest/bamboo.

We pass the word to the team members, "Meet in the middle at the radio." We're all trying to avoid making any noise, stealthily stepping with no sudden motion, but then... **Snap**!

A piece of bamboo snapped; in our minds it feels the same as a rifle shot! All enemy conversation ceases. (It's completely quiet.)

And then all hell breaks loose! Moya and Bumgardner initiate because they believe they'd been spotted by a couple of the enemy. This is grenade throwing and full-auto, the sounds of breaking contact. Forget squelch, I'm immediately declaring "Amber! Amber!", meaning, 'This is a life-or-death situation. We need immediate, emergency, hot extraction. We are in contact with the enemy.'

To be clear, the enemy is surprised, confused and terrified. They have no way of knowing our strength. With the number of accurately placed grenades, their estimate might be that they are being attacked by a company. But that's what a 'break-contact' procedure sounds like.

Cigar: "Choppers are on the way. I'll have F-100s (the North American F-100 Super Sabre fighter/bombers) on station in about two minutes. It looks like a hornets' nest. I think they are on both sides of you."

I tell everyone to turn our hats inside out. We have a bright orange, reflective piece of signaling panel sewed inside to let the air observer know who's who.

We're concentrating our fire primarily to the east and north of us, but now looking for the others reported to be to the west of us. I look up briefly. I spot the Cigar aircraft. He launches a 'Willie Pete' rocket that marks the enemy location for the F-100 fast-movers to place their ordinance.

In the middle of this chaos, the captain, our platoon commander, comes on the radio. I am completely surprised to hear him. He wants me to do something. With us feeling pressed on both sides, he's telling me his idea to call in fire from the brigade's battery of 8-inch guns on the enemy. The guns are a few miles away. The enemy is as close as 10 meters. I think it's too dangerous.

I tell him, "After we get extracted, then use the 8-inch guns." (The bursting radius of 8-inch guns is over 100 meters!)

He persists, trying to persuade me.

I refuse: "No sir. No guns. Not while we're down here." It's too dangerously close.

The captain is thinking of engaging the enemy. It feels like the emergency extraction of my team is not his priority. He persists in sharing his rationale.

I put an end to the conversation (with vulgarity added in) threatening him over the radio. "If I lose any of my people, I'm coming to kick your ass, you sonovabitch,"

We pass the word loud and clear, "Keep heading south to our extraction LZ! Help is on the way."

The enemy is now collecting their senses. They advance toward our position, still not knowing what they made contact with. That uncertainty continues to our advantage. Their advance is cautious. They are walking generally south, using automatic fire and hand grenades.

As we're moving and firing, I'm trying to talk to the extraction helicopter. I keep getting cut off by other people talking on my frequency. When word gets around about a Recon Team in Amber, a lot of high-ranking officers get helicopters to take them to observe. Thank God one of them is Brigadier General Smith, the commander of the 173rd Airborne Brigade. Like thunder, he says, "Everybody get off the air! The only people that should be talking are the Recon Team, Cigar, and the extraction chopper! Everyone else, stay off this frequency!"

As we retreat, we hear the helicopters, so things seem to be on track and on procedure. We can almost see the LZ, a brighter area ahead. And now, there is jet noise—truly the sound of freedom—our TACAIR F-100 Super Sabre friendlies, ready to bring Hell and Damnation upon my enemy.

As point, Moya leads us in our run toward the LZ, I'm watching the rear in retrograde. The shadows are getting long as the sun is going away. It's getting harder to see. Depth perception is not as good. I see a couple of crouching enemy soldiers to my right (east) in some thicket. I pause my run, crouch, and fire my M16 from the hip in full auto. My mag runs empty. I'm on one knee beside a tree and putting a fresh 20-round clip in my weapon. All the sudden, red tracers start zipping all around me. Two figures at this moment are running straight at me, head-on, knowing I'm reloading.

An unexpected, loud M16 really startles me. Reed Cundiff's barrel is right over my head. At least one hot brass casing falls into the gap between my ear and my collar, burning my neck. I reflexively cuss at him, "Goddammit, Reed!" Before I'm able to raise my M16, the barrage of automatic drops the two figures, dead. The hot barrel puts cordite smoke all around me in my nose and hair. My emotions continue to race. "You should be getting the team to the LZ!"

Then I look out and realize that the two dead bodies are only five meters from me. I look up to my left and see, standing over me, that Reed is grinning, out of breath, beaming with pride. That's the moment I realized that he had just saved my life. And Larry Cole, now right beside Reed, had been pinpointing the two machine gunners in the dusk with his tracers.

These were not the 'black pajamas' of VC. These were NVA regulars with AK-47s and with another step or two, they would have turned me into a bloody pile of meat.

The pursuit is still raging. The helicopter says, "Give us some smoke. We don't see you yet."

Image 82. M18 Smoke Grenades.

To mark our location while the choppers are still far off could be the kiss of death for them and for us, giving the enemy time to flock to our location. For a few endless, panicking seconds, it feels like a stalemate. No smoke = No pick up. The helicopter will be shot at, so he can only afford to be on the ground for a few seconds. He's got to know exactly where we are. This is where the O-1 Bird Dog forward air controller is irreplaceable. Cigar has been here the whole time and knows exactly who's who on the ground. He tells the helicopter where we are in relation to the white burning hot Willie Pete rocket that he just fired about 50 meters from us. Now the helicopter hovers nearer to us, but stays at altitude, out of range. We're hunkered down at the tree line. The door gunner is aiming his M60 right at our position in the trees, ready to cut us down if he believes we are the enemy. Per procedure, we 'pop a smoke' and immediately I say, "Throwing smoke! Authenticate!"

The chopper pilot tells us the color of the smoke he sees: "Purple." (This is standard protocol to ensure he's looking at the right smoke—the color and the fact that it is being popped right at that moment.)

I say, "That's us."

The chopper descends beneath the treetops into our LZ. He comes right to us as we break out into the open, running crouched per the SOP to give the door gunner a chance to fire over our heads. This is close suppressive fire. As our six-man team approaches, the door gunner is firing from left to right. We climb in and grab on. The doors stay completely open as the helo lifts off, moving forward; we begin a sweeping left bank, away to the

Image 83. Popping smoke for extraction.
A stock photo from Vietnam, 1967

south. Two of us are sitting at the right-side opening; two are on the left. The other two in the middle. All are sitting on the floor.

The Bird Dog pilot is helping us in every way possible. (Later, the story is that he was shooting his pistol out the window!) He's in here with us, God love him! Beyond this, the gunships are in tight, firing machine guns and 2.75-inch rockets and 40mm grenades. Beyond that, two F-100s are laying down strafing and bombs on the Willie Pete marker rockets burning between us and the east/west road to the north of us. It brought tears to my eyes thinking about what everyone was doing for us.

Image 84. A stock photo of a Bell UH-1 Huey outfitted
with a .50 cal machine gun for the door gunner.

As the choppers landed at our base camp, we walked
straight to the intel debrief with the 172nd Military Intel
Detachment guys. They said the indications were that this was
a main force unit of the Phu Loi region. They said the number
and types of people we described indicate this. The fact that
we heard someone playing a tune on a harmonica (Reed and
other guys tried to hum what the melody sounded like) was
helpful. It indicates that our opponents were not just a patrol.
They were acting at ease like they were the perimeter of a

main force. The harmonica's melody was a familiar tune of the Viet Cong Phu Loi regiment from the war zone north of Bien Hoa (see map below). We were outnumbered by something like ten to one. The O-1 FAC (Forward Air Controller) pilot reported he had never received as much ground fire or seen as many secondary explosions from air strikes.

Also, when Team 5, led by Sgt Rivers Evans (who was inserted at the same time, but to the west of us) returned a couple of days later, they told us what they saw. They heard the fire fight in the distance and monitored the radios. Hearing us report the east/west trail during our extraction, they decided to move toward it and spend that night monitoring it. They heard wounded being moved and a lot of talking, crying, and moaning. They couldn't see or count the wounded or dead, but they said there was a steady movement of people going back west for over an hour after the extraction. This indicates that this was the location of possibly a battalion or even a full Viet Cong/NVA regiment.

It was dark when I left the intel debriefing tent. The wind felt good. I could see my team. All of them were safe.

We'd just been through the fire. I had nothing but admiration for my team, these young soldiers. Man! --think about what they'd just accomplished. This is the American soldier. Fierce and fearless. Tenacity. Devotion. I committed to write them up for valor. But first, I had some unfinished business with a certain captain.

I took the long way back to our quarters area at the base camp. The rest of the LRRP Platoon was there (except for one or two teams out on patrol). They were all around us hugging and talking, so extremely happy that we all got out. I asked, "Has anyone seen the captain?"

Image 85. The Phu Loi area was in the thick of the Viet Cong Army's dominion. It is hand-written on this map just below 'IRON TRIANGLE.' 'BEAR CAT' was our launch point for this mission.

I guess Reed and some of the other guys knew I was fixing to step on my poncho strings. I'm telling you, as soon as those words came out of my mouth, they were like defensive tackles stopping my forward progress, making sure I didn't go anywhere, making sure I didn't say anything further, trying to divert my mind to some other topic. Someone handed me a canteen cup half full of something 100 proof. I drank it. It had its effect. In a few minutes, with an adjusted attitude, my mind was…

…looking for that damn captain!

But the defensive linemen prevailed. I made it through that night.

The next day, I was feeling a little less agitated and a little more professional. I heard from another team leader that the captain was considering pressing charges against me for:

- Insubordination,
- Threatening an officer,
- Behavior unbecoming an NCO, and
- Cowardice under fire.

Before I had time to lose my professionalism, I heard that Brigadier General Smith had an opinion on the topic. (I'm not sure, but maybe Lt Vencill and other team leaders and my team members had something to do with it.) General Smith had heard everything. He asked things like how many times I'd been sent in the hole (25-30 missions, which was about as many as anyone had) and when my 12-month tour of duty was scheduled to end. He apparently ordered that I'd pack my stuff and go back to Bien Hoa that night.

I figured I was going to the stockade [we called it 'Long Bien Jail' 'long be in jail' (LBJ)] but instead, a day later I was told I would be going back to the states in a few days as soon as I processed out of the 173rd.

This was all in the week before Christmas. So, it was time for some giving. I started writing awards and decorations recommendations for my guys. My team's performance was stellar. I wrote up a page-long citation on each team member.

Reed Cundiff, I put in for the Distinguished Service Cross. He saved my life. I would've been dead at 26. My two sons John and David would never have seen their father again. They would have only my name on the Vietnam Veterans' Memorial.

I wrote recommendations for Silver Stars for Larry Cole, Roger Bumgardner, Manuel Moya, and our RTO/medic. (Forgive me, I don't remember your name!)

I formally submitted the recommendations for citations at the orderly room.[14]

On Christmas Eve 1966, some of us went to Bien Hoa Air Base's 3rd Surgical Hospital to hear Hank Snow, the country singer who made the song "I've been Everywhere," a #1 hit record on the country charts. (Hank Snow's songs have sold over 80 million records. He had written songs for and mentored Elvis Presley.) I remember feeling pretty good from a lot of Christmas cheer. Hank Snow was signing autographs for everyone. I went up with some others from our unit and we thanked him and his band for giving up their Christmas back home and come to Vietnam to spend it helping us celebrate the birth of Christ.

We offered him a drink for a toast. It was a glass half full of some kind of whiskey. At first, he declined and said he was drinking soda. We said it would really mean a lot to us to be able to honor him with a drink. "Some of our friends did not live to see this Christmas. This is a very special occasion."

---

14 When you find out that a veteran has a certain award or medal, sincerely ask them to describe in detail the story of the events related to the citation. If the veteran doesn't want to talk about it, leave it at that. But let him know that you'd appreciate the honor of hearing it someday, if he/she ever decides they're willing to talk it through.

He did take that glass and drank it with us.

Soon after Christmas, I had my orders in hand for my return home, allowing me four weeks of leave before my report date to the 82nd Airborne Division at Fort Bragg.

Before New Year's Eve, I left Vietnam on a chartered commercial jet, knowing that many of my thoughts would, in some ways, remain there forever. Again, the stewardesses couldn't do enough for us. They knew all too well the differences between a group of passengers crossing the Pacific headed to Vietnam and those coming back from Vietnam. All have changed after a year, especially those wearing a Combat Infantryman Badge. I was so happy to be leaving, but also felt sad (maybe a mixture of guilt?) to leave our brothers who were still fighting and dying. I felt like I was deserting them. Somehow, I knew I would come back.[15]

As we approached the Golden Gate Bridge, the pilot came on and said, "Welcome home! Thank you for all you've done." The sight prompted a lot of hooting and hollering and clapping. Some shook hands across the aisleway.

We landed at San Francisco and were bused to the Oakland army terminal for stateside processing. Standard procedure, they issued every one of us a winter uniform. Remember how, when we were here last, they told us not to waste space packing anything but warm weather clothes? Most of us were wearing our short sleeve khakis. We got

15 In the final chapter, there's more about the importance of retaining soldiers who have Combat Experience.

our pay all squared away and got our travel orders and tickets back to our posts and our homes.

I didn't wait around in lines to get my issue of a green winter Class-A dress uniform. My Army windbreaker was good enough for me. I went to the airport for an early flight to Fayetteville.

Now, on the topic of getting any negativity being in uniform at the airport, I didn't have any problems that whole journey. In fact, some folks were down-right friendly. Someone even bought me a drink at the Atlanta airport. But this was still the early days of the Vietnam War. Things would turn bad later on.

Image 86. Staff Sergeant Jakovenko around 1967.
Notice the backing behind my parachute wings.
This color backing denotes the 325th Infantry.

26

Raider School

1967

While I was under the 'Repo' company (the 82nd Airborne Replacement Company), I was assigned to be an instructor at the 82nd Airborne Raider School. It was kind of a 'mini course' in the tactics taught at Ranger School. They needed Ranger-qualified NCOs fresh from Vietnam to be the cadre. My orders read that I was permanent party to Bravo Company, 2nd Battalion, 325th Infantry, as a Squad Leader but I was assigned special duty as an instructor at Raider School.

At Raider School, my First Sergeant was Tadeusz 'Ted' Gaweda. He impressed me as a professional. He immediately made me feel part of the team. He fostered a culture at Raider School where our priority was to train paratroopers in small unit Ranger tactics that would directly help them in their deployment to Vietnam. The course took about a month, and he wanted it to feel like the 9-week Ranger School at Fort Benning from Day 1. We had some of the most dedicated instructors, working 12-to-18-hour training days. All were Ranger qualified. All had been in Vietnam. First Sergeant Gaweda drove us to train the troops with the real tactics and to make it hard. We knew what awaited them in Vietnam. We made it personal. I was a primary instructor for Patrolling as well as for Hand-to-Hand Combat/ Unarmed Combat.

Image 87. Teaching unarmed combat.

We taught tactics for infiltration by parachute, including night jumps. We taught the newly developed LRRP six-man patrol tactics the Army developed through Project Delta and Recondo School at Nha Trang. I could describe the in-country training of the past year and give them some real-world scenarios from Vietnam that were not going to be found in a manual. I also walked lanes with students during the graded patrols. First Sgt Gaweda preached, "Your troops come first before your military career. Always lead from the front and they will follow."

Image 88. Raider School.

★ ★ ★

I took in a couple of renters. They were single guys going through Special Forces training. I'd served with them in 173rd LRRP. Both were NCOs. This really helped me pay the bills.

That summer of 1967, my old friend Gary Hamilton (who I knew when he was the leader of LRRP Team 6) was going through Special Forces training. He moved in as one of my renters. Three of his classmates used to study for tests at my house. It was Hamilton, Peterson, Corran, and Dix. Upon graduation, they went to Vietnam. I think they ended up in MACV-SOG in CCC (Command & Control, Central, headquartered at Kontum). Peterson was M.I.A., but was later declared KIA Corran remains M.I.A. Drew Dix was awarded the Medal of Honor for actions defending the province capital city of Chau Phu during the Tet Offensive of January and February of 1968.

Then, one inglorious afternoon in December 1967, everything changed for me. We were training a class that was about mid-way through their Raider School. The day was done. The class was doing pretty well. We were to the point when we'd soon parachute the students into a newly certified training area we'd developed at an auxiliary post a little north of us across the state line in Virginia. Then we'd be in the field there for a few days simulating being 'in the hole' (inserted into the area of operations).

Well, it was payday, and I was paying my bills before our deployment. I went to the 82nd Airborne club to pay my dues. The club was pretty much empty, but I did run into one of the machine gunners that used to be attached to my squad in Charlie Company, 2nd Battalion, 503rd Infantry at Bien Hoa. Well, I had to catch up with him. It turns out that he was there to clear his tab at the club. He was getting out of the Army.

He said, "Let's have a drink, for old times' sake."

I was in a hurry, but, what the heck. We walked down the hall and checked the bar. It was dark. Yep, they're not open yet. (I guess it wasn't five o'clock anywhere.) "Let's go to the Class-6 store (the package store on post)."

He went in and came back with a pint of 100-proof 'Old Grand-Dad' bourbon, and a cold bottle of Thunderbird Wine for a chaser. *This reunion is going to need a chaser? I guess this is going to be a little more of a commitment than I was originally thinking.*

I decided, *Well, I have no one waiting for me at home.*

[Advice for younger generations: This is a terrible mindset and a bad decision that sets off a chain of events.]

We sat by the 82nd NCO club under some pine trees. We were catching up on everything that we'd done in our careers so far, and pretty soon the pint of Old Grand-Dad had evaporated along with the bottle of Thunderbird Wine. I made a generous (read *stupid*) gesture in honor of my friend, "The next bottle is on me!"

I walked back over into the package store and returned with more whiskey and a bottle of Mad Dog 20/20. We covered a lot of war stories and pontifications. One of us told a funny story about a bar. That bar happened to be in Southern Pines, only 25 miles away. "Let's go check it out." We got into my sleek GTO, top-down, and started driving.

We never made it off Fort Bragg.

At the intersection of Butner Road and Collins Street, I did a sharp turn and collided with another car. It was a beautiful new Bonneville with two Drill Sergeants ('D.I.s,' Drill Instructors).

I apologized and said I would pay for the damages. The D.I.s were so mad that they decided they'd give me an ass whooping. *That*, I could <u>not</u> agree to. The fight was on. For whatever reason, my brother-in-wartime wasn't helping me at all. But I was actually doing OK, anyway.

Then a young MP pulled up in a jeep.

Somehow, this inspires my friend to pull out—note the genius caliber of my friend—a small, fingernail-cleaning, 2-inch knife. He commands the MP, "Stay out of this! It's two-on-one and he's doing alright!"

The MP ran back to the jeep and started calling on the radio. Whatever he said, we had a half-dozen MP sedans there in minutes, with red and white lights flashing everywhere. Special interest was shown to my friend with the knife. By the way they were yelling at him, I thought the MPs were going to kill him, using their night sticks to disarm him.

I couldn't help myself. I went in to help my friend who was now on the ground. One of the MPs hits me in my midsection with his night stick. My favorite disarming technique in unarmed combat was 'disarming a club attack.' It only took a second, and his arm was seriously hurting.

We trashed multiple MPs and even mixed it up with an officer. By the time the night was over, my friend and I were in the XVIII Airborne Corps detention cell. The Commandant and Command Sergeant Major of 82nd Airborne Division Schools were called to the brig to make a decision about me. They ended up getting me out before midnight. I was one of their Raider School cadre. They didn't want to lose me. They took me to our base camp, out in the forests west of Fort Bragg. They essentially hid me there for a few days until things blew over.

I spent the cold weekend out of sight at the base camp, recuperating from my encounter with the MPs. I had bruises on top of bruises. There was a day or two of waiting, out of communication with anyone. Then, my Raider School Command Sergeant Major came out to talk to me. He told me to report on Monday to my Battalion Commander.

They'd already talked to Sgt Gaweda and my Raider School C.O. (Commanding Officer). They'd already talked to the Battalion Commander. It would likely be an administrative Article 15 and a fine. [Due to my rank (E-6, for the time being), punishment had to be decided by a Battalion Commander.]

When I reported in to the Battalion Commander, I said, "I deserve whatever you decide."

After the counseling, he told me, "You'll have a hard time making any promotions in the 82nd. This went up the chain of command." I was given an opportunity to change units. I appreciate this help from the Battalion Commander. He'd spent time in Special Forces. He knew me and knew I should redeem myself. He arranged for me transfer to an SF unit to see if they could use me.[16]

16 Jakovenko explains that he's not proud of this one. Things escalated quickly and he should have de-escalated. He wishes he'd gotten the car out of the road and not allowed himself to get into a fight with the D.I.s. And far before that, he regrets ever getting into the car. On this day, the fighting spirit should have stayed corked.

27

The Green Beret

1968

I was scheduled to report to the SF headquarters building for an interview. It would be with Command Sergeant Major Ferguson, the Command Sergeant Major for all of Special Forces. He'd be making the decision.

Here's how the interview went. Arriving at the building that morning, I did have some things going for me. I speak several languages. I have combat experience. Still, I was very nervous. I went into the central reception area and noticed the name of the commander of Special Forces, Brigadier General Milley, my old 501st Battle Group commander. He took a stripe from me there in 1963. In counseling me on that occasion, he offered some career advice, given the temperament he observed in me: Maybe I should just settle in my mind that I'll be an E-4 for my entire military career.

When I was called, I walked down the hall to the office of Command Sergeant Major Ferguson and entered.

Command Sergeant Major Ferguson: "Sit down." (A stern silence followed.)

He eventually spoke. "Do you make it a habit of step-ping on your poncho strings?" (The word he used was not 'poncho strings.') I felt that for his sake and mine, I needed to inform him of my past encounter with now Brigadier General Milley, so I did, right up front.

As gruff as he was the whole time, the interview must have gone OK, because he had me do the Special Forces written test that very same day. It was the hardest test I'd ever taken. It took hours. As I finished, Command Sergeant Major Ferguson gave it to a Sgt 1st Class for grading and coldly told me to come back in an hour.

When I returned, I was immediately sent in.

Command Sergeant Major Ferguson: "Sit down." (Another stern silence followed.)

He eventually spoke. "You passed the written test by two points. When you get to the training group, they will assign you an SF MOS

[There were five MOSs for Special Forces:
- Intelligence (11F)
- Engineer (12B)
- Communications (05B)
- Medic (91B)
- Weapons (11B & 11C)]

"Looking at your test scores, I would not try for Intel though that's what they will recommend due to your rank.

Don't try Engineers; that will require you to add two plus two.

Don't try Communications; you can't hardly even speak English.

Forget Medical—enough said.

The only thing left is Weapons; it's mostly hands-on, so there you go."

For all his encouraging compliments, I thought about telling the Command Sergeant Major to shove it. God miraculously kept my mouth shut. When he was done, I politely thanked him for this (career-saving) opportunity, for his advice, and for "all the confidence you have in my potential." (I couldn't help but add that last part.)

I moved forward into this new challenge under less-than-ideal circumstances. I would do my best. In January 1968, I reported to the SF Training Group. This was my path to being awarded the 'S' designator and the 'full flash' on my beret. I would be assigned to one of the operational groups and assigned as a member of an A-team.

We started our training on Smoke Bomb Hill with a *lot* of classroom work. Special Forces have a primary role of teaching a country's indigenous forces military tactics, strategy, and doctrine for defending their country. So, a lot of our classes focused on how to teach.

Looking around at my classmates, the lowest rank was E-5. As far as the instructors, everything was run by senior NCOs. I observed that most Special Forces NCOs were not as rank-conscious as conventional NCOs. They mostly called each other by first names.

The bitter, cold, February and March of 1968 were spent out in the field at Camp Mackall, 20 miles to the west of Fort Bragg. There were no buildings, no tents. Everything we learned in the classroom, we had to put to practical use. The instructors broke our class into groups of ten and took each group to a remote area to set up our living locations. We had to establish our own leadership structure and responsibilities among ourselves. We had to improvise our own shelters. We were given minimal C-Rations, not enough to get us through the day. Instead, we were given a goat. We wasted no time. We butchered it and I was given the cooking responsibilities. We did what we could. I roasted it, baked it, barbequed it, I made stew, but it still tasted like goat.

In the field, we had more classes, but now, we each also had to *teach* classes. It could be survival-related, or it might be tactics. We had to improvise and come up with training aids.

Each student was given a mission to organize, brief, and carry out. We were further broken down into teams of three or four and then had to do compass courses. Some of these were at night. It was so cold and wet. But we drove on as a team.

If someone had a problem, we solved it as a team. We pulled together and would not let anyone even think of quitting. We encouraged each other with "They can smoke us, but they can't eat us." Now, there was no harassment from the cadre. There was no need for that. The terrain and the elements and the lack of sleep took their toll.

They put that 'Special' in each of us. They made it so easy to quit. Just walk up to the nice, warm, GP Medium tent where the cadre headquarters was and say the magic words, "I quit." They would give you a hot cup of coffee with a warm meal and then send you in a warm, comfy vehicle back to your warm, comfy barracks at the main post. No one would say anything against you.

Things never got better. Some got worse. For instance, one day we were coming back to our 10-man camp from a mission. The temperatures were below freezing when we came to a deep, sizeable stream. We spotted a log that bridged the water, and we began crossing it. It was slippery and I ended up in the stream, soaked to the bone. I had to keep moving to keep from freezing. Everyone was completely exhausted, but the team's only priority when we got back to our camp was to get me dry. The team made a huge fire and focused on getting me warm. The team pulled together for me.

At the end of Phase I, we were awarded the Green Beret with a crest, but there would be no flash at this point, since we did not know to which of the three SF Groups we'd be assigned. There was much more training to come. Next up was our SF MOS training.

Per the sage advice of Command Sergeant Major Ferguson, I took the SF Weapons Course. It would last 14 weeks across April – July 1968. On the first day of class, to my surprise, Tyrone Adderly was there. This period was so great. Tyrone has a wonderful wife named Gloria and, together, they have a life-changing impact from this point onward, as you'll hear through the rest of this book. We always ate our noon meal at Tyrone's quarters on post. Gloria was a heck of a cook and so hospitable. Tyrone and Gloria know the challenge that Army life places on a family. Together, they were a model of what an Army family can be.

Our course started with light weapons like pistols, revolvers, automatic weapons, rifles, shotguns, and submachine guns. We learned nomenclature of the weapons of the US, allies, and potential adversaries. We learned cyclic functioning and technical inspection and the repair of weapons, both American and foreign. We learned how to teach others the firing and maintenance of the weapon.

We learned how to improvise weapons with materials on hand.

[I was familiar with improvising firearms. Back in Jersey City, we made zip guns, and I almost was sent to reform school for it in 1955. The only thing that saved me when the police searched my locker was that the three zip guns they found were all missing their firing mechanism. I told them I was making toys for tots. It was December.]

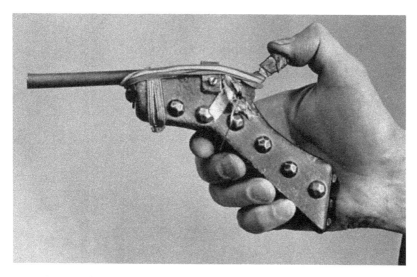

Image 89. A zip gun constructed of wood using a length of car antenna and a house key seized in New York City, 1959. The zip guns we made were never as nice as this one. Photo courtesy of Springfield Armory Museum.

Next phase was heavy weapons: .50 caliber machine guns, recoilless rifles (57mm and 106mm), mortars (60mm,

81mm, and 4.2inch). We practiced teaching people to lay mortars in and how to adjust mortar fire. We learned how to set up a firing center and direct mortar fire. We also studied defensive fire and interlocking fire. We did a lot of night firing.

After I earned my MOS in July, we began the field evaluation phase of SF Training. It's known as 'Robin Sage,' and it lasts about a month. It's a premier unconventional warfare exercise spread over many counties in NC and every SF student has to complete it. The name 'Robin Sage' was derived from the central town of the area, Robbins, NC, (where the first exercise was held in 1952) and a WWII expert in unconventional warfare, US Army Colonel Jerry Sage.

We were broken down into 12-man teams. Each team had two enlisted men for each of the five SF MOSs and two officers. The officers included one captain as team commander and one first lieutenant as team executive officer. We were to resemble an SF A-team. Our team was given a mission that involved making contact with a certain, hard-to-find guerilla chief, winning his trust, and securing an agreement with him that would enlist his guerilla band in the cause of the American allies to fight an enemy of the US. This was the Green Berets' specialty, unconventional warfare. We were immediately put into isolation in some training area barracks for a number of days to prepare a plan. We could ask questions of intel briefers, but no one else. We gave a briefing to our instructors explaining our mission plan, then we departed after dark from Pope AFB in a C-130.

At the jump point that we chose, we parachuted into our DZ. We set up an RON, and at dawn we linked up with a guerilla group per our mission plan. Intel had explained to us that this group consisted of about 30 indigenous people under the command of a hard-nosed guerilla chief. We began discussions with them to come to terms. They needed help, but we had to build trust that we were the right people to provide that help. It was give-and-take. We had to win them over. Through hours of difficult, cross-cultural conversation, we gathered what it was that they really wanted. Hard-nosed doesn't begin to describe them. They were very self-confident. They demanded so much. It was more than we were authorized to promise and more than we were willing to risk for them: their pet projects, their vendettas against rival tribes, and their outright corruption.

We went away to talk by ourselves over and over and made our decisions about what we were prepared to do for them. We had our mission to accomplish, which was to train, equip, and help the guerillas prevail against our common enemy.

Each team member was graded individually on their performance. Grading related to their specific roles and specialties and their ability to work as a part of a Special Forces A-team. Over two weeks in the field, operating on our own, with no input from instructors, the team covered all the trained skills and taught them to the indigenous forces. We made it to our extraction point, we received immediate critique there in the field, and then the instructors decided upon grades that would be recorded for personnel files. We were bused back to Smoke Bomb Hill. All our issued equipment was cleaned, accounted for, and turned in.

This graduation ceremony in July of 1968 was very special. We now had our assignments to an operational

Special Forces Group. We were extremely proud to have a full flash on our berets. We were full-fledged Green Berets. After the ceremony, standing there on the parade field, I was able to congratulate many of my friends—my brothers—who had triumphed together for this moment. Some were from my time in the 82nd Airborne back when I first arrived in 1962. Some were with me in the 173rd in Vietnam. Some now wore the red flash for the 7th SF Group, which had a special focus on the countries of Latin America and South America. Others wore the green flash for the 10th SF Group, specializing in Eastern Europe, the Middle East, and North Africa. I had red/black flash of the 6th SF Group, focusing on Southwest Asia (i.e., Iran, Iraq) and the parts of Southeast Asia other than Vietnam and so did my great friend Tyrone.

The core element in Special Forces is the 12-man A-team. 'A-team' is short for 'ODA Team' (Operational Detachment—Alpha, which is meant to imply 'the fundamental operating unit.') A-teams become a very close-knit family.

[From the term 'A-team' evolves the term 'B-team,' which refers to a Company Headquarters, commanded by a major. This unit is comprised of a number of A-teams. The 'C-team' then is the Battalion Headquarters, commanded by a lieutenant colonel. This unit is comprised of a number of B-teams (companies).]

When I'd settled into my SF Group at Fort Bragg in July 1968, one of my duties was as a member of the demonstration team at the Gabriel Demonstration Area. We constantly were giving demonstrations to dignitaries on the capabilities of the Special Forces. Part of my demonstration included giving an introduction in Ukrainian to show the audience the linguistic capabilities of Special Forces. We were a 12-man A-team specifically focused on explaining how an A-team operates. On that team, we also had guys fluent in Czechoslovakian, Thai, Mandarin, Spanish, French, German, and Arabic. We'd explain the features of our specialized weapons, we'd rappel from towers, and the Golden Knights freefall team would jump into DZs. You can see an example of this in the John Wayne movie, *The Green Berets*. The opening scene has the Gabriel Demonstration Team giving their presentation to dignitaries.

28

Special Forces Underwater Ops School

1968

Then, in August 68, I was promoted to E-7, Sgt 1st Class, and at last had an opportunity to do something I'd wanted to do since I was a teen. The SF has an underwater operations course which takes seven weeks. After one week of physical testing conducted at Fort Bragg, we headed down to Key West, Florida, for six weeks at the SF Underwater Operations School. I have to say that it was the most challenging course for me, physically and mentally.

First, let me describe the physical. At 0-dark-thirty each day, we had to run a fast mile. The requirement was for us to be at a 6-minute mile. After a few minutes rest, stretching and some pushups, we'd begin 'SCUBA P.T.' which was patterned after that of UDT/SEALs. The runs were a killer. If you dropped more than six feet behind the formation, you had to do remedial runs in the evening. The instructor could run backwards, and we'd still have a hard time keeping up with him as a formation. It was an amazing study in conditioning. The runs go better toward the end of each week.

In the week we graduated, there was one event where we did a 5-mile run and I don't think they slowed down that much from the 6-minute mile.

Now, the mental. We studied the physiology of diving and ways to deal with various injuries that you might encounter underwater. We studied the respiratory and circulatory systems. The written test was tough. But then you also had to successfully perform an oxygen test at a depth of 60 feet breathing pure oxygen for 30 minutes.

Image 90. The Special Forces Underwater Operations School.

We started with over 30 students in our class, and nine graduated. ...but I was not one of the nine. In late September, in week five of training, I had completed my open-circuit qualification. Now, we began training with the closed-circuit Emerson rig which we'd be using for the final three weeks. Unlike compressed air tanks, 'closed-circuit' means that your exhaled air is captured in a tank. In combat, there are times when you don't want bubbles giving away your location. With the Emerson rig, there are no bubbles.

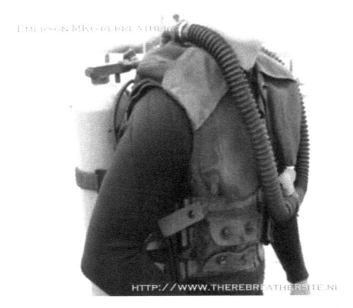

Image 91. The Emerson Mk6 re-breather, recognizable by the fact that two tubes meet at the mouthpiece.

Image 92. My Emerson rig.

Well, on our introduction swim, my manifold regulator malfunctioned. The oxygen hose blew off and, with over 1000 psi, hit the side of my head. It put a hole in my eardrum and almost knocked me out. With a perforated eardrum, I would not be able to swim for many weeks. I had to terminate the course. I was the last one to wash out of the class.

It broke my spirit but there was nothing I could do about it. By early October 1968, I was back home at Fort Bragg back on the Gabriel Demonstration Team for at least a few weeks, until my ear had healed.

[I did go back in 1971, completed the whole 7-week course, and did qualify for closed-circuit diving rigs. I received an assignment to be the team sergeant on a SCUBA team and most of my team were going to SF Underwater Ops School. My battalion commander said, "I know you've been through just about the entire course, but what are you going to do here with your team gone?" I could not come up with a good answer and ended up going through the whole seven weeks with the team as a student. I caught a lot of extra attention from the instructions and did enjoy most of it, especially the closed-circuit Emerson rig training.]

29

Special Forces in Vietnam

1968

Most of my classmates from Special Forces School were coming down on orders for Vietnam. I thought about volunteering to go back. Tyrone Adderly said he was on orders for Vietnam and his wife Gloria was taking it pretty hard this time. When I was visiting their home, we would all talk about it. She was afraid that he may not make it back this time. He'd already served his time there, and he had a Silver Star and two Purple Hearts from 1966 with the 101st Airborne Division as a testimony to how much he'd already done for the cause. As another sobering message to their family, Tyrone's brother, William, was wounded while serving with the 173rd Airborne Brigade in 1966, and he was disabled as a result.

There in their kitchen, I felt the gravity of Gloria's misgivings. At this point, I was making up my mind to do something.

I told Gloria, "I'll go with him. We'll stay together and we'll come back together."

I made a phone call to a lady I knew who handled Special Forces assignments at the Army Personnel Center. "I would like to get on Tyrone's orders."

"That levy is full, but I could send you a few weeks sooner and then you could link up with him in Nha Trang."

That sounded good. I said, "Let's do it."

Before October had ended, I was on my way to Vietnam. I told Tyrone I would connect with him in Nha Trang. I left all my belongings and all the details to the care of a lady friend with the instructions that, if I did not make it home, she would find my sons, John and David, and make sure that they would get everything of mine. I gave her Power of Attorney, and I made a Will specifying all this. My lady friend took me to the Fayetteville airport in my 1968 GTO convertible. I wanted her to use the GTO while I'd be gone. She gave me a hug and said "It will be here waiting for you when you come back. Take care of yourself. Write once in a while."

I wore my uniform on the flights. These were dark days for the military. Many Americans took their frustrations out on us soldiers. Some of us were verbally abused. On this trip, I got some hard looks, some whispers, and mean stares. But that's all. I'd made up my mind that no one was going to insult me or this uniform. If they wanted a confrontation, I could definitely oblige them.

It was a civilian flight from Atlanta to Seattle/Tacoma. There, we took a bus to Fort Lewis to do the processing for a couple of days. We then flew a chartered commercial flight from McChord AFB to our final destination, Nha Trang.

I processed in at 5th Special Forces Group headquarters. It was late October 1968. In these first couple of days, I came across numerous Special Forces guys I knew from

Fort Bragg. All were talking about assignments, the good ones and the ones to stay away from. Many were going to SOG (MACV-SOG, Military Assistance Command, Vietnam-Studies & Observations Group), especially CCN (Command & Control, North). CCN had recently gotten hit and took a lot of casualties, more than 20. For the first time, SOG was not focused strictly on volunteers. Instead, they were, for the time being, assigning people directly to CCN. I had no problem if I had to go to CCN. I guessed that SOG would be similar to our LRRP, six-man recon teams in 1966. I thought I might want to join II Corps' Mike Force or try to become an instructor at Recondo School right there in Nha Trang.

Around the beginning of November 1968, I ran into a friend from 501st, 82nd Airborne. He was wearing civilian clothes and I asked him about that. His reply was that he sometimes wore 'black pajamas' as his uniform (this was the typical uniform of our enemy, the VC). He said he could bring me in to work with him, but that he couldn't say much until I was to become "one of us." At that, he raised his shirt to show me that he was packing a pistol. He would not elaborate on what he did or who he worked for, but he did say it's called 'P.R.U.' I was hesitant. I didn't think I was ready for this cloak and dagger intrigue. I was still new to Special Forces, and I wanted to put into practice what I'd learned about operating as an A-team and my experience in weapons and small unit tactics.

[Later, I found out more about P.R.U. It is the Provincial Reconnaissance Unit, working for the CIA alongside South Vietnamese paramilitary groups. I regret that I couldn't join when he asked. They definitely did some very exotic and challenging covert operations. But my priority was to link up with Tyrone so we could serve together.]

In early November 68, I had to go to in-country training, two weeks at 'Entre Island' just off the coast at Nha Trang. There, I went through some good familiarization training, the latest Dos-and-Don'ts that will keep you alive.

[My belief, though, is that when your number comes up, all the training in the world is not going to keep your heart beating. It's your time to go.]

By the time I got back to Nha Trang, Tyrone was there. He got direct-assigned to MACV-SOG CCN. I said, "I'll go volunteer now. We will go together to CCN."

I told him I was really thinking about the P.R.U. but I said, "Mike Force is the way to go." Tyrone said not to worry about him. He believed his assignment was changing to a 12-month tour at Nha Trang.

To make sure, I went to the personnel office to volunteer for CCN. I knew the personnel sergeant from Fort Bragg. For my own good, he tried to talk me out of volunteering for CCN. He told me, "I hear you. I know that's what you want to do. But look, it's late in the afternoon. I've got a lot of other orders to process. Talk to your friends. Talk to people at the club. Sleep on it. If you still want CCN tomorrow, I'll help you get there."

Late that afternoon, I saw Tyrone for a few minutes. He was busier than a one-eyed tomcat watching twelve rat holes. He told me, "Jake, my orders have changed and now I'm not going to CCN. I've now been assigned here in Nha Trang."

I said, "Well then, if you don't mind, I'm going to try for Mike Force up in II Corps at Pleiku." Tyrone gave me his blessing.

The next morning, I went to talk to my friend at the personnel office. He said, "You're on a list for assignment to Bravo Company up in II Corps. Do you still want to change that to CCN?"

I said, "I'd like to join the Mike Force and they are part of Bravo Company, so let's just stick with that."

I got a full set of equipment issued while still at Nha Trang. They gave me an M1A1 carbine (not a machine gun). I said, "Thanks, but I'd rather have an M16."

"No deal. You can get that from the unit if they have them."

When we got to Pleiku in mid-November 68, there were six of us. We each reported in to Bravo Company and were told the base Command Sergeant Major was going to welcome us. I've forgotten his name, but looking around at his fancy office and air-conditioned accommodations, it seemed like his primary concern was, "Would you like to buy a watch?" Seriously, he made it clear that he would sell you a Seiko watch. I figured some Command Sergeants Major suffered from 'air-conditioning-and-starched-jungle-fatigues' syndrome. They were probably hell on wheels as E-5 to E-8, but once they make that Command Sergeant Major E-9 rank, it seems they have a tendency to lose perspective looking from the ivory tower down upon those in the foxholes. A man smarter than I said of Command Sgts Major, "Most of them are driven by the three *p*'s: perks, privileges and politics." (Forgive my cynicism.)

We soon met the C-team Command Sergeant Major, and he asked each of us to tell him what we expected from our tour of duty. I told him that I was hoping to become part of Bravo Company's Mike Force.

He asked, "How many of you have served in a border A-camp in Vietnam?" Two raised their hands. (An "A-camp" is a forward operating base where an A-team manages/assists a South Vietnamese unit for border surveillance.) He said, "As far as I'm concerned, if you haven't served a tour in a Special Forces A-camp in Vietnam, you are not truly qualified in what you were trained to do—and *expected* to do. That is the tip of the spear. And that is the 'point' of Special Forces." (At this moment, I could see that my chance of going to Mike Force was zero.)

He looked at me and asked me my SF MOS
"Weapons."

"Good! I have just the camp for you. They just held off an NVA regiment and took more than 1000 rounds of incoming mortar and 120mm rockets. They have no Weapons man. It's team A-245 at a border camp called Dak Seang. The only way to get there is by helicopter. All the bridges along Highway 14 have been blown up by the NVA. A-245 sure will be glad to see you."

I thought, *Yeah, and I'm looking forward to meeting them if their still alive when I get there.*

As I packed my gear, I asked everyone I saw if they had heard anything about Dak Seang. (I had to write 'Dak Seang' on my hand. I couldn't remember the name.) No one had anything positive to say about Dak Seang. They said, "Who the hell did you piss off?"

It's in the tri-border area (where the borders of South Vietnam, Cambodia, Laos come together). It definitely qualifies as a fighting border camp.

Image 93. Dak Seang, A-245, is the red circle closest to the Tri-Border with Cambodia.

The next morning, I reported, bag and baggage, with my M1A1 carbine. I had one small concern. I'd asked for ammo for my carbine at Nha Trang and I'd never gotten it. So, I went over to Bravo Company's supply and told them what I was needing. They asked me, "Why do you have a carbine?"

"That's what they gave me at Nha Trang."

They rolled their eyes and gave me a few boxes of ammo. I was told I'd get an M16 when I got to our B-team (company-level HQ) at Kontum. I spent only a couple of hours on the ground at Pleiku.

I caught a UH-1D helicopter to Kontum. It's about a half hour flight. We were about 3000 ft AGL (above ground level). I could see the highlands coming up. It was a beautiful area, green with small villages and rice paddies.

But then you started seeing bomb craters.

At Kontum, I hitch hiked a ride aboard a jeep to get to the admin area for my B-team, B-24. I reported to the Sergeant Major and immediately liked the guy. He could not do enough for you. Anything I needed, he got for me. I don't remember his name, but he definitely acted different from the other two I met in Nha Trang and Pleiku.

At Kontum there was good food, plenty of drink, and it was free. (At Nha Trang and Pleiku, you had to pay for everything.) I stayed at Kontum for a few days. I got briefed and got more equipment issued to me, including an M16 with ten magazines. Everybody wished me Godspeed. Our B-team's weapons supply man told me, "The one good thing about Dak Seang is that all your friendlies are inside the camp. All surrounding villages have been wiped out by the NVA. That means that you have a free fire zone. Anything outside of the camp perimeter is considered bad guys.

Image 94. Kontum Army Airfield, the
headquarters of our B-team, 'B-24.'

Image 95. I went by air from Nha Trang to Pleiku to Kontum
to Dak Seang. Highway 14 was not passable due to guerilla
sabotage of bridges, mines, ambushes, and booby traps.

I caught the re-supply helicopter going to Dak Seang. The pilot said, "We don't hang around the runway. It draws mortar fire. We drop off, pick-up, and we're gone. We don't shut down. A few helicopters and C-7 Caribous have been shot down over the years trying to re-supply Dak Seang. It's a badass camp. Some of the re-supplies they do by airdrop."

I was told that Dak Seang was a new camp. The old camp was further north in the valley. That old camp, called Dak Sut, had been overrun by the NVA back in 1965. The flight took about 45 minutes. Our flight path took us over Dak To (a camp very similar to Dak Seang) where one year earlier, 361 Americans had died under siege from the NVA and not much remained there. I didn't see any villages or crops. Just bombed out and scarred ground from tons of munitions dropped. You could see Highway 14 but there was no traffic on it with all the bridges down. I could see the Dak Poko River on the east and good-sized mountains coming up. The pilot was giving me a pretty good tour and briefing me all the way. He said, "Look to the north. That's Dak Seang there."

As we circled our camp to align on the runway for a tactical arrival, I thought, *Who the hell would build a camp on a slight plateau in a valley? High ground all around and a river less than a mile to the east. It's nice for farming. It's hell to defend tactically.* The camp was built rectangular, and it did not look much larger than a football field.

Coming to a stop on the runway, we were just outside the fence. I could see people on top of perimeter bunkers watching us land—soldiers, yes, but also lots of women and kids. I could see no villages around the camp. All these

Image 96. Dak Seang Special Forces Camp,
home of our A-team, A-245, July 1968.

families lived inside the camp with the Americans. Inside the camp, they had safety and security and paid work. A jeep was waiting for us. The second we touched down we unloaded our people and things, and immediately other people and things were loaded to go to Kontum. This is the only link to civilization. Nobody moved by land. The helicopter did not waste time leaving. True to his word, the pilot landed, unloaded, reloaded, and lifted off in a matter of minutes.

We hurried inside the compound. There was no gate, just several six-foot sawhorses covered with barbed wire.

I've never been on the surface of the moon, but the kilometers surrounding the camp sure did resemble it, with lots of craters and holes. As far as the eye could see (even beyond the border into Cambodia and Laos which was about 18 miles away), most of the vegetation was dead. Our border camps were the release point for the defoliant Agent Orange, all the way into Cambodia and Laos. This was to help us, by denying the NVA the cover of the jungle. We reduced one hazard (enemy mortars raining down upon us) and increased another hazard (hazardous chemicals raining down upon us).

Image 97. Notice that the field of fire outside the fence is free of vegetation. The dependents' quarters are just inside the perimeter bunkers.

30

The A-Camp, Tri-border Area

1969

The camp's perimeter line was always kept clear of vegetation, lined with tactical barbed wire and numerous defensive bunkers. Looking in from the gate, much of the camp was below the ground level, trench warfare, underground bunkers. We went straight to the team house, which was the center of operations. Commo (the communications center) was dug down below the team house. So was the TOC (Tactical Operations Center).

Above ground inside the team house was the dining area with kitchen and a good-sized bar fully stocked with whiskey, beer, and soda. We generated our own electricity from several gasoline-powered generators for our refrigerators. The base had a small canteen where people could buy soda, beer, and cigarettes. This made a small profit that we used to pay for some good things we could get on the Vietnamese economy.

Of course, the Army supplied us with food. We had a cook, and we had a regular re-supply of foodstuffs in from our B-team at Kontum, but we also had an alternate supply chain, the USAF C-7 Caribou aircrews that flew into our small airstrip regularly. We made deals with them for certain things we wanted. We traded war souvenirs for certain foods that they had access to. Generally speaking, anything that the Air Force crews ate and had access to at the various bases they landed at, we were able to get through them. If we acquired a communist SKS semi-automatic rifle (and we regularly did) it could be traded for several cases of steak and other perishables.

All told, we had around 1500 people in our camp. This included:

- US Army Special Forces,
- ARVN (Army of the Republic of Vietnam) Special Forces, and
- the CIDG and many of their wives and children.

The CIDG is the Civilian Irregular Defense Group. In our case, our CIDG was comprised of Montagnards (pronounced 'mon tan YARDs') the indigenous people of the surrounding mountain region. This is a primary role of Special Forces, training the people of a country in the best techniques for defending themselves. If having the families live inside the camp with us seems strange, watch the John Wayne movie *The Green Berets* and you'll get a sense of life at a camp with Montagnards. We loved the "YARDS."

Many of the perimeter fighting bunkers were built with family living quarters attached. Having the Montagnards' dependents in camp had its blessings. For one, we had a steady labor force. We paid the dependents for any work

Image 98. The Montagnards, (from the French 'mountain dwellers') were the largest ethnic minority in South Vietnam. They saw the North Vietnamese communists as enemies but due to poor treatment by the South Vietnamese government, they were no friends with South Vietnamese either. They were strong allies of the US, and reluctant allies with the South Vietnamese.

they did. For another, it made the defenders fight a lot harder because their families were right here in the camp. The families would have every reason to help us fight. Thirdly, the Montagnards did not have to worry about their families' safety. If the Montagnards' families had lived off-post and the NVA were to attack the area, then the Montagnard soldiers would be tempted to run to defend their unprotected village. Most of the time, the surrounding area was threatened by the NVA, and the safest place was inside the camp.

Image 99. The perimeter. Notice the dependents' quarters (under the tin roofs) are right beside the perimeter bunkers where their husbands/fathers would be fighting off the NVA attackers.

On my first day, I met most of the SF A-245 team members. Two were on a company-sized strike force of about 120 Montagnards. CIDG strike force operations were called 'C-operations.' Each C-operation would have at least two American Special Forces and at least two Vietnamese Army (ARVN, Army of the Republic of Vietnam) Special Forces. They are referred to as LLDB (Luc Luong Dac Biet). It's sad to say, but the relationship between the American A-team and its LLDB counterpart was often antagonistic in a lot of border camps. Here in Dak Seang, it seemed somewhat workable.

I was briefed, shown my living quarters and assigned duties. My first priority was to learn what to do in case the camp were to be attacked. I would man the 81mm mortar and provide defensive fire. Next, over the coming weeks, I would be prepared for the role of "providing assistance" to a Montagnard company that defends one of the camp's four sides. As a third priority, after a few weeks, I'd be prepared to go on C-operations.

I was introduced to the Vietnamese commander and the LLDB team. Formally, he was the commander of the camp. The Americans and the Montagnards were allies hosted at the camp by the Vietnamese Army. We inspected the entire 360 degrees of the camp perimeter, and he introduced me to some of the Montagnards responsible for various posts.

I could see right away that the camp defensive positions needed repairs and improvements, urgently. Since I'd not be going on any combat operations for a few weeks, I could focus on my responsibility to improve defensive positions for best use of our weapons and ammunition.

Image 100. Here we are training on the assault with M16s.

Image 101. With the Montagnards, we are running down the
Dak Seang airstrip on the way back from our M16 range.

I did an inventory of all weapons and ammo. We needed:

- 'pre-stocked' ammo (only to be used during an attack on the camp) and
- operational ammo for combat strike C-operations.

I coordinated with our A-team's engineer and came up with a list. We needed to harden our fighting positions. We needed to build some new, better defensive features to make our kill zones more lethal. We needed to increase the amount of barbed and concertina wire. We needed more machine guns. We needed to improve our mortar pits, which had become weathered over the rainy season. We needed to install Claymore mines in certain, more vulnerable points. We needed to create some fougasse barrels (pronounced 'foo GASS) around the perimeter (I'll explain these weapons later.) I loved this job the way an architect loves his job. In my thoughts, *It may take time, but when we finish, this will be one of the best border fighting camps in Vietnam.* I was the camp's 'Weapons Guy' and now you're starting to see what the weapons guy does in a Special Forces A-team. This was the reason I was needed at Dak Seang.

Image 102. A mortar position at Dak Seang. This is a 4.2-inch mortar, 'the big boy.' The red lines that I'm sitting on are aiming lines.

We made our requests to our B-team at Kontum. They gave us a high priority because they knew we were rebuilding from the last attack. In a few days, CH-47 Chinook helicopters started coming in with our requested lumber, defensive wire, weapons and ammunition. We paid the family members to go out and cut bamboo for punji sticks and help fill sandbags and mix cement. We worked from morning til evening on improving our perimeter defensive positions.

The main gate, opening up to the runway, was a defensive nightmare. If the enemy mounted an advance from that direction, our mortar rounds and other H.E. (high explosives) weapons might fend off the attack, but in doing so, we might also tear up our own runway. That's the reason the design put our camp at the end of a runway, rather than at the mid-point. We built a bunker large enough for a .50 cal and an M60 machine gun. The .50 cal locked down that whole flank of our camp, which included the first 200 meters of the runway, the length of two football fields.

Each corner of our rectangle had a bunker with three .30 cal M1919A6 machine guns, one each for the left and right flanks and one in front with interlocking fire of the left and right. Each corner bunker also had a 57mm Recoilless Rifle on top of it, protected by a wall of sandbags. Due to its huge back-blast, it can't be in the same pit as the other guns.

Each of the four sides had five bunkers in between the corners, each with a .30 cal M1919A6 machine gun and a 60mm mortar pit. They mostly were sighted to fire H.E. rounds to land in the kill zone (the area between the outlying concertina wire and the inner fence, which was the wall of our camp).

Around the perimeter we installed trip flares, booby traps, and punji sticks. We also installed over 100 Claymore mines on engineering stakes about 12 inches above ground. Each Claymore had a white phosphorus grenade secured in front with a crisscross of barbed wire.

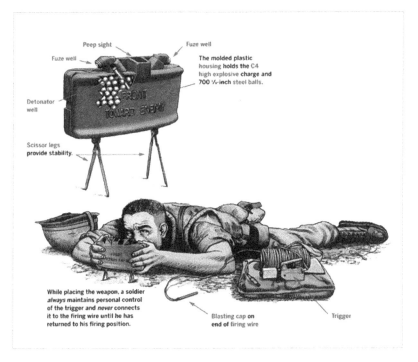

Image 103. The Claymore Mine.

Now, about the fougasse. We also buried in the ground, at an angle, about 12 fougasse barrels. It acts like napalm. It's an M1 thickener mixed with gasoline. It has a two-pound kicker charge under the barrel with a white phosphorus grenade tied at the opening. It's all connected with det cord (detonating cord) and detonated electrically from one of the bunkers. The Americans assigned to each of the four walls knew which bunkers had the firing circuits for the fougasse barrels. When detonated, it would create a hellscape of sticky flames about 150 feet wide and about 150 feet forward all the way across the kill zone beyond the outermost barbed wire. This would be activated if a sizeable enemy unit (more than just a handful) made it to our main fence.

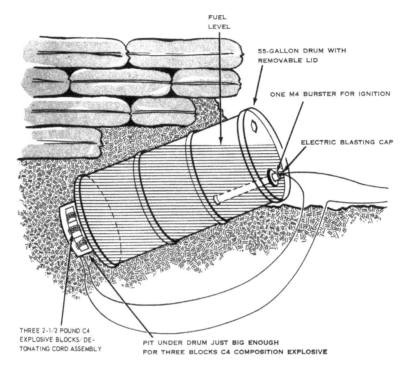

FUEL
LEVEL

55-GALLON DRUM WITH
REMOVABLE LID

ONE M4 BURSTER FOR IGNITION

ELECTRIC BLASTING CAP

THREE 2-1/2 POUND C4
EXPLOSIVE BLOCKS/ DE-
TONATING CORD ASSEMBLY

PIT UNDER DRUM JUST BIG ENOUGH
FOR THREE BLOCKS C4 COMPOSITION EXPLOSIVE

Image 104. We created twelve of these fougasse weapons.

We also had two 105mm howitzers. They were primarily the responsibility of Sgt 1st Class Jerome Jacob. We had
pre-planned target concentration areas along approaches
we expected the NVA might use in attacks.

For all indirect-firing weapons (mortars and howitzers),
there were certain target areas that we'd already registered
the coordinates for:

- All high ground near the camp and
- All dead space (not solidly covered in the kill zone)
  around the perimeter of the camp.

During an attack, it would be quick to call for mortars to drop on any of these locations as needed.

We also built an interior perimeter that would be our hold out if the main wall/fence was overrun. Inside it was the American SF Team House, which included the communications bunker beneath it, the TOC (Tactical Operations Center), the supply room, the ammunition bunker, the medical bunker, and our living quarters.

We had a security force of Montagnards that was assigned to the fighting positions of the interior perimeter. There were six M60s, two .50 cal machine guns, two 4.2-inch mortars, two 81mm mortars, a 106mm Recoilless Rifle on the east side, and we had another 106mm Recoilless Rifle mounted on a jeep to maneuver in support of any wall that was in need. The primary plan for this last Recoilless Rifle is to fire a flechette round (shooting thousands of small, wicked, metal darts) with the expectation that this would be the most likely to stop the enemy inside the wire. The two 4.2-inch mortars could fire either H.E. or Willie Pete rounds or illumination rounds (a flare that slowly descends with a parachute) for camp under attack. To round out our defensive position we used two 81mm mortars. These mostly fired H.E.

Image 105. A 106-millimeter Recoilless Rifle
being loaded. Recognize the holes that allow
the backblast to eliminate the recoil.

How flechettes work

M546 APERS-T **105mm** shell

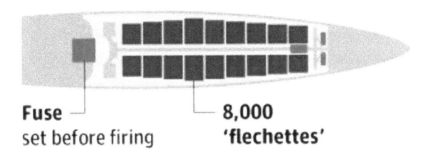

Fuse
set before firing

8,000
'flechettes'

Tank or field
gun fires shell

Shell bursts
when timed fuse
detonates

Flechettes
spread out
in a cone

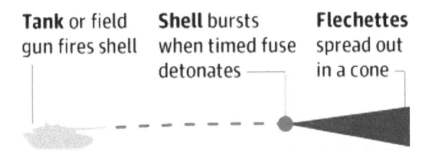

One of the 8,000 steel flechettes
each about 25mm long

Fins
help level flight

Long body
loses rigidity on impact

Image 106. Flechette, anti-personnel round.

[Here are three types of ordnance that we dealt with: High Explosive Rounds, Marking Rounds, and Illumination Rounds. H.E. are designed to destroy things. Marking Rounds are designed to land on a target and put out smoke and/or light as a visual reference for subsequent munitions. Illumination Rounds are sent high overhead and often descend on a parachute to provide a couple of minutes of light for an area.][17]

Lastly, we had the escape tunnel. The tunnel entrance was at the bottom of the team house, went under the camp's east wall, under the entire kill zone, outside the outer wire, and exited not far from the Dak Poko River. Only the Americans knew about this tunnel. All A-camps had an emergency escape plan that could be put into operation if the camp were to become totally overrun.

After a few weeks (this is now December 1968), I'd been on a few short C-operations to kinda get the feeling of working with a company of Montagnards. The Yards were no problem, but our LLDB (ARVN Special Forces soldiers) were a big disappointment. I found out that they definitely did_not want to make contact with the enemy. And, if we did make contact, they would make all kinds of excuses for why we should *not stay* in contact. I learned one thing real fast. If you let the LLDB get their wishes, you might

---

17 This is some of the Science part of Skills as described in the retrospective chapter, "Soldiers."

as well stay in camp. The Montagnards, on the other hand, will follow you. They didn't respect the LLDB. If you give in to the LLDB, the Yards will lose faith in you.

Image 107. Sgt 1st Class Jakovenko, December 1968, at Dak Seang's central building with the bar. Below ground here is the communications area.

Americans had two bargaining chips that would always persuade the LLDB:

- air support and
- artillery.

The Vietnamese couldn't call for the American air and artillery. Those calls could come only through us. So, we'd listen to their input and take it into account to make our best decision. Then we'd tell the LLDB what we planned to do. If they were threatening to go against the plan, we'd eventually have to remind them that if we don't know where they are, we might mistake them for the enemy and call in TACAIR or artillery on their position. Most Vietnamese knew if they separated from the Americans, they would not have the means to survive contact with the NVA.

On one C-operation that lasted a few days, we made light contact with the NVA early on, then things were calm for the rest of the patrol. We let the Yards do some hunting and fishing. This was a kind of a reward for a job well done on the operation. The Yards bagged a few game animals and gathered various types of vegetation and fruit to bring back with them.

They had a unique way of fishing. They would come to a stream and put some people in the water downstream with these utility nets that we issued them. Upstream they'd throw a grenade in the water. The fish would float right into the nets, belly up. I was uneasy the first time I saw the Yards do this, worried about security, but they knew what they were doing. They would secure the whole area before the first grenade. Only a small detail did the hunting. The rest were in a defensive position.

Image 108. One of our C-operation patrols.

We didn't stay long in any one place. We would hunt on the move, on the way back toward camp. When we got back, we had plenty of everything. It would be a happy feast for the families.

31

The Defense of an A-Camp, Vietnam

1969

By now our camp was looking good. We'd put a lot of work into our fortifications. I believed we now might be the best armed fighting border camp in Vietnam.

Image 109. Our improved mortar pit with a "big boy" 4.2-inch mortar. This is how deep a mortar pit should be. Down here, a mortar crew can focus for better efficiency and precision.

Then, we got an order from 5th SF Group at Nha Trang, that all A-camps must have a 20- to 30-foot tower and must install a .50 cal machine gun at the top. Once again, you can see what it looked like in the John Wayne movie, *The Green Berets*. We called it "the John Wayne tower" (the movie had come out just a year prior to this). When ours was completed, it was exactly as we thought: it would be suicide to be the man at the top of it during an attack.

Image 110. The view from the John Wayne Tower.

[Sure as hell, in April of 1970, long after I'd left, the first thing that got hit during the NVA's month-long siege of Dak Seang was the John Wayne tower. The lieutenant manning the .50 cal machine gun at the top survived, but the tower was completely destroyed.]

We had our full complement of new M16 rifles. We conducted a two-day training class with the Yards. This included classroom instruction, maintenance and zeroing of the weapon, and scored firing.

At any given time, we tried to keep a third of our strike forces out on a C-operation and at least 300 strikers in camp for defense. On one C-operation, we intercepted a sizeable NVA unit at a creek near the Laos border. With over 100 soldiers, we were spread out down a good stretch of river. After the engagement, it became clear that three of our Montagnards were missing. Just like with our American soldiers, we would never leave a fallen soldier behind. When we were sure that we'd repulsed the NVA and the valley was secure, we searched up and down the creek and eventually found the lifeless bodies of each of our three missing men.

Two were along the riverbank, and the bodies had clearly been searched and stripped of weapons and ammo. The third, we found a little further down on a sandbar in the middle of the stream. This body had all its weapons and equipment. He was lying on his back, arms folded neatly on his chest as if laid in a casket. We held everyone away because we suspected it had been booby trapped. Often, the enemy would pull the pin of a grenade or two and put them under the body. If the body was moved, the grenade would explode.

We created a large loop with parachute cord, and I crawled to the sandbar and secured it around his leg. I backed away about 100 feet and then we pulled the body with the cord. We waited. Nothing happened.

We brought the three bodies back to Dak Seang. Though their native village had been abandoned due to the NVA attacks, we arranged a small operation to take the three bodies to that village for their burial, per their family's custom.

We thought of ourselves as someone to be reckoned with. The NVA was always watching us. Just in case they ever thought they wanted a piece of Dak Seang, we sent them some clear messages. Every few weeks, we'd put on a fire power demonstration for our adversary. At dark, we'd sound a practice alert. Our defensive positions were quickly manned. On signal, all weapons in camp would exercise firing their FPF (Final Protective Fire). We called this, a 'Mad Minute.' This exercise did two things. It showed the deadly fire power of the camp, and it rotated ammunition, so we always knew we were loaded with good clean ammo.

The LLDB had been proving themselves to be a sorry excuse for soldiers. They would not extend any respect to the Montagnards, so the Montagnards found it hard to respect the LLDB. We all perceived that the ARVN (the South Vietnam army) higher echelons of command were just as sorry. There was incompetence, corruption, bribery starting right at their top headquarters at Nha Trang. The problems trickled all the way down to the place most crucial for success, the A-camp.

Image 111. In Dak Seang, 1969.

Our counterpart relationship now deteriorated to a point where most of us team members carried sidearms on our person around the camp–and it wasn't because of the enemy threat. Before I arrived at Dak Seang, there had been an incident. The LLDB team got so heated that some of their members had turned a .50 cal machine gun and shot up the American SF team house. As I understand, no one was killed. I think both teams were replaced, the Americans and the Vietnamese. Well, now it was starting to feel like that kind of animosity could flare up again.

Our Vietnamese LLDB commander evidently notified his chain of command in Nha Trang, and their general asked his liaison, an American SF colonel, to visit us. Well, now the panic button was pushed, and 5th Special Forces Group commander sent his inspection team, which is headed by his deputy commander. We all knew this inspection team as "the hatchet team," because when they'd descend on an A-camp, heads would roll.

That's exactly what happened. After the inspection, our team basically disintegrated. Our commander, Captain Reeb, was an outstanding officer and a good leader. He and a few others got reassigned. He went to A-244, Ben Het, which was about 10 miles south of Dak Seang.

As you expected, I made my small contribution to the situation. They came up with a genius decision that the counterpart relationship at Dak Seang would be improved if we were to tear down the interior perimeter (around the team house). I told them I'd rather keep the interior perimeter and invite the Viet Cong to come live with us before giving it up to "live in harmony" with the LLDB. That didn't go over well with the inspectors.

They also said the .50 cal machine gun on the north wall was not utilized to its full potential. It didn't have long-range fields of fire. My response was that it was there to protect the front gate and the airfield. It had good grazing fire over 200 meters. The weapons man on the inspection team condescendingly asked me if I knew what the maximum effective range of a .50 cal machine gun was. I said, "5000 meters."

He said, "And you're using it for only 200 meters?"

I took time to show him the design of our defenses. I had two 105mm howitzers, plenty of 4.2-inch mortars and 81mm mortars. I've had the long range covered. He insisted I move the .50 cal or get written up.

I did not make friends with them. "When you Nha Trang commanders decide to spend several days and especially nights in a fighting border A-camp, then I might listen to your suggestions on how to defend it."

Needless to say, I got written up.

[But I honestly believe that if I had cooperated with that inspection team's direction, Dak Seang very possibly would have been lost in the siege of April 1970. That is the gravity of the decision. Some of the camp was overrun, but the interior perimeter held, and the enemy never did take the front gate or the airfield. And it was because of that bunker with the .50 cal and the M60 machine guns. My tour was over before that siege. Captain Udo Walther, whom you'll hear about in the Son Tay Raid, was there. I take great pride in the fact that our defenses held and that one A-team member, Sergeant Gary B.

Beikirch, was awarded the Medal of Honor for his actions defending our camp.]

Image 112. Dak Seang Camp, 9 May 1970, after successfully fending off a month-long siege by the NVA. After that siege, a *Stars and Stripes* reporter described Dak Seang, "Scores of NVA corpses lie in the camp's barbed wire fortifications, some within 30 yards of the camp's bunkers."

I started thinking about what assignment I'd ask for at the end of this, my second tour in Vietnam. I was seriously considering extending for options like Mike Force at Pleiku. During one visit to Kontum, I took the opportunity to walk over to CCC (Command & Control Central), the MACV-SOG guys. We talked late into the night, considering what it would be like if I were to extend my tour and come to CCC. They are a hell of a good bunch of people. I had already met a lot of them at Dak Seang as they often used our runway to land their teams, 'riding the strings' from across the border. This was a very common situation for MACV-SOG guys. On long range patrols into Laos, they'd make contact with the NVA, then be hot-extracted with no LZ. In that case, the helicopter would hover just above the jungle canopy, lower 'the strings' (ropes, sometimes ladders), the team members would grab on, and then be pulled vertically out of the jungle. They'd then need a clear, safe location to descend so that the guys could get off the ropes.

In March of 1969, we got our new team members. They were Second Lieutenant John Kubit, and a new team commander, Captain Udo Walther, coming from a year as a Special Forces advisor in Thailand. Captain Walther was arriving at a very difficult time.

America had built an alliance with the Khmer Krom, an ethnic group in Cambodia. A company-sized unit of Khmer Krom with dependents was assigned to Dak Seang. They seemed to have a good relationship with the LLDB. Specifically for that reason, the Montagnards immediately did *not* like them.

Now, the Cambodians were not ready right away to conduct operations in the mountains, and I completely understand that. They were flatlanders, not mountain people. But over a few weeks—when you'd expect some progress in their soldiering—this unit seemed to spend a lot of time in garrison. They simply did not want to go on combat operations. The Cambodian unit liked to go out with the Vietnamese because they always avoided contact with the enemy. They seemed to languish with no progress throughout the weeks of the spring.

Time was moving on and in May 1969 I heard from my attorney. He sent me my final divorce papers. My marriage was finally over.

I had no forwarding address for my two sons.

===

32

Fatal Lies, Tri-border Area

In the summer, the LLDB told Captain Walther that they wanted to send out a long-range patrol comprised only of 30 Cambodian soldiers. The LLDB said the Cambodians were ready to conduct operations. Captain Walther was a little surprised. "There would be no LLDB and no Americans? That will be considered a P-operation."

There were three types of standard operations:

- P-operations, which were platoon-sized operations utilizing 30 or 40 Yards, typically having a couple of LLDB but having no Americans (which were rare because the LLDB never liked going on operations without the Americans),
- Recon operations, which were small with typically no more than 20 Yards and no Americans or LLDB.
- C-operations, 100 strikers or more and at least two American A-team members. (As far as Montagnards are concerned, nothing got them more excited than a C-operation. They typically got to do the hunting/

fishing, they got paid more, and they were with soldiers they respect.)

This P-operation was approved. Our apprehensiveness about the Khmer Krom's readiness was allayed by the fact that we did have a scheduled C-operation launching in a few days with a full complement of two Americans and two LLDB. So, if the Cambodians made contact, we were already fully prepared to support.

Image 113. Departing Dak Seang on a
C-operation with Montagnards.

The P-operation of Khmer Krom launched. We watched them walk out of camp headed southwest, toward the tri-border about 30 km away (20 miles).

We got back to our preparations for our scheduled strike force C-operation. We'd have 120 Montagnards and Captain Walther and I would be the A-team members. The mission called for recon of an area we knew well that was less than a click (1 km) from the Laos border and about 20 miles northwest of Dak Seang. It was just southwest of Dak Pek, our northernmost A-camp in these highlands (see the map on Image 95). It would be a heliborne assault. (This is the combat story that you read in Preface 2.) I was about to learn much about combat, about people, about the fear of having made a terrible mistake, and about the deepest feelings of betrayal I could ever have imagined.

Over the coming days, we issued the food, ammo, and equipment for our ten-day C-operation. This was going to be the first combat operation in Vietnam for Captain Walther. (Remember that his experience to this point had been at a post in Thailand.) We discussed tactics for the air assault, for which the Yards had little experience. We had to take the high ground for a defensive position. We'd be so close to the border that we'd require TACAIR and artillery to be on call. I would go in on the first lift and secure the LZ at the wood line. I'd have two M60 machine gun crews on the first lift, Captain Walther was to have another two M60 machine gun crews on the second lift. The second lift would come in immediately, even if we happened to be in a fire fight. We'd maintain commo with the second lift and utilize smoke to mark our flanks and positions so that their door gunners could be effectively firing even as they were arriving.

A couple days prior to the scheduled launch of our C-operation, we had a formal briefing for the Montagnard leaders. We covered helicopter procedures and checked our commo with them and the LLDB.

We had been getting nightly updates about how the Khmer Krom P-operation was progressing. They were not on our radio frequencies, but every night the LLDB gave us the RON location of the Cambodian operation. They were deep into their mission and had made no contact with the enemy.

Our helicopter support would come from combat assault aviation (52nd Combat Aviation Battalion, 17th Combat Aviation Group, 1st Aviation Brigade) out of Camp Holloway, near Pleiku. This unit used the call signs "Gator" for the Huey slicks we'd be riding and "Crocs" for their Huey gunships. Their Hueys had been upgraded to the more powerful 'UH-1H' models to deal with the higher density altitudes (air pressure/temperature/altitude combinations) of mountains like those we'd be facing on this C-operation.

The night before launch, Captain Walther and I were in the TOC with maps spread out on the table. Somewhat in passing, he told me we would have some additional Americans accompanying us on our C-operation. They'd be from the combat assault aviation unit. That seemed very strange to me. "Guys from an aviation unit on patrol with us? What's their mission?"

"I'll explain it tomorrow. Don't worry, they won't be in the way." The captain evaded my question some and tried to change the subject.

I persisted, "Captain, this is going to be a bear of an operation. The Laos border is a hornets' nest. I don't need any surprises."

Captain Walther was a little miffed (not just at me) as he explained, "The aviation Battalion Commander at Camp Holloway (at Pleiku) is friends with our B-team Company Commander (at Kontum). The aviation commander said his companies' pathfinders (guys who get off the choppers and assure safe, secure LZs) were not being used enough. They want more action. So, they've decided that the pathfinders will do some patrols with us A-camps whenever we're using helicopter assaults. The pathfinders (there will be six of them) will be on the first lift to help you set up the landing zone."

I was not happy. "Well, that may sound like a really good idea, sitting at a table for two at the officers club in Pleiku, but I can tell you, it's a really bad idea at an LZ in the mountains bordering Laos."

The LZ's no bigger than a football field, and we'd be landing six helicopters at the same time. We'd already have 30 Montagnards landing plus Captain Walther and me. Now we had to worry about six more from a different unit.

We continued discussing the mission plan. We always had radio problems going into this certain valley. In the mountains, our PRC-25 radio just did not have the range. So, we decided to put a radio relay on top of a mountain we knew as 'Nu Yak' about 3km north of our camp, elevation 3,000 feet. We'd set up the relay with 20 Yards and A-team member Sgt 1st Class Cook. If you were going to be that close to the border, you had to have constant commo with our camp. It was our lifeline if we got into a fire fight.

The next morning, we were doing our final preparations. Sgt 1st Class Cook was ready with his Yards to set up the radio relay on Nu Yak Mountain. We checked in on the radios with the other camps nearby and explained our operation to make sure the operational area was clear of friendly troops. We checked with the LLDB and got the latest coordinates of the Cambodian Khmer Krom P-operation. Last night's check-in indicated that they were over 15 clicks (15km is about 10miles) southwest of Dak Seang. I remember making a comment about how far they are from camp.

We broke the Yards into loading orders for the choppers. My lift was ready to go. Sometime in the first half of the morning, the 18 helicopters arrived. It was quite a sight: 12 lift choppers ("Gators") and 6 gunships ("Crocs"). They came in quickly and landed on our Dak Seang airfield.

We went inside the TOC and had a quick briefing about our plan of operations. This is where we first got to talk with the six pathfinders. They explained their plan to land ahead of us while we orbited for as much as 10 minutes. They would set up the LZ and then call our choppers to come on and bring the first lift in. I disagreed, "You'll compromise us that close to the border. Ten minutes of helicopter noise will alert the enemy and give them time to organize."

Captain Walther said that this is the way it's going to be. "Sgt Jakovenko, we're going to let them secure the area, set up an LZ, and then bring us in."

I made it clear that didn't like the idea.

We then explained that we needed them to put our radio relay team (over 20 soldiers) on top of Nu Yak Mountain three clicks north of camp. We said we have to set up our radio relay before we do anything.

The helicopters' commander explained, "That's no problem. We'll have my gunships soften it up before landing."

To that, our A-team heavy weapons man Sgt Jerome Jacobs said, "I can do better than that. At 3km, I can easily put suppressive fire on top of Nu Yak before the choppers land."

Image 114. At Dak Seang, preparing for a
C-operation with Montagnards.

The flight leader agreed that was even better.

So, we turned both of our 105mm howitzers. We already had the pre-planned registration on that mountain. We told the LLDB and the Montagnard strikers and dependents about the massive fire mission they were about to hear. (Truly, the noise is shocking and terrifying to anyone in our camp who wasn't warned about it ahead of the first shots.)

The first round would always be a marking round (which only explodes with smoke and is also called a 'safety round') in case there might possibly be any friendly troops in the area that we hadn't heard about. A smoke round landing on your position is not as bad as an H.E. round.

We fired the first round with a thunderous boom. A couple of seconds went by as it sailed.

We saw it explode into white, but there's no sound. With a smoke round, you don't really hear much of a "crack" as it hits its target. The smoke round landed dead center on top of Nu Yak Mountain!

The next order to fire was proximity-fuzed rounds (H.E. with fuzes that have radio wave sensors commanding detonation while still above the ground) that would ensure any enemy personnel in the area would be wiped out, but not put a crater in our planned LZ. The command was given and both the 105mm howitzers commenced firing. Everyone in camp was plugging their ears because of the deafening noise. After just the first few rounds, you could no longer see the top of Nu Yak for all the pummeling explosions and brimstone plumes.

After several more rounds, a couple of the LLDB came running over yelling, "No more shoot on Nu Yak! Cambodians on top!"

In the deafening thunder and excitement, their words seemed irrational. We couldn't believe what we were hearing. We immediately yelled for the guns to cease.

"What are you screaming about? You told us they were 15 clicks southwest of us! Nu Yak mountain is 3 clicks northwest of us!"

The Cambodians had lied about their location. They had been giving the LLDB false reports of their coordinates each night. In reality, they'd only moved 3 clicks from our camp and had been loitering there for days.

We started launching our helicopters, but with the primary mission being MEDEVAC. I went on the first lift. When we got there, it was a total disaster. There were at least ten of our own Khmer Krom soldiers dead. Most of the rest of them were wounded.

The survivors said they called the LLDB when the first smoke round exploded. They said that they screamed on the radios, "Don't shoot! Don't shoot! We're on top of Nu Yak Mountain!"

The bumbling LLDB were angry and arguing, yelling on the radios and yelling at each other for a couple of minutes—deadly minutes. In my opinion, these idiots failed to act decisively at that crucial moment. We were well into a firing mission before they notified us. The LLDB had plenty of time (about three minutes) between the smoke round and the first of the H.E. rounds. All those rounds of high explosives landed on top of our Cambodians.

I was so damn mad at the Vietnamese LLDB. I made up my mind I would not extend my tour if I had to work with the LLDB.

Captain Walther was now *not* going on our C-operation. He now had a friendly fire incident on his hands. There would be a big investigation by the high echelons of command. To add to the exasperation, we heard a rumor that some of the Cambodians blamed the Americans for the friendly fire and were considering killing Americans in reprisal. I told

Captain Walther, "Sir, don't you think our priority right now needs to be taking care of business in our camp. The North Vietnamese can wait."

"Negative. Your operation is still going. You'll be the senior advisor. Lieutenant Kubit will go with you."

33

The C-Operation with Lt Kubit, Vietnam

1969

I really liked Lt Kubit. He always had a smile and a good attitude. (But he'd only been in country a few weeks, and this was his first mission.) He came running over, gung-ho that he was going on a combat operation. He called me "old man" even though I was only 29. He was 23. He was sharp. (He later became a professor at Syracuse University.)

He and I went over our plan of operation. I would still go in on the first lift. Lt Kubit would come with me. I could really use him working the radio on the LZ. I would immediately get to work setting up the perimeter. Lt Kubit would keep contact with the helicopters and Dak Seang through our radio relay on Nu Yak Mountain.

I still did not like the idea of pathfinders going in before us. That had the potential to stir up a hornets' nest. But I was overruled.

Even with the delay caused by the friendly fire incident, there were still several hours of daylight remaining.

The radio relay was finally established on Nu Yak, so we lifted off for the area known as Dak Rolen Valley on the Laotian border. It only took about 20 minutes to get there. The pathfinders went in on one Huey slick with three Huey gunships flying cover for them. It took almost 15 minutes before they gave us clearance to land.

We're going in. We now descend out of orbit, along a ridge line, and approach our mountain saddle LZ at tree top level. The pathfinders throw yellow smoke. They perform the authentication SOP for positive identification. We come in low and hot. As we touch down, we burst out of the chopper and run for the wood line to set up our perimeter. The first six helicopters shortly lift back into flight to bring us another load of our Yards. The other six Hueys are now descending out of orbit and will be landing in this tight LZ momentarily.

Crouching just inside the protective shade of the jungle canopy, I tell Lt Kubit to set up here and maintain constant communication with the incoming helicopters. I give him a few Yards along with our interpreter. "I'll send back some guides once the perimeter is ready to bring the other lifts in."

I head out around the perimeter of the LZ with all the Yards, assigning them sections. This feels different. We have no LLDB with us. They stayed back at camp for the investigation. I kinda like it this way. I have no problem communicating with the Yards.

I've set up about five points around the perimeter spread out nicely, covering more than 180 degrees around the LZ at this point. The other flight of six is coming now. I see the pathfinders coordinating with them. Smoke is out, this time purple. All is going well and then...

…all hell breaks loose! Full auto fire coming at us from somewhere in the jungle! There's also heavy fire targeting the landing helicopters! I can't tell the size of enemy unit or exactly where they are. We fire back in the general direction. It's not clear how spread out they are. We look to the gunships for some cues as to where the enemy concentrations are. The lift helicopters seem to be taking some hits. A couple of the Hueys are only a few feet above the grass, but they just can't land. Some of the Yards are jumping out several feet above the ground. One of the Yards that I stationed at a perimeter position comes over to me saying, "Trung úy!" ("Lieutenant") pointing his finger at his midsection and pulling on me to follow. I have a bad feeling.

I run around the perimeter toward Lt Kubit's commo position. From 50 feet away, I can tell he's been hit and he's lying flat on his back.

Right as I reach him, a gunship comes in just above the trees on a loud, heavy gun run firing straight outward from a hover right over our heads. He's letting loose with the M60 machine guns and his rockets. The terrible thought does pass through my mind. *That gunship is the enemy's prime target at this second. They could get hit and come crashing down upon us.* But the actual feeling in me is one of security, of power, and of trust. These men are standing up beside me, tall, taking the blows to the face and dealing the same to the enemy. They are shoulder to shoulder with us in the fight. They are above us, beside us, with us. They have the horsepower to escape to safety, yet they have no interest in running. They want to be here with us in this fight. They know us, even though we've never met.

I check Lt Kubit. Yes, he's been hit in his left side. He's still conscious but looking like he's going into shock. I open his jungle camo shirt and pull up his T-shirt, which is soaking up blood from the left front to the left back. He keeps asking, "How bad is it?"

*That's a **lot** of blood.* I grab his left hip and pull him forward so I can see if there's an exit wound on his back. (There is.) The round entered from the front and exited his back missing his left kidney. "Nothing but a scratch" is my answer as I start giving him first aid. I rip open one of the packets of gauze in my medical kit hanging on my LBE. I shove some into the dirty mess of a bullet hole. Most of the blood is coming out the back. Keeping the Lt balanced on his right side, I push a wad of gauze into his exit wound, trying to apply pressure to stop the bleeding. He's still talking to me. I don't think it tore up a major organ or his spine, because he's still able to move.

A Yard has brought the bigger medical kit, full of bags and needles that I need. I try to give Lt Kubit some blood expander. The blood expander is a pressurized canister with an I.V.-type of hose with a needle. In the dirt and sweat and combat noise, I'm kinda fumbling around with the needle & hose and have a hell of a time spotting any vein I can stick. I worry that the round might have damaged his intestines. But the gauze seem to be holding back the blood (they're not drenching through now), so I bandage him up and tape it off securely. I take the cap off the needle and eventually find a vein in his left arm, just below the elbow and secure it with tape.

I pick up the PRC-25 radio. The frequency has just a lot of static. "Gators, come in!" No helicopters. Nothing but static. It dawns on me that I've not been hearing any chatter on the radio since I landed. I check the frequency. It's the right freq. My concern is to get Lt Kubit MEDEVACed to a hospital.

Image 115. A stock photo showing a PRC-25 backpack radio/telephone.

He's shaking slightly, kind of all over his body. He's turning gray in his face. His lips are blue. He's fully into shock now. I call on the radio, but no one is replying. I feel like Lt Kubit's life is in my hands. It's a hell of a feeling. Make all the right decisions learned in training and he may live.

Someone pops green smoke about 75 feet away from me at the tree line. A helicopter is coming in. It's now steadying to land about 100 meters from us. I start dragging Lt Kubit toward the helicopter even before it lands. I see two pathfinders getting ready to board. It's clear that they're not even aware of Lt Kubit's situation. I realize now that they must have gone to a backup frequency.

The fire fight is raging. A lot of fire is directed at this helicopter, which is facing to the right as I'm looking at it. I'm dragging the Lt at a running/limping pace. My left hand has a death grip on his LBE at his left shoulder; my right hand is trying hold all my gear and my weapons on me. I hear rounds over my head and sometimes kicking up dirt nearby. It feels like a hundred bullwhips chasing me. The louder the crack, the closer the bullet. I can tell that they're not shooting at me. They want to bring down the chopper. I hear explosives, but I can't tell if it's incoming NVA RPGs (rocket propelled grenades) or our gunships' suppressing rockets.

This is the purpose for all those years of grueling P.T.

I'm still 50 meters from the helicopter. *Dammit, do they see me?* I wave my rifle trying to get their attention, while still trying to make progress dragging Lt Kubit. Dammit, it looks like the pathfinders just got on board. Come help here! I think the helicopter is going to leave. A thought crosses my mind…

[*If they try to leave, I'll let go of the Lt and shoot the tail rotor off. They'll be able to set it down. No one will be injured. They have plenty of firepower to keep the enemy out of the LZ. A lot of priority effort would immediately be made by other helicopters to rescue the crew and pathfinders…and Lt Kubit.*

But on the other hand, that right-side door gunner with the M60 machine gun would instinctively cut me in half with one sweep before I put more than a few bullet holes in his sheet metal.]

The helicopter engine noise changes to more a powerful sound. *He's lifting off?* I'm shouting vulgarities at them with a cursing anger, "Don't leave without Lt Kubit! Lord Jesus, stop them!" I know he'll die.

This is the most desperate moment. Life and death.

The helicopter pauses just 10 feet above the ground and then sets back down. "Thank you, Lord!"

The bullets hitting the helicopter every few seconds sound like shooting at a 55-gallon drum. The two pathfinders jump off and come sprinting straight toward me, running fast with everything they've got. God bless 'em. They're panting and sweating, and they each grab a shoulder's worth of Lt Kubit's LBE and quickly drag him, putting him on the helicopter. I come along behind them. I'm still standing on the grass, so they yell, "GET ON! We're the last helicopter!"

I say, "What about my Yards?!"

"There's nothing we can do for them right now!"

I tell them, "I can't leave my Yards!" I turn, crouch down, and zigzag back toward the perimeter.

Back at the radio, in the shade and concealment, I look at the helicopter gaining altitude, heading southeast down a valley toward Dak Seang. We still have sporadic fire, but not as bad as it was. The enemy is probably trying to figure out what's going on. The helicopters left even though we still have more than 30 of us on the ground. The enemy unit is large enough that they fended off our helicopters, so it's certainly large enough to finish off those of us that remain.

Our Yard radio operator hands me the handset. I can hear our radio relay, Sgt 1st Class Cook, asking me for a status.

"We have multiple wounded. Lt Kubit got hit. He's coming back on the last helicopter. We're still taking fire. I'm going to need TACAIR. See if you can get the 175mm or 8-inch artillery out of Dak To."

I give him a registration point on some high ground about a half click west of me toward the Laos border, "Stand by for my call. I want you to arrange an extraction or at least reinforcements and re-supply. We're running low on ammunition."

Sgt 1st Class Cook informs me, "They're planning to try to reinforce you. Hold on to your LZ."

I move along the perimeter with our interpreter telling the Squad Leaders, "Give me a count of all ammo and casualties. Conserve ammo. Only shoot if you positively see your target. Pull the perimeter back to the tree line. It will give us easier communication for a tighter defense."

Then it starts to rain.

The gunfire dies down somewhat. The sound of the rain drops replaces the sound of gunshots. The rain gets heavier.

Then it really starts to pour.

Waiting.

Hunkered down.

Many minutes pass without a shot being fired.

After nearly an hour with no sign of the enemy, I sit up on my rucksack against a tree and try to light a cigarette. No one is talking. No one is moving. Our minds are working hard just to listen through the heavy raindrops. I'm reviewing the last few hours. We got Lt Kubit out, and for that, I'm thankful. But the Americans left me and my Montagnards behind. I was so disappointed. I just could not believe that they flew away without us.

It's now about 5pm and there's about an hour of daylight remaining. Everywhere is muddy. The heat and humidity weigh around our necks. We wish for one more lift to arrive. We don't need the lift to remove us; we just need them to *resupply* us. If they would bring us the rest of our strike force and take our handful of wounded Yards, we would have a strong vantage point for the night.

Then our hope runs even lower. We hear sporadic gun fire. I'm sure they're moving in to finish us off. The firefight erupts just as before, and explosions are everywhere. My buddy with the radio suddenly shoves the handset to my ear. I take it and hear a clear voice asking me to identify myself: "Do you need assistance?"

I say in the clear, "My name is Jakovenko. I'm from Dak Seang, the Special Forces A-camp south of here. I have less than 40 Montagnards. Some of them are wounded. We're under fire and low on ammo."

The voice comes back, "I see a lot of movement on the ground."

"That's not us. That's the bad guys."

He says, "Mark your location with smoke."

"Popping smoke now."

He authenticates, "I see yellow smoke."

"That's me. My perimeter is within about 50 meters of the smoke."

The voice says, "Well, they're all around you. Get low. This is gonna be close support."

All of a sudden (I've not heard their engines at all up to this moment), a Cobra helicopter is right over our heads, about 25 feet above the jungle canopy treetops. He is firing his nose-mounted miniguns precisely down onto the heads of the enemy. A second Cobra materializes right beside him and this one begins firing rocket after rocket, pummeling every location of the enemy that I am aware of (and more that I hadn't seen). The empty casings from the Cobra gunships are raining down around us.

Then, an unseen, unheard A-1E Skyraider passes from right to left. I'm telling you, he comes down so low that I see the profile of the pilot's helmet. He states over the radio, "Keep your heads down. This is going to be danger close." Then with pass after pass, he comes around again, with guns and bombs. I would think that he must have gotten everyone in that first pass, but he keeps this up. I ain't never seen such fire power.

Then, a voice says, "I can't see much movement. We've got to head out, now. Take care down there."

[To this day, I don't know who those Cobra gunships and A-1E Skyraiders belonged to. I don't know how they got on my frequency. Some friends of mine in MACV-SOG tell me it sounds like their support package used during insertion and extraction of their teams "across the fence" (into Laos). I was close to the border. That's my best theory. Whoever they were, I owe them my life.]

The engine noise fades down the valley like the last trickles after a dam burst. There's silence, even the animals—no jungle noise at all. No rain. Some humid fog sticking to the jagged valleys and draping the nearby mountains.

We wait a few more minutes. Nothing. It's getting late in the afternoon, maybe 5:30pm by now. With only a half-hour of light remaining, I'm starting to move us to some higher ground, easier to defend, with more concealment. Carrying the wounded and low on ammo, we are vulnerable. We find the right spot after only a few hundred meters and start setting up a good defensive position for a RON.

"Shh! –did you hear that? Is that a helicopter?" We wait in silence.

(No helicopters.) We look at each other, perfectly still, listening. (There's nothing.)

Then the radio squelch breaks and then loud and clear in a commanding voice: "Juliet, come in." ('J' is for Jakovenko, so phonetic alphabet 'Juliet' is my call sign.) It's Captain Walther and with him is the rest of our strike force. "Give me the status. We're gonna need you to mark the LZ."

"We have the LZ secure. There's no enemy fire at this time."

I take eight guys from our RON knoll, and we run down the hill to the LZ. It's just the easiest and fastest and happiest sprint. As the eight choppers approach (six Gators, two Crocs), I pop purple smoke. The flight lead says, "I see purple smoke."

"That's me."

Captain Walther is the first man off the first Gator. Efficiently, the 30 soldiers offload and within a minute the

Gators are headed back to Dak Seang. We employ each
reinforcement to bolster security on the LZ. Two more lifts
happen just as efficiently and now we have a complete
company of 120.

We now move the entire company to our high ground.
We dig in and set a few Claymore mines on the approaches.
If they do hit us, we'll make them pay for this high knoll.
Just before dark, the rear security platoon leaves the LZ
and comes up to our defensive position for the night.

By 7pm or 8pm, things are calm and pitch dark. There
are just the jungle noises to listen to, and that's reassuring.
If the jungle goes silent, that's when you have to worry that
the enemy might be on the move nearby.

Let me pause the story to tell you what I found out days
later about how Captain Walther got here. By reinforcing
us, he was disobeying an order to remain in camp for the
friendly fire investigation. He had gotten into a heated dis-
cussion with the flight leader about how to get us out. The
choppers were beyond their authorization regarding rearm-
ing the gunships and flying this mission. They said they
were asking for authorization from command. His birds
had too many bullet holes and too few bullets.

He came out here to reinforce me, putting his career on
the line to help an enlisted man. He has his priorities, and
his priority was us. He said to me, "Lt Kubit got hit and that
should have been me. Kubit took my bullet."

I said, "Captain, if right now a bullet flew right up
between us and asked us both, 'Who wants to die?', I'd

probably point right at you and blurt out 'him!' Nobody wants to die. In war, someone's gonna die. When it's your time, there's not much you can do about it."

He told me, "Well, Lt Kubit is on his way to the U.S. Thanks to (Staff Sgt) 'Doc' Nelson (our senior medic on our A-team) and your MEDEVAC work, he'll make it."

He explained that Doc did more work on Lt Kubit than the typical medic can do. A lot of times, medics can't do much for team members who are that severely wounded. But this was life or death. When they finally got him to Pleiku Air Base for surgery, the surgeon said Doc Nelson had saved his life. Doc had actually gone inside to find the source of the bleeding. That stabilized him for movement."

Right then, Captain Walther awkwardly changed the subject, "I got those pants you asked for."

That's when I noticed that my crotch area was ripped wide open and totally exposed because I had no under-wear. I'd ripped my pants open earlier and told Sgt 1st Class Cook on the radio relay that I needed a pair of the tiger stripe camo pants sent out for me. Now, I'll continue the story.

At first light (about 5am), we post the normal 30-minute Stand-To, 100% alert. We send our small clearing patrol around our perimeter. We change the people on listening posts (tactical positions outside our perimeter). Everything is quiet. No enemy. We decide to sweep the Laos border area per our originally planned mission. We perform a commo check and tell the A-team members back at Dak

Seang that we need them to stand by to provide supporting fire in case we make contact. Ammo is distributed while everyone eats their morning meal. Movement orders are passed to the platoons.

As we move out, Captain Walther stays up front and I remain in the middle. We move along the border for several hours. This is intense, but we're starting to get a little comfortable.

But suddenly, the quiet jungle erupts in automatic fire somewhere on point. Everyone faces out to the flanks and rear. It sounds like Captain Walther and his platoon are in substantial small arms contact. I tap our M60 machine gun crew and start to move up front. As I go, I tell the interpreter to tell the Yards' squad leaders, "Be prepared to support in case we make contact. I'll tell you when."

I make it to Captain Walther and the firing is dying down. We determine that it was our Montagnards, no incoming fire. No sweat. It happens. But with the language barrier, nothing is ever perfectly clear, especially in a combat zone.

American soldiers are in countries all over the world. Foreign languages and cultures. Plenty of gray. Challenging uncertainties. This is why we created the Special Forces.

Let's be sure. We decide to sweep the area of contact. We send two platoons around. We actually do find some equipment and some blood trails.

And that's the way the next several days went.[18]

---

18   When you get a veteran to trust you enough to tell you a story, just listen. Appreciate the soldier and their Spirit. Maybe don't even try to make any of your own points or share any of your own lessons. Just listen and understand the lessons that the veteran might want you to learn from the story. Know that it's good you, for them, and for all of us.

It was time to start our return to camp which would take more than three days. No contact. Great intel gathered. Good learning. We cleared an area, at least for the time being. About a day or so out of camp, we let the Yards do a little foraging, hunting and fishing.

When we got back to Dak Seang, we had visitors from the aviation battalion. It was the two pathfinders. They wanted me to be witness to some valor awards for them and the crew that got Lt Kubit out. To this day, I wish I would have been a little more understanding. I guess I got pretty indignant. I cussed and told them they left me.

But in truth, it was my choice to stay behind. They did get Lt Kubit out. They did show bravery. I wish I'd have written a recommendation. I was wrong. They did deserve the recognition.

This was my last operation.

Extending for another tour in Vietnam? I never thought about it again. I was fed up with the ARVN and the LLDB. I didn't want to be part of turning over the A-camps to them. In my mind, these LLDB had disqualified themselves from expecting the loyalty of the Montagnard people. The'd proven themselves unworthy to assume that role without the adult supervision of the American Special Forces.

[Before I close this story, allow me to summarize Capt Udo Walther's career assignments from around this time. It will be useful in our later story about the Son Tay Raid.

- Thailand from March 1968 to March 1969: He was an Infantry Company Advisor with the 46th Special Forces Company.
- South Vietnam from March to December 1969: He was Executive Officer and then Commanding Officer of our Detachment A-245 with Company B, 5th Special Forces Group at Dak Seang.
- South Vietnam from December 1969 until he returned to Fort Bragg in June 1970.
- Fort Bragg in August 1970, Bull Simons selects him for the Son Tay Raid.

Captain Walther was born in Germany in 1947. His family immigrated to the US in 1956.]

34

The Son Tay Raid, Hanoi

1970

By November 1st, 1969, I was back at Fort Bragg. I was assigned to Charlie Company, 6th SF Group and the first couple of weeks at Bragg were occupied with processing back into my unit. I was able to take a month of leave through the Christmas/New Year holiday. I spent a lot of that time in Jersey City catching up with my parents and friends.

In January 1970, I got assigned again to the Gabriel Demonstration Team and served there through the spring and summer. I kept in shape by doing the Ass Kicker workout I'd learned at SF Underwater Ops School. Give me a minute to describe it. The 10 exercises work your body all the way from your neck to your toes ending with two tough runs. I'd do 500 pushups in the morning and another 500 pushups in the evening, 100 sit-ups, 100 flutter kicks (on your back, feet off the ground, kicking as if you had fins). Then run three miles.

One late afternoon in August 1970, I was at the company headquarters building, drawing my sidearm for guard duty that night. (At the Gabriel Demonstration Area, we had quite a "VC Village" range that even had a lot of exotic animals native to Vietnam and other countries that SF might deploy into. Those ranges and those animals had to be guarded. Every couple of weeks, I'd have to pull guard duty, making sure the animals were OK and that no miscreants tried to pull any pranks.)

Our Battalion Commander was in the hall asking our Battalion Command Sergeant Major, "How many more volunteers do we need?"

"We need two more." As I walked by, I heard the Sergeant Major say, "Well, there's a volunteer if I ever saw one."

The captain said, "Yeah, put Jakovenko on the list."

The Sergeant Major starts writing. "How do you spell your last name?"

I said, "Wait a minute, I speak English nowadays. A 'volunteer' is an individual who volunteers, and I did *not* volunteer. What am I being volunteered for?"

Writing my name he says, "J...A...K...E, got it. Be at 'The White House' (the JFK Special Warfare Center and Special Forces HQ building) in the morning and you'll find out from Colonel Bull Simons himself."

I'd only been in Special Forces a short two years, and I'd been at Fort Bragg for only half of that, so the name "Colonel Arthur D. 'Bull' Simons" was not a name I knew. But everyone else seemed to be inspired to hear him talk about volunteering for an important mission. I agreed to go to the theater—if the Sergeant Major would get me out of guard duty tonight.

"Get your ass out of here! Yes, you still have guard duty tonight and yes, your butt better be seated at the theater in the morning."

My butt was there shortly before lunch. The place was packed. There were probably over 500 soldiers. All were wondering what this mission was.

The Commanding General of Special Forces, Major General Edward M. Flanagan, walks onto the stage, front and center. He stands there looking at us for a few seconds while we are still at attention. More seconds pass before he eventually says, "Today is a day when I wish I was an enlisted man."

I will never forget those words. It meant something to me. *Now, I've just gotta know.*

He introduced Colonel Simons, who walked on stage. In contrast to the general's Class A dress uniform, Colonel Simons was wearing fatigues. He was kind of on the ugly side (like an ogre). But there was something about his manner. The way he looked at us seemed like he was eyeball-to-eyeball with everyone in the audience. When he spoke, you listened.

Image 116. General Flanagan   Image 117. Colonel Simons

"I need men for a moderately hazardous mission. This will be temporary duty away from Fort Bragg. At this time, I'm not going to tell you what the mission is. I also can't tell you for how long you'd be gone. Plan on being gone through Thanksgiving or Christmas. Once you're in, you'll have to stay with us for the duration no matter what."

He added, "There will be no TDY pay, no extra money. If you're interested, report back here to the theater at 1300 and bring your 201 File." (Your 201 File is your personnel folder. You'd have to pick up at the personnel office.)

Now I was curious. I stood in line at personnel and picked up my 201 File. Arriving back at the theater, I ran into Tyrone Adderly and saw that he had his 201 File. "You gonna volunteer?"

"I'm here."

"So am I."

We walked in and found seats in a row about halfway down. What is it that motivates a man to volunteer, knowing that a man like this just told you it's going to be hazardous?

We were told that Colonel Simons will personally interview candidates. It took about three days to interview us all. When I was called, it was Colonel Simons, a Lt Colonel Cataldo (a doctor who would be going on the mission), and two Sergeants Major (Pylant and Davis). Many questions didn't seem to me to make any sense. They asked for certain skills, certain weapons, certain experiences in combat. You could not figure out what you were volunteering for. "What kind of survival training have you had?"

"Does time spent in Auschwitz as a kid count as a survival school?"

Colonel Simons gave me a look I'll never forget: surprised, yes, and then he gave me a slight 'really?' with his eyes.

After quite a few more questions, "That'll be all. You'll be notified."

A week later, Tyrone and I were both notified that we'd been selected. Still no details.

Around dawn on Wednesday morning, September 9th, Tyrone and I and about a hundred others met at Smoke Bomb Hill in the parking lot of the JFK Special Warfare Center's 'The White House' building. There were a few wives, hugs, and tears. Gloria knew the game plan. She'd been through this many times before. Wills and Powers of Attorney were complete. You don't know where they're going. You don't know how long they'll be gone. There's always a momentary thought, *Will this be the last time I see him?*

Three long Army buses (45-passenger capacity) drove us a couple of miles to Pope AFB's flightline where two C-123s awaited. We quickly boarded and took off, and we didn't know where this plane was taking us.

We landed at Eglin AFB, FL, which is the largest base in the Air Force. We were ushered immediately onto three buses, which took us out into the forest 15 miles north of the airfield to a remote part of Eglin's testing ranges.

It felt like security was especially tight at this austere, hidden military facility. It was referred to only as "Auxiliary Field #3." We were miles away from any civilian roads.

There was a small airstrip and a few wooden operations buildings, including WWII-style barracks. For 360 degrees, we were surrounded by tall pine forests.

The next morning, Thursday Sept 10th, 1970, we immediately hit it hard and heavy. It was Day 1 of training. And training was unforgiving, day after day, rain or shine, weekday and weekend, each day started with PT before breakfast. We'd wake at 0500. Apart from everyone else, I'd do a streamlined version of the Ass Kicker workout. 100 pushups, 100 sit-ups, 100 flutter kicks, 100 Hello Lil' Darlins then run two miles.

During that first morning, I'd spotted a familiar face, Captain Udo Walther, my old commander at Dak Seang. We were so excited that we naturally hugged each other. Think about seeing someone you'd been in combat with. He was now the Commanding Officer of Detachment B-42 with Company D, 6th Special Forces Group at Fort Bragg. Yet he was plucked out of that important job to command one of the three small assault force groups on this secret mission. It sank in more and more that this is an unprecedented mission, maybe even historic. I tried to ply him for information, "You know anything about what this is all about?" Whether he knew anything or not, his reply was, "Nothing." (I knew he wouldn't tell me, but I had to try.)

Through the weekend and into the following week everything, including your P.T. is serious. There are over 100 competing and only about half of us will be chosen. All are being scrutinized and evaluated. Everyone is in top shape. We are trying to be the best because we know that not everyone will get to go.

Looking around our group of 100 men, I can see Master Sgt Pappy Kittleson, an iron man at age 46, who is a legend in Special Forces for having been with Bull Simons storming Papua New Guinea and the Philippine Islands in WWII. (More about him later.)

There's a short stocky 20-year-old Sergeant named Terry Buckler who had achieved a perfect score on the Army Basic Training Physical Fitness Test. Young "Buck" is chomping at the bit to win a spot on the actual mission, whatever it ends up being.

Tyrone Adderly is now a Sgt 1st Class and, beyond our combat experience in the Dominican Republic, he is a Purple Heart veteran of combat at Dak To Vietnam from 1966. His second Purple Heart came later that year and required him to be MEDEVACed to a hospital in Japan and then back to the states. Remember that he then had *another* Vietnam tour in 1968-1969. He is a serious, lightning-fast boxer that no one wants to mess with.

I've already told you about Captain Walther in combat. Well, there is also Captain Dick Meadows, a special operations legend throughout the branches of the military. He fought as an enlisted man in the Korean War and served with the British S.A.S. special ops unit. In Vietnam, Meadows received a field commission directly to Captain by General William Westmoreland for his secret missions behind enemy lines.

Sgt Frank Roe is about the toughest man I've ever met. He's a combat veteran of Vietnam in 1968-1969.

Master Sgt Herman Spencer's combat experience includes the secretive "White Star" missions with Bull Simons early in the Vietnam conflict. He was on the A-teams in Vietnam in

1966-1967 and his personality makes you think he was always a hair-trigger away from getting into a fight with you.

Something similar can be said for Sgt 1st Class Don "Pete" Wingrove. He was in Africa during the Congo Crisis of 1964, was in combat in the Dominican Republic in 1965, and had two combat tours in Vietnam.

Throughout the week, we are given briefings about operational security and communications security. We are told the terms of our isolation. We are not to call home except when given express permission. In conversations, we are not to divulge where we are or any of our activities. If we come across anyone we don't personally know, we are not to discuss any aspect of our training or anything we've seen while on this facility.

We are issued CAR-15s (similar to an M16) and begin daily range firing where our scores are recorded.

On the morning of Friday, Sept 18th, the first cut was made. Out of the 103 soldiers brought, 51 were selected for the mission, and an additional 10 men were identified as backups. We were broken down into three groups.

'Blueboy Assault Group' had 14 members.

'Redwine Security Group' had 15 members.

'Greenleaf Support Group' had 22 members.

Beyond these, there were others in the Ground Force Command Group.

We had to move all of our belongings so that each of the three groups lived separately from the others. Greenleaf got its own two-story barracks building, as did the other two groups.

Tyrone was selected to be an M79 grenade launcher on Redwine.

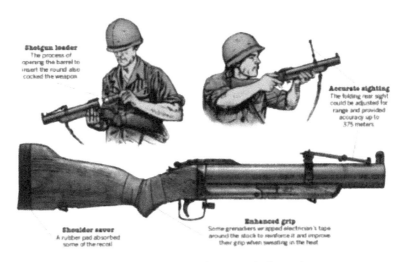

Image 118. The M79 grenade launcher.

I was selected to be an M60 gunner on Greenleaf. Why the M60? I don't know. I wasn't given options, I was just told, "Here's your assignment." I was just happy that I'd made the cut. As you've already seen in multiple stories above, in Vietnam, I always believed in having an M60 crew added to my A-team. I attached an M60 crew (always two or three men) on my C-operations. But, for this mission, there would be no crew. Each M60 would have just one guy. It fires a 7.62mm diameter round, rather than the 5.56mm round of the M16 and the CAR-15. And it is a heavy gun, so, I stripped it down. I reduced weight in every way that I could. This included discarding the bipod. I'd fire from the hip, kneeling.

On Blueboy, the M60 was the 46-year-old iron man, Master Sgt Pappy Kittleson. He had been on the Cabanatuan POW Camp Raid in the Philippines in WWII with Colonel Bull Simons, which freed 512 Americans from their Japanese captors. Because we both had M60 roles, we got

Long reach
The adjustable rear sight enabled accurate firing out to 1,200 yards.

Cool touch
The carrying handle kept the gunner's hand away from the hot barrel and receiver.

Easy loader
A hinged feed cover swung open to load the belt or clear a jam.

Sling
The gun strap was one of the most important parts of the M60. The heavy weapon was hard to carry very far in the field without the sling.

Vital partner
An assistant gunner carried ammo and ensured a smooth ammo feed.

Stable shooter
A bipod stand provided stability when the weapon was fired.

Reliable feeder
Disintegrating links connecting the rounds reduced jamming and accelerated loading.

Fire ready
Ammo boxes contained 200 rounds each.

Image 119. The M60 machine gun.

to know each other a bit. He was a sincere Christian man, and I really admired him as a leader. We'd pass each other on the P.T. morning run, and he'd always say something encouraging. He told me he was going to place an order for '100% tracer rounds' for his M60. I asked him to place an order for 1,000 rounds of that for me too.

Maybe you've noticed a theme. I believe in ammo. I'm the weapons guy.

Ammo is good. More ammo is *more* good.

This ammo comes in boxes of 100, on a belt. For this mission, I ended up putting 100 rounds locked into the M60, then eight boxes in pouches on my LBE, and then I asked my teammate Sgt 1st Class Leroy Carlson to help me out by carrying an extra box of 100 rounds for me. Each pouch could hold 100 rounds, so with that many, I found that the snaps that hold the pouch closed sometimes would get knocked open. So, I created a flat wooden wedge with a hole to protect the snap from being brushed against.

That day, Friday, Sept 18th, each of the three groups loaded up into their group's respective deuce-and-a-half truck and were driven out five miles east, deeper into the heart of the hundreds of square miles of remote forests controlled by Eglin AFB to keep civilians far away from the aerial gunnery ranges and bomber targets. Arriving at Range C-2, we dismounted the trucks, and we laid eyes on a maze of 2x4s and target cloth constructed to represent buildings and roads. There were a couple of helicopters on their landing areas and a couple of A-1E Skyraider aircraft loitering overhead. The sandy soil had been carved out with the bulldozers to create a full-scale mockup of a small town in the middle of an open range about a half-mile square. We were told, "This is the building complex we are going to assault." It had a 'Main Road' down the middle running North/South. At the North end, they had constructed a 100-foot-long wooden bridge that arched up just a few feet above the flat ground enough to show vertical supports. (These were apparently for practicing installing explosive ordnance and eventually, detonating it.)

Most of the 'buildings' were to the west of the Main Road, but about four were along the east side. 'Flowing' westward from under the bridge at the north end, a 'river' had been bulldozed out which turned sharply southward to run alongside the westernmost structure, a 'Walled Compound.' Captain Walther was chosen to be the commander of Greenleaf. He explained to us that this Walled Compound was the primary objective of our mission. At last, we are hearing something about what we're gonna do.

Redwine and Greenleaf were to neutralize buildings outside the objective and provide security around it, sealing off the nearby roads and access. Blueboy group would subdue the interior of the Walled Compound. We now knew that we were going to be rescuing people from cells. Who we'd be rescuing and where we'd be doing the mission was not divulged. Over the coming weeks, we thought it most likely was something in Cuba.

Day after day, we would do three or more walk-throughs of our roles, with every man timed to arrive at designated points in such a way as to create kill zones without ever being exposed to friendly fire. We'd always have our full gear on. The M60 is 23 lbs, and eight boxes of ammo weighs about 50 lbs, so we were carrying about 80lbs on our person. That's enough of a workout on its own and we got used to it with that many rehearsals. We'd dismount the truck then walk our element through the mockup, clear buildings full of guards, secure the access routes, then we'd execute a secure rear guard in retrograde, then re-board our trucks. Our responsibility was to neutralize all guards in the buildings east of the Walled Compound and blow up the bridge to eliminate access from the north.

These first walk throughs let us see how spread out (or close together) we'd be and how our fields of fire must be controlled to ensure no friendly fire incidents. Colonel Simons thought using blank ammunition was a waste of money with very little training value. So, we did a lot of 'bang, bang' by voice for a few days.

By Wednesday, September 23rd, we were ready to build more realism and more confidence into our steps. We started using live ammunition. Our steps and our firing angles were choreographed such that we ensured (and proved) that no one was in a line of fire. Every person had to act with the serious professionalism required for every movement, every shot, every angle. We had to know the movements of every other person in our area.

Now, the helicopters were added to our run-throughs so that we could try out various orders of exiting. Greenleaf Group would ride aboard an HH-53 Super Jolly Green Giant. Captain Walther was our commander, but Colonel Simons would be aboard our chopper with two RTOs (Radio Telephone Operators), Staff Sgt Walt Miller and Staff Sgt David Nickerson, so that he could be in constant communication with the generals. Our helicopter would land just south of the Walled Compound facing east and we'd exit the tail.

I was a part of Greenleaf's Demolition Element commanded by Captain Glen Rouse. From the chopper, we'd run north between the Walled Compound (to our left) and the Guard Barracks (to our right), running by the Water Well between them. We'd see two small buildings immediately on our left which we would clear (neutralizing every person inside.) These two small building were the kitchen and the mess hall. We'd then move north along that eastern wall of the Compound to the Main Gate. There, we'd rendezvous with First Lieutenant George Petrie's element (part of Blueboy Assault Group, operating inside the Walled Compound) which included him, Master Sgt Tom Kemmer and Sgt 1st Class Pete Wingrove. Then, we'd clear the Communications/Admin Building, ensuring the enemy could make no calls for reinforcements. We'd then move quickly up to the North Bridge to set 40 pounds of C-4 to blow the bridge, eliminating any chance of reinforcements.

We had four demolition experts setting the charges on the structure: Sgt 1st Class Earl Bleacher, Sgt Frank Roe,

Staff Sgt John Rodriguez, and Sgt Keith Medinski. While they were working, I would set up in the middle of the bridge and cover them with my M60. Once all the others were done and had activated the timer, they'd move back to our side of the bridge and back 200 yards behind me, while I repositioned to the middle of the road on the south side of the bridge to ensure no one crossed. Just a couple of minutes before detonation, I would then run back as far as I could before the huge explosion was to occur. This is the reason that I am wearing hearing protection in the photo of Greenleaf in Image 121 below.

Lastly, Sgt Marshall Thomas was our Medic to patch us up, should the worst happen. Marshall carried a CAR-15 and was our Forward Air Control guy to be in contact with the A-1Es to call in air support as we needed it. The A-1Es would be loaded with 100-lb White Phosphorous bombs and strafing available within about 60 seconds of our asking.

The aircrews were very professional, and we were kept separate. The helicopters were not hangared at Aux Field #3. They always flew from Hurlburt Field to Aux Field #3, where we would board, then they'd fly us to Range C-2 to practice approach and landing at the mockup and exiting the aircraft and running our mission at full speed.

Once we were able to run the mission consistently at full speed, we were ready for the next step. By October 1st, we began running the mission at night. We would go through the entire operation three times before sunrise. We had to get to the point where we could do this in our sleep. We had spent some after-dark hours on the shooting ranges. Since shooting accuracy decreases at night, Captain

Dick Meadows introduced a new technology, The Armalite SinglePoint Sight.

[To read more about this with photos and first-hand experience using the SinglePoint sights, I recommend you get, *Who Will Go: Into the Son Tay POW Camp* by my friend and fellow Raider, Terry Buckler.]

On Monday, October 19th, our Greenleaf Demolition Element was taken to a building we'd never been in before. Captain Walther introduced us to 'Barbara,' a perfectly detailed scale model of the objective area, on a board about 5ft x5ft. It really opened our eyes. It had amazingly realistic detail so that, at long last, we could see all the buildings, walls, streets, every tree, bush, ditch, light post and telephone pole. We could see every window and door on each building. We saw where each helicopter would land and where every one of our raiders would be running and their field of fire.

Image 120. 'Barbara.' This is oriented such that we are looking to the northeast. The LZ is in the foreground.

Captain Walther had us each use a periscope-type device that let us see the view from the ground level. I put the periscope in each location I would be in and I had an extremely clear view as if I was inside the complex. I took my time looking at the views...

- from the LZ,
- to the Water Well, the Kitchen, and the Mess Hall,
- coming up to the courtyard where I'd first be able to see my approach to the Admin Communications Building, and
- around the corner of the Admin Commo Building to the street.

Over the next couple of weeks, we spent time in that room, discussing risks and making improvements to our plan. It had been created by the Defense Intelligence Agency and was Top Secret. The intelligence community deserves a lot of credit.

We rehearsed over 170 times. We fired thousands of rounds. We brainstormed improvements to our sequence. We devised innovations to our gear to minimize weight. We got everything we asked for. We experimented with goggles and night scopes and night sights. The enlisted men brought years of combat experience.

We were what Special Ops should be.

We formalized our final order of battle and then learned the other groups' missions so that we could be their back-up in case their helicopter didn't make it to the objective. There were three Alternate Plans:

'Plan Blue' was how we would operate if Blueboy Group did not make it to the objective.

'Plan Red' was how we would operate if Redwine Group did not make it to the objective.

'Plan Green' was how the other two groups would operate if we did not make it to the objective.

We knew our plan.
We knew all Alternate Plans.
We knew what each other man on Greenleaf Group was doing and where they would be at all times.
We were ready to launch.
This is how it should be done, a textbook of planning, preparation, and execution still studied in Special Ops units around the world.

[To read the most authoritative book on the Son Tay Raid with much of the planning documentation, please read *The Son Tay Raid: American POWs in Vietnam Were Not Forgotten*, by my friend and fellow Raider, Colonel John Gargus.]

Image 121. Greenleaf Group at Aux
Field #3 around Oct 20th, 1970

1. Richard Valentine 2. Jack Joplin 3. Robert Nelson
4. Marshall Thomas 5. Jimmy Green 6. Jake Jakovenko
7. Walt Miller 8. Keith Medenski 9. Gary Keel 10. John Rodriguez
11. Frank Roe 12. Udo Walther 13. Don Taapken 14. Eric Nelson
15. David Nickerson 16. Leroy Carlson 17. David Lawhon
18. Glenn Rouse 19. Earl Bleacher 20. Sal Suarez 21. Dan Jurich

Image 122. Blueboy Group at Aux Field #3 around Oct 20th, 1970.

1. Bruce Hughes 2. Anthony Dodge 3. George Petrie
4. William Tapley 5. Billy Moore 6. Lorenzo Robbins
7. Tom Jaeger 8. Pat St.Clair 9. Tom Kemmer 10. Don Wingrove
11. Pappy Kittleson 12. Dick Meadows 13. Kenny McMullin

Image 123. Redwine Group at Aux Field #3 around Oct 20th, 1970

1. John Lippert 2. Freddie Doss 2a.(behind 2) Ron Strahan
3. Greg McGuire 4. Joe Murray 5. Noe Quezada
6. Tyrone Adderly 7. Terry Buckler 8. Billy Martin
9. Joe Lupyak 10. Dan Turner 11. Don Blackard
12. Herman Spencer 13. Charlie Masten

Now I need to pause to tell you about "Friday Night Fights" at the "Hook & Jab Club." At Aux Field #3 (today its name is Duke Field), one of our buildings was a club where we could have a few drinks and relax on Friday nights. The training schedule was tight and, typically, each weekday was a successively more complex mission, working up to the biggest, most time-consuming event Thursday night. From October onward, it was all nighttime, so we'd be up the entire Thursday night until dawn Friday morning. After getting some sleep during Friday daylight hours, everyone would be wide awake come Friday night. A few times, they even brought in a band.

As you'd walk in, there was the bar area with a classic jukebox. You'd have plenty of barstools but also a few tables and chairs. To your right was the dance floor and a stage for the band. You had even more tables with chairs there (about 40). It was dark and it smelled like beer and wood. In other words, it was perfect.

The nights at the Hook & Jab Club were long and hilarious. The guys were opinionated and gregarious. The stories told were sensational. These were characters—with an ego. Eventually, someone would get on someone else's nerves, an insult would be spoken, and tempers would escalate. "The Hook & Jab Club," we called it.

I'd say that Master Sgt Herman Spencer was in every fight, even if he had to join in someone else's fight. There was the time Spencer sucker-punched Sgt 1st Class David Lawhon. I could list a few, but I'll summarize by saying that, in some of the fights, Herman did not come out the winner. And that did not deter him from joining in next time.

Image 124. Aux Field #3. The runway is in the background.
Our barracks (for Greenleaf) was the near building. The bottom
floor was for equipment and offices, including the Commander's
office. Upstairs was an open bay with rows of beds on left and
right that could sleep about 50. Just beyond our barracks and
on the right out of the photo was the "Hook & Jab Club."

One Friday, Herman and I got into it, one on one. I
almost bit his thumb off. Here's how it went. So, there is
one sausage left in the jar at the far end of the bar. There's
no fork, so I start to fish it out of the jar with my fingers.
It's about 10pm. There are about 20 guys in the bar. I have
it in my hand, I'm turning around (my fist is stuck in the
throat of the jar), and I hear Spencer say, "You're paying
for that whole jar." He's making a Clint Eastwood squint
trying to look like a tough smartass. He's standing only
a couple feet from the end of the bar and a couple of feet
from me.

I say, "Oh, so what are you? An employee here?"

He steps toward me to intimidate (it's only one or two steps), and he sucker punches me, no warning, while my fist is still in the jar. I catch the punch on my left shoulder, and it glances off and lands on my left ear, which kinda hurt. I reflexively knock him down with my right fist now free from the jar. (I should've left the jar <u>on</u> my fist.) Only a second more and I send Herman crashing into the tables and I tackle him to the floor. A couple of guys in the club pull me off him. They tell Herman that he'd better leave. I say, "Herman, it ain't over." I go after him.

As he's reaching his barracks, there's a small, enclosed porch with one lightbulb overhead. Herman sees me coming for him, so he smashes the lightbulb out and waits there to ambush me. He gets me by the head, gouging my eye with his thumb. I jerk my head and his thumb releases my eye and now I have his thumb right next to my mouth and I bite it. Herman recoils from the pain and some Redwine guys separate the two of us. Herman ends up at the dispensary getting his thumb checked out. For the next few days, my eye was red, and Herman has this huge bandage wrapped around his thumb.

The next morning, word got to Colonel Simons about Herman being in yet another fight. He called Herman to his office and said, "Herman, I want you on this mission. But if you so much as raise your hands above your waist one more time, you'll be off the team."

Sergeant Major Pylant got us together and made us shake hands, with Herman's bandaged thumb. We actually became pretty good friends after this.[19]

---

19 Righteous indignation, sufficient self-restraint, leaders who know how to mete out discipline where needed. These bar fights are nothing to be ashamed of.

One Friday night, an Air Force bus pulled up to The Hook & Jab and a group of about eight women walked into our watering hole. They knew we had a Country & Western band playing that night. They danced and talked with the guys and joked and mingled. We suspected they were agents trying to find out if any of us were security risks, talking about the mission. We had been briefed by a Major Max Newman (Nickname "Blue Max" as a nod to his Prussian heritage). He was in charge of Operational Security for our mission. We could imagine that he selected these female agents, "Get 'em drunk and make 'em talk, Ladies."

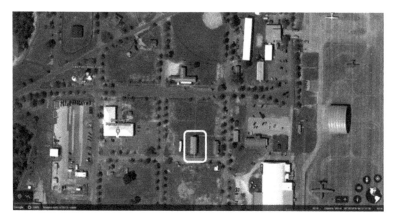

Image 125. Above, you can see the location where our barracks and the TOC and "The Hook & Jab Club" used to be. Notice the sidewalks we traveled between the old WWII buildings. And you can see the one remaining 2-story WWII barracks building we used (the centermost building in the photo, circled). This is a very secretive base where very few have ever been. Some of America's most classified Special Operations around the world originate from the seclusion of Duke Field. One-of-a-kind, civilian-looking aircraft, specially modified with wicked rockets, sensors, guns, or hellfire missiles reside on their flightline, far from photographers.

Beyond that particular night, there were two women who were there pretty regularly. One wore these tight white pants with red Coca-Cola bottle logos on them. Every guy from thenceforth knew her as "Coca-Cola Pants." We figured they were giving Blue Max detailed reports of everyone and every word. But they were fun.

At this point, it had been two months sequestered at this secret facility and one Sunday afternoon, I called my parents in New Jersey. Keep in mind that my parents spoke fluent Ukrainian, but only <u>broken</u> English, so naturally, our conversations were in Ukrainian. The next day, a sergeant comes to me and escorts me to a building I'd never been in before. 'Chief of Operational Security' it said on the office door. The agent inside asked me to sit down. Major Max Newman had agents in civilian suits observing our comings and goings from unmarked sedans around the base. Now, we suspected that all the phones were tapped, but it surprised me when the agent asked, "What language are you speaking?"

Look at it from their perspective. I'm in the heart of a Top Secret operation in the heart of a classified military compound in the heart of a huge, secure military reservation and I'm the guy making an off-base phone call, speaking the language of a Soviet republic. So, I understood why they'd be suspicious. Still, I had to take a jab at them, "What, you guys don't have anyone who speaks Ukrainian?"

Before the sun came up on Tuesday morning, November 17th, we loaded onto buses with everything we were bringing for the mission. The buses took us through the black, desolate forest to the barely-lit flightline at Eglin Air Force Base right up to a waiting C-141 Starlifter with its tail ramp fully open. In the pre-dawn dark, there were some pinpoint taxiway lights, but otherwise, the only thing you could see was the surreal sea-foam green glow of the plane's cargo bay interior. Its four engines were not on, but there was jet-noise from its auxiliary power unit that runs the avionics. The loadmaster gives us a questioning look but dared not ask, "Who are you guys?" We wore no insignia or any identification on our uniforms. Soon, the engines were starting up and the ramp was rising to close us in.

28 hours later, at 3am on November 18th, that same door was lowering onto a hangar floor. We didn't know onto what airfield or even into which country we were stepping. Vans took us to single-story dorms, and we got about five hours of sleep until the sunlight awakened us. We had a briefing to tell us our schedule, including equipment checks and team meetings planned for the next couple of days. We could only guess by the temperature and aromas that it was somewhere in Southeast Asia.

[Years later, we now know that we were at a secret CIA compound at Takhli Royal Thai Air Force Base.]

On Friday, November 20th, we were told to get some sleep after lunch and to be at the theater at 1800 for a briefing.

It's there that Colonel Simons finally told us our mission. "We are going to recue 70 American prisoners of war, maybe more, from a camp called Son Tay. This is something

American prisoners have the right to expect from their fellow soldiers. The target is 23 miles west of Hanoi."

We were so excited. It was the greatest mission we could have imagined. Everyone stood up, applauding and cheering. "Let's go get 'em out!"

Colonel Simons then added, "You are not to let nothing—nothing—interfere with the operation. Our mission is to rescue prisoners, not to take prisoners. If we are walking into a trap and they're ready for us when we arrive, don't even dream about walking out of Vietnam. I want to keep this force together. We'll back up to the Song Con River and let them come across that damned open ground. We'll make those sonovabitches pay for every foot."

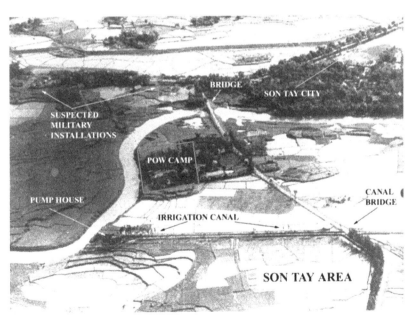

Image 126. A reconnaissance photo of
Son Tay in 1970, looking north.

We loaded onto the vans with our gear, weapons, equipment, and ammo. The sun had fully set, and the stars were shining in a clear black sky as we boarded. They took us straight to the flightline to a C-130 with engines running, tailgate down.

We landed 30 minutes later at Udorn Royal Thai Air Force Base where we boarded the helicopters that we'd become so familiar with over so many rehearsals at Eglin. My seat was on the left side, about three seats down from the left minigun at the front, manned by USAF Master Sgt Harold Harvey, the PJ (pararescueman) who is right behind the cockpit.

A few minutes later, at 11:17pm local, all the engines of our six helicopters accelerated for liftoff. The lead, an HH-3 Jolly Green Giant, code named *Banana* lifted off first. All the other five choppers were HH-53 Super Jolly Green Giants, which lifted off in trail formation, climbing to 3000 feet to form up with two HC-130s, *Lime 1* and *Lime 2*, circling overhead that would lead us to the border of North Vietnam. Our HH-53 had the code-name *Apple 1* and the remainder were *Apple 2* through *5*.

I say 'code name' rather than 'call sign' because there was no need for call signs at this point. There would be no radio transmissions. And there'd be no use of exterior lights. And no use of navigational beacons. Our helicopters now had to fly in formation behind HC-130s *Lime 1* and *Lime 2* for two hours in radio silence. There was no procedure and no precedent for flying six helicopters in formation. And they did this for three exhausting hours with simply their eyeballs and the light of the quarter moon. In fact, that quarter moon determined the window of dates that the mission could be run. The mission planners wanted the moonlight to be just enough so that our pilots could safely see the other aircraft in their formation, but not so much that it would make the aircraft easy to see from the ground. The pilots' experiments at Eglin had proven that the optimal would be a quarter moon.

Lime 1 and *Lime 2* were HC-130s, the only type of aircraft with the capability to refuel helicopters. This gave these helicopters unlimited range, making this mission possible. At the North Vietnam border, topped off with fuel, all six helicopters then slid over into formation with an MC-130, *Cherry 1*, at 6,800 feet which is 1000 feet above the mountaintops. *Apple 3*, the gunship, was on the right wing of *Cherry 1*. Behind *Apple 3* was our chopper, *Apple 1*. Looking out the port window, I could, at times, see the MC-130 and the HH-3 (code named *Banana* with Blueboy Assault Group aboard). Off the left side of the HH-3, there was *Apple 4* and *Apple 5* (two spare HH-53s). Off our right was *Apple 2* (with Redwine Security Group).

Now in formation with *Cherry 1*, we're driving 30 minutes eastward into the enemy's airspace, approximately 1000 feet above the ground. We're dropping in altitude as we hug the descending slopes of the mountain range into the flat coastal plains of Hanoi. There's a cloud deck draping the mountains. It's "H-10" ('H minus 10') which means 10 minutes prior to the 'H-Hour.' The variable 'H' is the moment our MC-130 *Cherry 1* is required to be directly over the Son Tay POW Camp. At that moment, *Cherry 1* will drop four Mk24 illumination flares (2 million candlepower each) to light up our objective area and will state

Image 127. I was in *Apple 1* with the Greenleaf Support Group aboard. *Apple 1* is the middle helicopter off the right wing of the MC-130 *Cherry 1*. Never had helicopters flown in such an elaborate formation. The aviation achievement of air refueling helicopters had been invented only in 1965 with the introduction of the HC-130N. This, for the first time, gives helicopters unlimited range and made this mission conceivable. Think of the risk of a dangling hose full of fuel. Then imagine approaching the tail of the aircraft with your rotor blades reaching far out ahead of the cockpit. Now do it at night with no lights and no radios.

on the radios, "Alpha, Alpha, Alpha!" announcing to all our air and ground crews that the mission sequences have begun. With more than 100 aircraft involved, each has calculated their timing based on the H declared by the commander, Brigadier General LeRoy Manor (the H-time/date was announced yesterday via a coded messaging system known as 'Red Rocket').

[NOTE: The details in the following timeline are made possible by Cliff Westbrook's research of After Action Reports, recordings of the actual radio transmissions, and interviews with Raiders.]

H-10: Inside the HH-3 *Banana*, the Blueboy Assault Group opens and jettisons the Plexiglas windows in preparation for each man to be able to fire out the ports when the time comes for *Banana* to descend into the courtyard of the walled POW camp. The formation breaks out of the bottom of the cloud deck at 4,800 feet. Visibility is unlimited, and the clear sight ahead of them is the bright city lights of Hanoi and the surrounding metropolitan area. Son Tay is on the near side of those lights.

The loadmaster aboard the MC-130 *Cherry 1* completes his final checklist for fuses on the flares and napalm markers. They are on pallets that he will drop via parachute out the back. The tail is open. Our formation is 500 feet above the ground at the IP. The Initial Point is the key navigation point that ensures you approach the POW camp from the correct angle. We are 11 miles west of the Son Tay POW camp.

H-5: Captain Bill Guenon (pilot on *Cherry 1*) announces over the radios, "Papa November, Papa November." This is the first use of the radios for any of our aircraft since we started engines over three hours ago. This is the only way to let every aircraft know that 1.) there are five minutes until we are at Son Tay and therefore, 2.) it is time for the soldiers to stand and prepare to dismount. Captain Walther tells us to perform our Final Checklist. I stand up and stow the seats up flush against the helicopter wall. I

H-6 (2:12:41am): Cherry 1 at the IP. Intercom confirms this is the moment passing over the river.

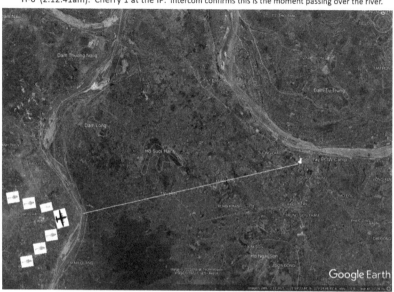

Image 128. In this graphic, the yellow line shows the 11 miles from the IP to the POW camp. The aircraft are not to scale.

check the security of my five grenades. On my M60, I load the starter round of the first 100-round belt. I put my red/ amber goggles on.

H-2: Captain Bill Guenon announces, "Zero Seven Two, HACK," over the radios. This pre-planned radio call is the opportunity for the helicopters to hear what heading is optimal inbound to the Son Tay POW camp. The MC-130 has the benefits of 1.) state-of-the-art special operations avionics, FLIR (forward-looking infrared optics) and radar for precise low-level navigation and 2.) multiple navigators to do the calculation of the wind-drift-corrected heading. For these remaining 3.5 miles, the helicopters are to fly heading 072 degrees. At this moment, *Cherry 1* climbs and accelerates, leaving our helicopters to navigate on our own. *Banana* now moves ahead of us, and I can no longer see him, since we are now required to fall into trail formation about a half mile behind him in the final approach. We've been at 105 knots the entire trip, but now we slow to 80 knots. Our tail ramp (on *Apple 1*) is open, and we can see *Apple 2* about a half mile in trail behind us.

H-2 (2:17:32am): "072, HACK" 3.5nm from POW Camp, the Start Climb Point.

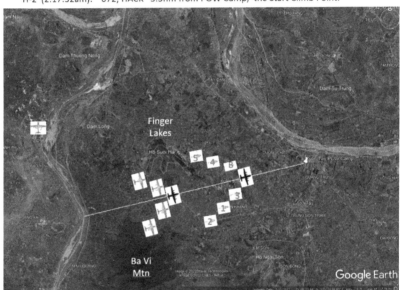

Image 129. You can see the position of other aircraft. *Cherry 2* is an MC-130 leading the Strike Force of five A-1E Skyraiders, *Peach 1* through *Peach 5*.

H-Hour (0219 hours, 2:19am local time): Captain Bill Guenon broadcasts, "Alpha, Alpha, Alpha!" The four flares drop out the tail of *Cherry 1*, lighting up the POW camp. But there are no helicopters! At this moment, *Apple 3*, the gunship, which was supposed to be coming over the west wall of the POW camp, is 400 yards south of the objective at a military facility with a similar shape to the POW camp. In target study, this group of buildings was referred to as The Secondary School. The wind had blown them south of their planned course.

H+30seconds (2:19:35 local time): Immediately, *Apple 3* recognizes the huge flares and banks hard left in a hairpin S-turn to re-approach the POW camp from the correct direction. From the view that *Banana* (Blueboy's helicopter) has, *Apple 3* appears to be executing his planned mission, and does not understand that *Apple 3* is in the wrong location.

2:19:35am: Apple 3 hovers overs the Secondary School then turns left.

Image 130. The helicopters are shown in red. The HH-53 gunship *Apple 3* (shown as '3') is the first helicopter to arrive, but it's at the Secondary School. The HH-3 *Banana* (shown as 'B') is arriving in trail, behind *Apple 3*.

H+50seconds: Blueboy's chopper, *Banana*, descends to what looks like the POW camp, the gunners naturally open fire at the northwest and southwest corners of the walled compound. The pilots, seeing that there is no courtyard to land in, realize this is the wrong place and now swing left to head to the POW camp.

2:19:50am: Banana fires on the Secondary School then turns left, following the same path as Apple 3.

Image 131. The helicopters are in red. *Banana* is over the Secondary School. Our helicopter, *Apple 1*, is in trail behind him, but now focuses on the ground cues for landing. Redwine's chopper, *Apple 2*, is in trail behind *Apple 1*.

H+1minute (2:20:15 local time): Having seen *Banana* (Blueboy's helicopter) descend and then open fire, *Apple 1*'s (our) pilots now are fully focused on executing the landing. They don't see that *Banana* has departed to the north. I'm standing right next to our PJ/gunner, Master Sgt Harold Harvey.

2:20:15am: Apple 1 lands at the Secondary School. The door won't open, due to a berm. Apple 2 sees Banana bank to the left. Apple 2 recognizes the real POW camp now.

Image 132. The helicopters are in red. Our HH-53 *Apple 1* (shown as '1') is now on the ground (not realizing this is the Secondary School). *Apple 2*, with the best vantage, sees that *Apple 1* has landed in the wrong place.

Per instructions, Harold opens up on the barracks on the left side of the chopper. The noise is deafening, a minigun firing 4,000 rounds per minute!

Image 133. As we are landing, this is roughly the view that
I had. (This photo is of a modern variant of the HH-53.)
Master Sgt Harold Harvey was the left side gunner.

Image 134. Here is the view looking toward the tail,
fully opened up for a tactical landing like ours. (This
photo is of a modern variant of the HH-53.)

As we land, something strange happens. The tail ramp rises about halfway. We've landed on something that is forcing the tail up. Greenleaf tries to exit, but it's taking a while, since every guy has to basically stoop down very low to squeeze out! A rice paddy dyke at the Secondary School has forced the ramp up, making it very difficult for anyone to exit out the tail.

Image 135. In this view, the tail ramp is up about the amount that it was up as we first landed. (This photo is of a modern variant of the HH-53.)

While I'm crawling out the back—somehow lugging an M60 and the bulking gear attached to my LBE—the helicopter surprises me by lifting up a few feet and moving forward. Well, this makes it very easy for me now, so I just jump out and land on my feet as the helicopter moves forward about 15 feet. Now, I'm running with Captain Rouse and our Demolition Element north to a

4-foot-deep ditch between us and the nearest building, a barracks.

I see that this is not the right place. In training, we absolutely knew what the barracks building was going to look like, and this ain't it! But our 22 Greenleaf soldiers are running to their positions. Our helicopter lifts loudly away just 40 feet behind me and within seconds it is long gone.

The only sound now is our gun battle with grenades and automatic fire. To my right, one team has secured the eastern entryway/alley. Captain Eric Nelson's team has headed past that out onto the north/south road.

Captain Rouse tells us to hold up. This clearly is not the place. There's no path for us to proceed up. There's no Walled Compound camp to the left. There's no Water Well. Instead, there's a building running north-south. Nothing looks like what we had rehearsed. Looking north, there is a courtyard formed by these buildings. ALL of us know that this ain't the right place, so everyone is holding back and not going beyond visual range of Bull Simons, who is to my left, about 50 feet south of the barracks, coordinating with his two RTOs and with Captain Walther.

[I was not aware at the time, but here is more of the story of what's transpiring at this moment. Captain Eric Nelson, commander of Greenleaf's Security Element, and his men had been stacked along the very back of the starboard side of *Apple 1* and had exited the tail ramp turning to their left to run up *Apple 1*'s right side per the plan. Their route ran them out away from the nose of the chopper. From what they could see, things seemed to fit their planned

route that they'd studied at Eglin. They immediately
began their run to the north-south road just outside
this compound. But as they turned and ran north-
ward up the road, there was no bridge in sight. And
the buildings don't fit. And the road is curving to the
right. They run a hundred yards up and then hold up,
taking a defensive position for the time being.]

H+2 minutes: The dyke that propped *Apple 1*'s tail ramp
up is part of a long trench/ditch that now becomes useful
to us. It provides about five feet of depth, so our element
can take cover in it, but I pull my M60 to my hip, take a
knee, and set up shop on the near side of the ditch. None of
Greenleaf is passing near my kill zone. To my left, a team
including Staff Sgt Bob Nelson, Sgt 1st Class Dan Jurich,
and Sgt Frank Roe secures the left side (the west) exit of
the barracks. To my right, Captain Walther, Sgt 1st Class
Sal Suarez, and Sgt 1st Class David Lawhon secure the
opposite end. They are dropping everyone that shoots at
them. These two teams both recognize that we are all at the
wrong place but have to deal with this hornets' nest. They
clear a room or two but resist going in further than needed
to subdue enemy fire. Standing near me are Colonel Bull
Simons, his RTO, Sgt Walt Miller, Sgt Gary Keel, Sgt Noe
Rodriguez. We don't bother going into buildings or clearing rooms, but whoever comes around the corners quickly
finds themselves dead. There are many more enemy soldiers here than we expected to be at the POW camp. All of
the sudden, out of the darkness, an enemy soldier pops up
out of the ditch and then ducks back down. The language
that he's yelling is not Vietnamese. I tell Staff Sgt John

Rodriguez, "If he pops up again, shoot the sonofabitch—but don't fire automatic! We're too close to everyone else." The enemy pops up again and Bull Simons raises a weapon and drops him with a short burst.

H+3: Colonel Bull Simons tells Captain Walther to begin disengaging and then to prepare for extraction. Within a minute, everyone gets that message. Now our job is to hold out until our *Apple 1* helicopter comes back to pick us up. Sgt 1st Class Leroy Carlson and Sgt 1st Class Don Taapken are firing their M79 Grenade Launchers. Over the time at this facility, Carlson puts 26 rounds into those windows, each one flashing for an instant with a huge BANG, one every 5 or 10 seconds.

H+4: By this time, we've killed at least ten enemy soldiers, and maybe quite a few more. We're not sticking around to count. (In our After-Action Reports, the evidence and statements were corroborated, indicating this number of confirmed enemy losses by this time.) One thing that is not clear is who these soldiers are. From my two tours in Vietnam, I can recognize that these are not Vietnamese. They are larger in height and weight.

> [Later, strong evidence indicates that these are Chinese soldiers studying the real-world application of the Russian SAMs (Surface-to-Air Missiles) that are used by both the Vietnamese and the Chinese.]

Sgt Walt Miller, Colonel Simons' RTO, calls to LtCol Elliott "Bud" Sydnor on the radio, "Wildroot (Sydnor's

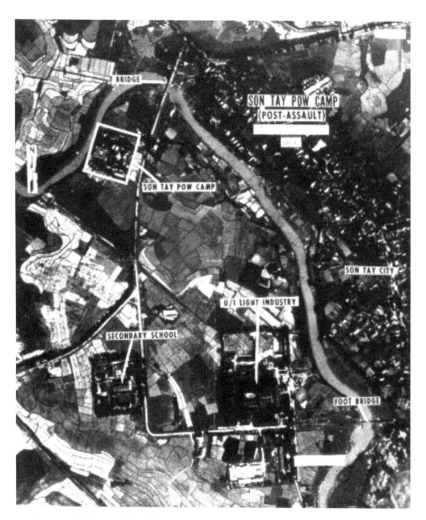

Image 136. In this SR-71 reconnaissance photo, you can see
the Son Tay POW camp as well as the Secondary School.

callsign), this is Axle (Simons' callsign). We're set down
on the wrong side." Sydnor and Redwine Security Group
have just exited *Apple 2* at the correct location, the POW
camp about 400 yards north of the Secondary School. *Apple
2*'s pilots hear this radio conversation between Simons and

Sydnor since they are in the air with line-of-sight to both of them. *Apple 1*, on the other hand, is on the ground at the waiting point, an island on a small lake a mile away, so his radios don't pick up this radio signal clearly.

H+5: *Apple 1* has now gotten the message and broadcasts over the radio, "*Apple 1* is going back to get the force." On the ground at the Secondary School, all of Greenleaf has withdrawn from the buildings. Four enemy soldiers now run out of the left side of the barracks. The kill zone is clear of our guys. I open up with a barrage. All four are dropped. I now begin firing on full-automatic (the M60 is ALWAYS automatic fire) all along my designated arc, the entire length of the barracks building. From my hip, in the darkness I'm 100% tracers, blazing a digital dashed orange line through the black air. Udo Walther had given me the name "Hoseman" for this reason. The kick of an M60 is not like the recoil of semi-automatic. It's more like a steady force, pushing you backward. I lean in a bit to muscle it forward, keeping every enemy head down.

H+6: Withdrawal of Greenleaf to the LZ is well underway with just about all members at the LZ. The helicopter says on the radio, "Give us a signal and we'll come pick you up."

Sgt Walt Miller replies, "Roger. Here's a Marker Signal NOW." He activates a strobe pointing it west toward the sound of the helicopter. I keep firing, protecting my team rallying just 30 feet behind me at the LZ. The tracers bounce off the walls, sometimes ricocheting left or right or straight up in a reddish-orange streak.

H+7: Captain Eric Nelson's Security Element runs in from the street, confident in an M60 providing a red/orange wall of cover. Withdrawal to the LZ marshalling area is complete. All 22 Greenleaf members are accounted for.

I keep firing. Every now and then, one of my orange tracers bounces off a concrete surface and ricochets way up into the air looking just like a bottle rocket. *Apple 1*, approaching but not yet certain which light is us, sees my tracer rounds and comments, "OK, is that your signal, Axle. –with the tracers?"

H+8: Out of the western blackness now approaches *Apple 1* rectifying our situation. "Set it down right there, *Apple*," says Captain Walther on the radio. *Apple 1* loudly settles on the ground now and our members immediately begin boarding. I keep firing, full-automatic, protecting my team as they board.

H+9: Everyone is aboard except Captain Walther and me.
I keep firing, on full-auto, of course.
Captain Walther: "Alright, get on the helicopter!"
I keep firing. My barrel is getting really hot. (At this point, I'm afraid to stop. We seem like a sitting duck. Plus, my finger is frozen in the KILL position.)
Captain Walther grabs my neck and shoulder: "Jake, get on the chopper, NOW!"
I stand with my M60 still leveled. I run to my left to the tail. Captain Walther pushes me the whole way as we step up onto the helicopter's ramp. The PJ/gunner there at the tail says something on his headset and within five seconds, the helicopter lifts off. Master Sgt Harold Harvey at the left side window, lets loose his minigun's fateful lightning.

With that, every head will stay down until we are out of range of their small arms. The pilot executes a sharp right bank which swings us south of this compound, then west of it, then rolls out headed north toward the POW camp.

H+10: In the roaring, dimly lit interior, we're gathering our wits and shuffling back into order. I'm careful to keep my barrel from touching anyone. It's glowing dark red/orange. All 22 of us are standing. All are calm, a little frustrated, but immediately re-focusing as each leader rallies their stallions for 'Take 2.' Now, we're back in order. We have about 60 seconds to catch our breath and look over our equipment. I notice that I have only two boxes of my ammo remaining. Wow, I've used up <u>600 rounds</u>.

We're already there. Out Harold Harvey's window, everything looks just like the Barbara model. Harold is not firing. There are 34 Green Berets already on the ground in among those buildings. We've got to be smart. Everything has changed. We have to adapt to this unrehearsed scenario. (Plan Green was if we were taken out. No plan had us being put back in.) We've got to be sure we're not shooting at one of our brothers.

Apple 1 settles onto the originally planned rice paddies just south of the walled POW camp. We dismount and immediately spot the Water Well, but there's no need to run to it—Redwine already neutralized it.

H+11: We paused and got the word that Colonel Simons is telling us not to proceed any further. (The North Bridge will now, under Alternate Plan Green, be hit with incendiaries by the A-1E Skyraiders. It is no longer safe to approach the bridge.)

Image 137. The best image of the Son Tay POW camp. This photo was taken by a USAF Buffalo Hunter reconnaissance drone in July 1969 when there were unconfirmed suspicions that it could be holding POWs. This view is looking north.

LtCol Sydnor: "Greenleaf (Captain Walther), this is Wildroot. In your area there's part of Redwine's forces. Have your forces cease fire until you make contact with us."

Captain Walther and Sgt 1st Class Sal Suarez are at the east end of the Barracks and flush out an enemy soldier. Master Sgt Herman Spencer drops him at the northwest corner of the Barracks. I set up on one knee with my M60 at the Air Raid Trench.

Captain Rouse, John Rodriguez, Keith Medinski, Frank Roe, and Marshall Thomas set up at the west entrance of the Guard Barracks. They see approximately five soldiers inside and go in with concussion grenades followed by a standard clearing.

A soldier fires an AK-47 from the Communications/ Admin building, so Leroy Carlson, standing just outside the Guard Barracks, fires multiple M79 grenade launcher rounds in, eliminating that threat.

H+12: LtCol Sydnor broadcasts on the radios, "There are negative Items in the compound. Standby to withdraw normally." (The heart-breaking significance of this statement takes time to absorb. It's hard to believe that there are no POWs.)

From my current position with Earl Bleacher and Leroy Carlson, I'm already at the LZ. LtCol Sydnor is within 50 feet of us with the Ground Force Command Group, which includes Staff Sgt Paul Poole (RTO), Sgt 1st Class Marion Howell (RTO), Captain Jim McClam (MACO, Marshalling Area Control Officer), and LtCol (Doctor) Joe Cataldo.

H+14: Captain Rouse, John Rodriguez, Keith Medinski, Frank Roe, and Marshall Thomas arrive from the Guard Barracks. Our entire Greenleaf Demolition Element is now together at the LZ. There is still sporadic gunfire. The sound of a round from a LAW (Light Anti-Tank Weapon) is heard out on the north/south road. Redwine is still out there, and they are engaging a military convoy coming up the road.

H+15: LtCol Sydnor calls the A-1Es on UHF (Ultra High Frequency) radios, "*Peach*, Wildroot on Uniform."

Peach 1 (Major Jerry Rhein): "Go ahead, Wildroot."

Sydnor: "We want you to take care of the Big Bridge—I say again, The Big Bridge—now."

Peach 1: "Ok, we'll take care of the Big Bridge for you."

This is the North Bridge that our Demolition Element was originally planned to destroy.

H+16: LtCol Sydnor announces on the radio that the LZ is marked and ready for the extraction, "*Apple 1*, this is Wildroot. We have the lights. You're cleared in. You're cleared in."

Apple 1 (LtCol Warner Britton): "We're about 30 seconds out."

H+17: *Apple 1* requests, "Wildroot, *Apple 1*. Give me a flare."

All of our Greenleaf Support Group is now with us at the LZ.

H+18: LtCol Sydnor launches the flare and initiates authentication with *Apple 1*, "Did you get my flare?"

Apple 1: "Got it."

Apple 1 lands. This is the HH-53 that brought us in, but it is not the helicopter that we will extract on.

LtCol Sydnor: "Alright, Blueboy and Redwine. Blueboy and Redwine, move to the aircraft and load. Blueboy and Redwine. Over."

I'm a little surprised, but I like it this way. My psyche likes being the last one out. I have the M60.

H+19: The first SAM (Surface-to-Air Missile) launches in the Son Tay area. It's a fantastically huge orange ball of fire brighter than the illumination flare that kicked off this whole operation. And much more blinding than the flare that LtCol Sydnor fired a minute ago for *Apple 1*.

H+20: Another SAM launches just east of us. Those F-105 SAM killers are going nose to nose with those SAM sites so that we can make it home on our helicopters.

H+21: *Apple 1* lifts off. It has almost all of Blueboy Assault Group and almost all of Redwine Security Group. Captain Dick Meadows, Master Sgt Billy K. Moore, and Sgt 1st Class Tony Dodge are still inside the walled POW camp connecting the time-delay fuze for the charge that will demolish the *Banana* helicopter intentionally crash-landed to get Blueboy inside the Walled Compound.

The MACO, Captain Jim McClam asks *Apple 2*, "Do you need a flare to get to the Lima Zulu?"

Apple 2 (LtCol John Allison) says, "Give us another flare, just to make sure."

H+23: *Apple 2* smoothly feathers in, settling into the rectangle of "Bean Bag Lights" that outline the LZ. His tail is open. The smell of the exhaust and jet fuel is in the whirlwind. Just about everyone is boarding except Sydnor, Bull, and McClam.

H+25: Captain Meadows, Moore, and Dodge arrive at the LZ. They confer with Sydnor, Simons, and McClam. They're still waiting for someone. I'm not sure who.

H+27: Three shadowy figures are running toward us and the helicopter from the east, from the north/south road. The first posture is to figure out if they are enemy. Captain McClam raises his Night Vision Starlight Scope and identifies them as our last element that we've been waiting for. They are Sgts 1st Class Don Blackard, Freddie Doss, and Greg McGuire, the farthest-flung element of our entire unit who guarded the southern approach and had fired the LAW.

All run aboard.

We're off the ground.[20]

We were headed home…but the POWs were not. It started to really sink in. There were no POWs.

We had executed the mission without losing any of our team, but no one felt like celebrating. We were emotionally drained. We dominated that battlefield. Certainly, we should not come back empty handed. Guilt weighed in our minds.

President Nixon and Chairman of the Joint Chiefs of Staff, Admiral Thomas Moorer had weighed the possibility that there would be no POWs on the day we went in—there was evidence of POWs and evidence against. They had made the command decision to proceed with the raid because 1.) it was worth the risk and 2.) it would send the right message, even if there were no POWs. But as far as

---

20   The public likes to talk about the generals and the President and the command posts. But, when you earn the trust of a veteran to the point that they are willing to share their story, choose instead to be primarily interested in their personal experiences, what they personally saw and heard and felt. For you and for them, those conversations will be some of the most profound, real, and edifying.

us, the raiders, our minds had been completely focused and confident that we were going to have those prisoners back to enjoy Thanksgiving dinner, 1970, with their families.

We returned to Udorn RTAFB (Royal Thai Air Force Base) and spent a couple of hours on the ground before flying to Takhli RTAFB. There we rested before a C-141 took us back to Eglin Auxiliary Field #3. Repeatedly, we were instructed not to talk about the raid. The news of the raid was on the TV, the radio, and the newspaper. The Pentagon press briefings will be the only source sharing information about this Top Secret raid.

On Monday morning, November 23rd, back at Aux Field #3, we went to the Base Exchange snack bar and saw the employee there that we all knew as "Mom." She'd always been great to joke around with throughout our three months there. We sat at our usual table. She came over smiling and said, "There are my favorite customers! I missed you. Where have you been?"

No one said anything. And we didn't joke around like we had before. I think I said, "We were training at a different location."

The TV was on. We were watching Colonel Simons answering questions about the raid at the Pentagon press briefing. With him was Melvin Laird, Secretary of Defense, Admiral Thomas Moorer, Chairman of the Joint Chiefs of Staff and Air Force Brigadier General LeRoy Manor, who commanded the overall operation.

Mom said, "Oh my God!" She put everything down and went around to each of us at the table and gave us sincere, tearful hugs.

Image 138. Secretary of Defense Melvin Laird, Colonel
Bull Simons, Chairman of the Joint Chiefs of Staff Admiral
Thomas Moorer, and Brigadier General LeRoy Manor.

The raid sent the message to the enemy and to the POWs, loud and clear. Americans will come for our own. Fearing more raids, the North Vietnamese government consolidated the prisoners into two POW camps deep in the heart of downtown Hanoi and closed all the isolated POW camps. At last, all the POWs were together and solitary confinement came to an end for so many suffering. The POWs were able to organize. They formed the 4th Allied POW Wing and were able to take care of each other. The Son Tay Raid gave them hope and raised their morale. They now knew that they were not forgotten by their country.

In the East Room of the White House, only four days after the Raid, President Nixon honored the Son Tay Raiders by having the following representatives in a televised ceremony in the White House's East Room.

USAF Brigadier General LeRoy Manor

Colonel Bull Simons

USAF Technical Sgt Leroy Wright (the representative of the aircrews) and Sgt 1st Class Tyrone Adderly (the representative of all of us Green Berets)

Image 139. Tyrone Adderly is second from the right. The White House, November 25th, 1970, four days after the Raid.

I was so proud to have Tyrone Adderly represent us there. Gloria was flown on a Lear Jet to Washington to be with Tyrone for the ceremony. In the Blue Room, she and Tyrone met with Colonel Bull Simons and his wife Lucille, Brigadier General Leroy Manor and his wife Delores, and USAF Tech Sgt Leroy Wright and his wife Shirl. The

Chairman of the Joint Chiefs of Staff, Admiral Thomas Moorer was there, meeting each of them. Wives of POWs were also there–this is for them more than anyone. The Blue Room is in the center of the White House and has the famous balcony where Presidents overlook large gatherings on the South Lawn.

President Nixon stood proudly with these men as he spoke to the nation: "This mission was carried out with incomparable efficiency. Even more important, it was carried out with incomparable bravery."

On December 9th, Secretary of Defense Melvin Laird came to Fort Bragg and we received our awards and decorations in a parade ground ceremony. A formal dinner was held at the officers' club in our honor. The guest speaker was the Chief of Staff of the Army, General William Westmoreland.

We were given 30 days of leave, so I spent Christmas and New Year's with my parents at their home in Jackson, NJ. It was a small community called Rova Farms with a lot of people from the old country. There, they had a lot of new friends who spoke their native language.

Image 140. Secretary of Defense Laird personally awarding us our Silver Stars. In this photo, I'm over Secretary Laird's right shoulder. Also in the photo are the following. Captain Dick Meadows is shaking hands with Lt General John Tolson, commander of XVIII Airborne Corps. Master Sgt Tom Kemmer is receiving his award from Secretary Laird. Next row (l-r) is Sgt 1st Class Marion Howell, Sgt 1st Class Don Taapken, and then me. The next row back (l-r) is Staff Sgt Paul Poole, Staff Sgt John Rodriguez, and then Staff Sgt Lawrence 'Tiny' Young. Next row back is Capt Tom Stiles, Capt Bill Stripling, Capt Tom Waldron, then MSgt Harold Harvey.

In January 1971, I decided to get involved in helping American prisoners of war and their families. I became an advocate, speaking on the topic of what could be done for the POWs to improve their treatment and secure their release. When I'd speak, I'd sell POW bracelets. That was a campaign to raise the public's awareness. Each bracelet had the name of one POW. Five million were made. Bob Hope and Martha Raye continuously used their celebrity for the public awareness.

1st Lt George Petrie, who was with the Blueboy element on the raid, was really involved as well. He arranged for me to get thousands of them.

I would go in uniform to schools and civic organizations and give a narrative on behalf of our POWs and their families. Very often, I would get a standing ovation and sell every bracelet I had, raising money for VIVA, the group of families lobbying the government to increase pressure on the North Vietnamese to stop the mistreatment of the POWs.

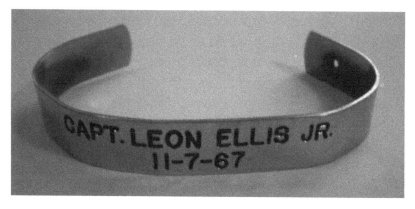

Image 141. Lee Ellis, Colonel USAF retired, was a prisoner at Son Tay POW Camp until the day they moved all the POWs out in mid-1970. We became friends through the reunions.

In July, 1971, the local newspaper in Fayetteville came to a Special Forces demonstration of rappelling. When the journalist talked with me, he decided to make the story about the Green Berets of the Son Tay Raid.

Image 142. The Fayetteville Observer, July 24th, 1971. Here, Dean Russell, one of my fellow demonstrators is strapped to my back to show how we can carry a wounded person down.

35

Combat Diver

Fort Bragg is the headquarters of our Army's Special Operations Command, so it's natural that Special Forces is headquartered there with global reach for missions by land, by air, and by sea. The "by sea" part is accomplished by Special Forces SCUBA Teams, based at Fort Bragg.

When I returned from the Son Tay Raid, I was ecstatic to be chosen right away to become a SCUBA team sergeant on the A-team known as ODA-594 in Charlie Company, 5th SF Group. I went back to Key West to finish out the Special Forces Underwater Operations Course. (I just couldn't get enough of this agony!)

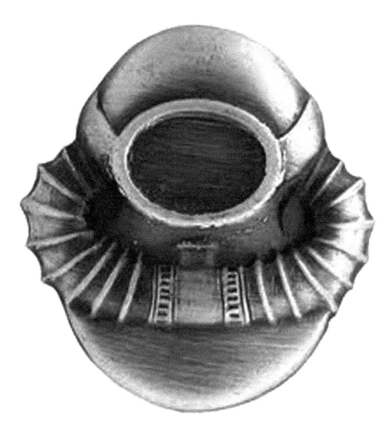

Image 143. The SCUBA Badge awarded to Special Forces Combat Divers. Notice that it depicts the re-breather gear.

The Army gives you a lot of responsibility and they prepare you well for it. Returning from Key West, I was sent in the spring of 1971 to the five-month-long SF O&I (Operations & Intel) Course, which is required of all team sergeants. We studied all aspects of mission planning and special ops intel techniques for unconventional warfare. Now, in life, you have some people that are really good at classroom work and other people that are really good in field work. Maybe you've figured out by now that I'm not the bookworm type. I owe my graduation from this course to two outstanding soldiers and good friends, Bernie Newman (my friend who'd earned the EIB) and Pat Martin. They burned a lot of midnight oil getting me ready to pass the numerous, difficult tests. I rate this as a great triumph, and I am thankful for my SF brothers, Bernie and Pat.

In the late summer and fall of 1971, our SCUBA team really began to gel. Like any other A-team, we were the tip of the spear. SF SCUBA teams are not limited to the sea, and throughout the fall we did a lot of our training in the mountains. In the winter of 1971-72, we were training for winter survival and for infiltration by cross-country skiing in Montana, Utah and Idaho. After 20 years, I was back in Idaho, our first home when we arrived in America. In some ways, I felt I was coming full circle in my American dream.

In 1972, the spring and summer found my team running desert training exercises in New Mexico, Arizona, Nevada and Utah.

October of 1972, coming out of our team's operational evaluation in the North Carolina mountains, I went straight to eleven weeks of the Advanced Noncommissioned Officer Course at Fort Benning. That capped off two very full years of fantastic training.

In early 1973, I was back at Fort Bragg. I followed the news about the American POWs. In waves through February and March, they returned at last. I watched these brave men step off the plane and see their families for the first time in years. I had tears in my eyes. I had such an emotional attachment to them and all that they represented about the

US military and about honor. I hoped to get the chance to meet some of them.

My wish was about to come true. In April, I received an invitation to be an honored guest at an event in San Francisco at the Fairmont Hotel along with all Son Tay Raiders and all POWs and their spouses. Everything was paid for by Mr. Ross Perot, a great American, a true patriot whom I've admired ever since. I consider him a role model for all Americans. Hollywood stars came to a gala dinner and ate with us at our tables. John Wayne, Ernest Borgnine, Red Skelton, Clint Eastwood, the Andrews Sisters. The city put us on street cars strung with banners that displayed our names as bands played in a full-fledged tickertape parade. The POWs were the true heroes that day.

[I have the great honor of knowing many of them. They are so gracious to express their appreciation for our effort that meant so much to them. I see them at our Son Tay Raider reunions and at their POW reunions.]

I had met a lady while I was at Fort Benning for the advanced NCO course and things developed over those coming months. We married in September 1973 and our marriage was good. We were happy. We felt like we could make a go of this Army family life, this Special Forces family life.

In June 1974, I went through HALO school (High Altitude parachuting with a Low Altitude Opening). HALO allows a stealthy tactical insertion. HALO school was at Fort Bragg and lasted a total of seven weeks. The first four weeks were freefall and HALO. The rest of the time was Jumpmaster certification.

Our HALO jumps were typically from a C-130 and were usually at about 15,000 to 25,000 feet, jumping right off the tail ramp. We'd have an onboard source of oxygen that we'd be using right up to about one minute before the jump. At that point, we'd transition to breathing from our own mask and bottle mounted to our harness. Upon exit, we'd freefall for a very long time, monitoring the altimeter you wore on your wrist. Staying together in freefall, we'd be able to deploy our chutes together and land together in a tight LZ, forming up immediately, keeping our force concentrated.

Image 144. One of our HALO jumps.

In late September 1974 our A-team went to Guantanamo Bay Naval Base for Submarine Air Lock training. The Navy's Underwater Demolition Team 21 was also training there at the time. They were great guys and we got along well.

Capt Dana Huseman was our Team Leader for ODA-594 and was there at Guantanamo with us. First, we trained on a diesel submarine and later on a nuclear submarine. 'Air Locking Out' (exiting a submerged submarine) and 'Locking In' (entering a submerged submarine) is done through the Airlock 'trunk', a small pressure-controlled room with a door that allows you to exit the side of the submarine. Standard procedure is never to be alone. You'd always operate as a 'swim team,' which is a pair of combat divers. For instance, Staff Sgt Ricky Thompson and I were a swim team once when we did a Locking Out using a balloon with a nylon ascent rope to swim to the surface.

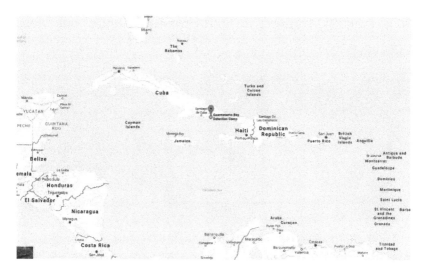

Image 145. Guantanamo is shown with the red marker.

The procedures were very similar for the two types of subs, except for a couple of things. The Airlock trunk area was <u>much</u> larger on the nuclear sub, which allows more teams at a time. Another difference is that a diesel sub can stop dead in the water during Airlock ops, but nuclear subs had to keep moving. However, for the safety of the swimmers, it was required that the speed must not exceed two knots.

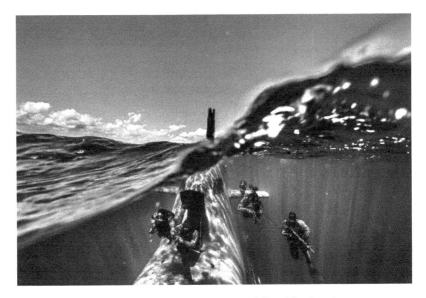

Image 146. A stock photo of 'Locking' out.

The procedure for a standard SCUBA Lock Out on a nuclear sub:

- The sub establishes a depth at which its Airlock trunk is 40 feet below the surface.
- From the inside of the submarine, three to four swim teams walk into the trunk (a 'swim team' provides redundancy for buddy-breathing, etc.) and secure the interior hatch closed.
- The Trunk Tender (controller) asks the Team Leader for permission to flood the tank to the 'bubble line,' which is about three quarters of the entire Airlock. (Throughout this operation, the Trunk Tender must

manage the oxygen level to keep carbon dioxide from building up. He must also not over pressurize and must ensure there will be no sudden changes in pressure. The lives of the swimmers are in his hands. A mistake can result in hypoxia, the bends, blown eardrums, and worse.)

- The Trunk Tender opens a valve that allows pressurized air to flow into the tank, matching the pressure of the ocean. At this point, the outer hatch can be easily opened by the swimmers.
- An ascent line's balloon is then released to the surface and the swimmers exit.
- The swimmers ascend to the Con Tower and attach the ascent line there. (This will be the 'lock-back-in' line.)
- Once everyone has made it to the surface, the Trunk Tender and the Con Tower coordinate to drain the trunk (the Airlock) and equalize the air pressure.

We learned to do this both with SCUBA gear and without. Imagine doing this with no SCUBA gear! To Lock In without SCUBA gear, you have to...

- Take a deep breath at the surface of the ocean,
- Hold your breath while you swim down 40 feet following the ascent line to the Airlock on the side of the sub (the hatch will already be open),
- Get inside the Airlock. (You'll be expecting to find the Trunk Tender has managed the oxygen content such that the air trapped inside the Airlock above the bubble line is breathable.)

- If anything goes wrong, you'll have to quickly swim 40 feet back up to the surface before you run out of breath. This is a life and death challenge.

If you have SCUBA gear, a group of combat divers can Lock In to a nuclear sub using this technique:

- We swim down to 40 feet and string a line horizontally. It's a 120-foot-long, nylon rope called a 'BUD line' and all swimmers secure themselves with carabiners spread out at certain attachment points.
- The rope has a sonar 'pinger' at each end and the submarine will steer precisely perpendicular to hit at the midpoint of your BUD line.
- On the Con Tower there are whisker poles that will snag your BUD line. As the submarine goes by, you're now being pulled inward and alongside, behind the Con Tower.

  [It is truly an awe-inspiring moment when, SCUBA diving with a thousand feet of ocean below you, out of the hazy distance comes a massive war machine right at you.]

- Now you pull yourself to the Con Tower and climb down the ladder rungs to the Air Lock hatch.

Piece of cake. But honestly, you have to be continuously alert. During my time on active duty status, there were fatalities with Navy SEALs, Marine combat swimmers, and our Army SCUBA teams.

In October of 1974, during our training at Guantanamo, I had the surprise of being promoted to Master Sergeant (E-8). A couple of captains from Fort Bragg came to Guantanamo for training and they brought my orders with them. They were part of other SF SCUBA teams that were training with us from sister companies Alpha and Bravo from 3rd Battalion.

The Navy training unit there at Guantanamo gave us outstanding support. The Navy divers filled our tanks and let us train on some of their equipment. While we were there, they asked us to help them do a hydrographic survey of one of their beaches. This is something the Navy UDT and SEALs did regularly as a primary part of their mission. US Army Special Forces are trained to do this, but it's not a primary mission. I don't know why they couldn't have utilized the UDT-21 team or scheduled a SEAL team to do it. We jumped at this rare opportunity.

The mission was to create a survey of the ocean floor along a 500-meter stretch of beach and reaching 500 meters out into the water. This has to be done regularly to ensure that we can accomplish things like an evacuation or an amphibious landing. This was excellent development for us, real-world. It took all three SCUBA teams.

Here's how it worked. We swam out to 500 meters and spread out our swimmers 25 meters apart in two-man teams. Each team had a slate clipboard for recording the data and a nylon string that had a small lead weight tied at the end. The nylon string had knots tied at one-foot intervals and a double knot every ten feet. The signal is given to dive, and we begin measuring the depth of the water and marking the obstacles in our

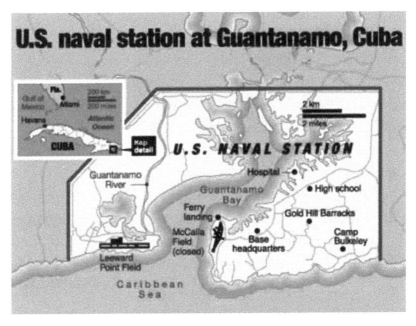

Image 147. Hydrographic surveys are needed
prior to amphibious exercises.

25-foot-wide area. One member of the team checks the
depth with the nylon string. The other dives down to
record the obstacles on the bottom that could interfere
with a boat coming ashore. When all swim teams were
finished marking their area, a signal was given to swim
forward 25 meters and repeat the procedure until you
reach the shore. All the information from each team is
transferred to a 500-meter beachfront chart.

All obstacles that present a danger must be removed by
demolition. 'Demolition' is the '*D*' in 'UDT,' and demolition in this case means a *massive* amount of explosives.
The station divers had a semi-trailer full of satchel charges
with 'Composition B' in them. They are very useful for
removing coral heads. They had everything we needed for

the big shot. Yes, we were going to clear all the obstacles at the same moment. We all had been through the training in underwater demolition, and we got some advanced training in SCUBA school. We even did some underwater demolition in our joint (Army-Navy) training with UDT-21's demolition men. It took us all day to rig the charges on every coral head that would interfere with landing craft such as the Navy's 'LST' boats.

Our demolition plant was complex, tying all the obstacles' branch lines of det cord (detonating cord) together. Tying each charge in would have taken a lot of time with the old-school method, using specialized knots. But the Navy divers had given us what they called "blue devils", small plastic connectors that bring together the det cord from all the obstacles. We put a 'Ring Main' into our demolition plant. It's the det cord circuit that ties in all the charges to be blown. It provides a little more assurance that ignition will reach all charges. This was going to be a 'non-electrical' detonation using a timed fuse set for three minutes.

All clearances were done with air traffic control and all appropriate agencies at Guantanamo were notified about the planned detonation time.

All preparations and precautions were taken.

We got the green light for the shot.

We pulled the primary and our "ring main" alternate.

Three minutes go by.

Suddenly, 500 meters of waterfront massively jumps 100 feet straight up! But there was not much noise. It was muffled by the water. The noise that you heard was more of a *bump* than a *bang*. It was the churning of water followed by the heavy raining sound.

The water turned dark. Some debris came down. Within a minute, hundreds of seagulls and pelicans were diving for the fish that floated to the surface. After verifying it was safe, we swam out and grabbed a bunch of fish for ourselves. We held a fish fry party that afternoon. We reserved the officers' beach. We invited everyone we knew for lobster and fish. The Navy divers provided the trimmings.

The beer was good.

The food was even better.

But the once-in-a-lifetime experience with our Navy brothers was the best.

When I came home in November 1974, I went to 12 weeks of the Spanish Language Course at Fort Bragg.

In late 1975, our team was deployed from Fort Bragg to Roosevelt Rhodes Naval Base in Puerto Rico to perform a salvage of an A-7 fighter jet that had sunk to the bottom of the Caribbean Sea just off the coast of Vieques Island, PR. Two A-teams of 12 men each worked it for three days. At the sea floor, the current was strong, working against us. We used these long canvass-like flotation devices that we had to latch onto the crane's straps and hooks.

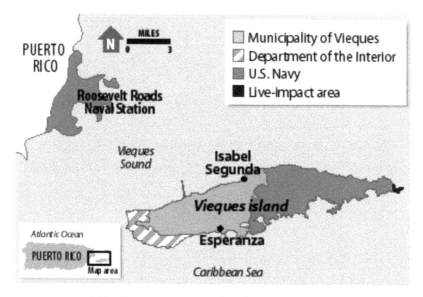

Image 148. For many years, the Air National Guard unit
at Roosevelt Roads' airfield flew A-7 Corsair IIs.

Image 149. My Emerson rig. For proficiency,
we used it as often as we could.

Image 150 and 151. Working the salvage
of the A-7 in Puerto Rico.

I had something on my mind in 1976. I decided to change my name from John Jakovenko to Vladimir Jakovenko. I had changed it to John when I became a citizen back in 1961. My mother was never happy that I had changed my name. She said, "Your father and I gave you that name. It's not right to change your Christian name, given at your baptism. When I die, you can be any name you want." I'd felt guilty all these years. In July 1976, I officially became Vladimir, the most common American spelling of Volodymyr.

Then, one day in the late 1970s, I'm sitting at the bar at Fort Bragg's Green Beret Club when I'm told that a captain has arrived looking for me. He comes up to me in a hurry. "General Mackmull has asked for you to come over to the Officers Club right now." Major General Jack Mackmull is the commander of all Special Forces. As I get in the captain's jeep, he explains that General Mackmull urgently needs an interpreter for a visitor that is on post today. The visitor is a Soviet three-star general.

As we pull into the O Club parking lot, it was a very strange scenario. I'm in fatigues, and everyone else is in dress uniform. There are four or five officers standing around an army staff car in which General Mackmull and the Soviet general are waiting.

As the captain opens the left side door for me, I find myself sitting next to the Russian and I can tell that there is an awkward silence. The Soviet general is not responding to any English. General Mackmull knows me well and introduces me.

"Jakovenko?" the Soviet general says, emphasizing that he recognizes that this is obviously a Ukrainian name. "так ти хохол? (So you are a Khakhol)?" (This is a derogatory cuss word that Russians call Ukrainians.)

Without hesitation, I reply, "Отже, якщо я хохол, то ти кацап? (So, if I'm a Khakhol, does that make you a Katsap?)" (This is an equally insulting cuss word that Ukrainians call Russians.) The Russian general gives me a surprised laugh. Now he knows I'm a true Ukrainian.

The conversation is entirely between him and me all the way to Pope AFB, where his flight would take him to the next stop on his tour. The general asks pointed questions, trying to appeal to my conscience with questions like, "In Vietnam, did you ever think about the fact that America might be killing people from the land of your birth who were only helping their comrades?"

As we step out of the limousine beside the waiting air-craft, he shakes my hand and pulls me near: "Volodya." (This was striking. He's using a term of endearment that only a very close relative would ever call me. The only person who would ever call me that is my mother.) "Don't forget who you are and the land of your birth." It's hard to explain the feelings that he's trying to tap into. He is clearly giving me the heavy pitch to appeal to and to tear at my loyalties. "How can you serve America rather than your true homeland?"

I equally lean into him: "Imagine a child whose bio-logical father left him at birth. The mother marries a man who raises that child through childhood, adolescence, and the teenage years into adulthood. Now, who would you say was truly a father to that child?" America is the true father that raised me.

After everyone says their goodbyes and the Soviet general departs, Colonel Norton (General Mackmull's chief of staff) says, "Did you put it to the Russkie?"

"Sir, I gave him the same respect that I give to any three-star general. I tell them what I really think."

Colonel Norton explains that this three-star is a top dog in the Spetsnaz, the Special Forces of the GRU, a Soviet intel agency. The 1970s was the time of Détente, the relaxing of tensions of the Cold War, with the U.S. and the Soviets getting to know each other. General Mackmull had been stressed from the moment the Soviet general had arrived today when it became painfully obvious that this Soviet general would be speaking no English and did not bring an interpreter. (My bet is that our intel knows for a fact that he is fluent in English. That's the only explanation for why no one planned an interpreter for him. This was only a short hour or so in which this general was away from his larger group for lunch and a limo ride to the airfield, so I guess everyone thought there'd be no need.)

I explain to General Mackmull everything that the Soviet general had been saying. He is very thankful that I was able to come help with no notice. His final summary to Colonel Norton and me is, "Well, at least we didn't start World War III."

[Later on, General Mackmull is promoted to Lieutenant General. I remember one time when I invited him to go out to lunch with me and Master Sgt David "Bear" Martin, one of my team members. We went to a popular BBQ place nearby. When we're giving the waitress our orders, we order good old barbecue plates, but Gen Mackmull just orders a salad.

Bear says, "You're just ordering a salad?"

Gen Mackmull replies, "I have been put on the Fat Man's Program."

Bear asks, "Who tells a three-star general to watch his weight?"

Gen Mackmull says, "A four-star general."]

36

Blue Light Hostage Rescue Counterterrorism

1977

In late February 1977 we had our A-team's annual performance test. Ours was to be a two-week-long, graded exercise in the swamps of Fort Stewart, GA. I got into a verbal confrontation with my Battalion Commander, LtCol Rod Paschall of 3rd Battalion, 5th Special Forces Group. We had succeeded in our performance test, with plenty of time spent in the freezing cold creeks that feed into the Savannah River and yet my ODA team captain was getting chewed out in our debrief over the tactics we used. Some of the evaluators/debriefers had already imbibed some Jack Daniels (as had wc). I learned really fast that you don't win a confrontation with your battalion commander.

I kinda butted in to come to my captain's defense. I was loud and angry saying something to the effect that he shouldn't be getting chewed out. We had accomplished our objectives while, "for two weeks standing in the swamp water, my frozen balls had retracted up into my throat…"

LtCol Paschall cuts me off, "At ease!" to which I retorted, "At ease, my ass! Let's do this debrief later, when your staff is not half-drunk."

I think he was considering some kind of disciplinary action after we got back to Fort Bragg. So, I had to report to the battalion headquarters on March 10th, I figured this might be an Article 15 (an administrative punishment that goes in your permanent record that will be seen by any promotion board). I reported in. He looked deadly serious.

He caught me totally off guard when he asked, "Have you been watching the news?"

On March 9, 1977, twelve Hanafi Muslim terrorists, heavily armed with rifles, shotguns, pistols and machetes had stormed into three buildings in Washington, DC. One person was dead, three were wounded by gunshots, 149 people were taken hostage. The terrorists said that if their demands weren't met, they would start throwing heads out of windows.

LtCol Paschall says, "I've been directed to choose three of my A-teams to conduct a possible hostage rescue operation in Washington, DC. Yours is one of the three."

Am I shocked that he isn't going to discipline me? Yes.

Am I surprised that he'd choose our team? No.

Companies Alpha, Bravo, and Charlie each have one SCUBA team and LtCol Paschall picked these SCUBA teams for this mission. That afternoon, all three SCUBA teams meet at station 10 of the Gabriel Demonstration Area where we are briefed.

We are ordered to develop a plan that may need to be executed today or tomorrow. The three buildings that the terrorists have are:

- The "District Building" on Pennsylvania Avenue,
- The Islamic Center on Massachusetts Avenue, and
- Offices of B'nai B'rith on Rhode Island Avenue.

Each team is responsible for one of the buildings.
We will wear civilian clothes for this operation.
"There are no rules of engagement at this time."
Is there a plan that you want us to execute?
"No. You develop it yourself. You know your abilities."
Are there any specific weapons or tactics that we are not allowed to use?
"No. If you believe you need something, ask for it. Don't ask for anything that's not available today. There's no time to order something."
We talk about getting onto roofs and entering a high rise building through windows. We get a UH-1 helicopter that day and practice fast-roping onto platforms there on the range. That helps us brainstorm which type of climbing ropes, Swiss Seats and gloves.
LtCol Paschall explains, "Flying from Fort Bragg to Washington, DC, you'll have to bring whatever you need to accomplish the mission. Don't count on anything being provided there."
Ricky Thompson is a sniper, and he asks, "Can I bring my own scope rifle? At these distances, I'll be better with my own rifle than with the team sniper rifle, the M21." (This is the old M14 with a scope added.)

LtCol Paschall says, "Bring whatever will work for you."

Our logistics captain says, "Sir, I don't think you can let the men bring their own private weapons."

LtCol Paschall snaps, "Let me worry about the ramifications of what they bring." It's clear to us that LtCol Paschall's orders are coming from outside the Army, from the highest echelons of civilian command. But the logistics captain is right. The Army would never allow the approach that LtCol Paschall is leading us toward. And the Constitutional legal issues involved with the use of the US military against US citizens on US territory are immense. The civilian leaders are trying to think of something—they are scrambling and thinking outside the box. We can see that our government is caught flat-footed, unprepared to deal with terrorism. No good answers could be given. They looked to our Battalion Commander and these three Special Forces A-teams.

We are told to decide upon our plans, prepare, and stand by on alert. As of this moment, we may be called upon any minute.

My team finalizes our plan. We decide to break our A-team down into four shooting elements of three men each. Each element will have:

- Two primary shooters to prioritize neutralizing their assigned targets and
- One focused on broader situational awareness (area security, directing the hostages out of danger) and communications.

We will get building floor layouts once we get to DC. To open doors, we'll use a battering ram, or an 870 shotgun with number 9 shot to blow out the door lock and hinge area, or small platter or ribbon charges. Under certain circumstances, we will enter through windows. For distraction, we have smoke bombs and concussion grenades.

My guys get their equipment and weapons and meet at my house. That's where we will be when the commander calls. Here we are, going into a shooting situation with no rehearsal and no 'brief back' to a commander for approval.

You'd be amazed how relaxed everyone was as we discussed our plan. These are among the most well-trained, committed, disciplined, and versatile soldiers. My guys slept in my living room.

Before sunrise on March 11th, the telephone rang. I was expecting it to be, "Go." Instead, we were told to stand down. The terrorists were coming out of the buildings and surrendering.

It was a best-case scenario. I was happy that all the hostages were safe. The terrorists would be brought to justice.

But it was only just beginning. Terrorist plots were clearly increasing in their sophistication. This was bigger than any civilian authority could handle.

We, as special operators, must learn from this. When the terror struck, we were the ones that our national command authority called upon. We must never be caught unprepared. We must plan. We must prepare.

Our team took this personally. We started working on concepts, tactics and equipment for counterterrorism. We developed and refined plans for:

- Weapon system kits for urban and rural operations,
- Tactics for friendly territory and for enemy-controlled,
- Carrying our weapons and equipment for various modes of infiltration (military free fall, static parachute, or SCUBA),
- Functional uniform requirements,
- Close quarter battle techniques in close proximity to hostages,
- Varied scenarios and objective areas (i.e., buildings, buses, trains, and airplanes).

As a team, we started to think about counterterrorism as one of our regular missions.

I gained a lot of respect for my commander, LtCol Paschall. We had our difference of opinion on some matters, but that day in March 1977, he kept his feelings in check as he chose me and our A-team, empowering us to provide a solution to this national event. He was entrusted with an immense responsibility. He knew we were ready to go into harm's way at his command.

[LtCol Paschall would later make full bird Colonel and be chosen to succeed Colonel Charlie Beckwith as commander of Delta Force. So, allow me to give the background of Delta Force. International terrorism was increasing throughout the 1970s. President

Carter looked to the Army. Colonel Charlie Beckwith had proposed a solution. He had taken part in an exchange program with the British S.A.S. (Special Air Service) in 1962, which specialized in commando raids. When he later was the commandant of the Army's Special Forces School, he was finally given the opportunity to create an S.A.S.-style unit. The climate was right in 1977. Beckwith was authorized to create Special Forces Operational Detachment-Delta ('Delta Force'). Delta Force would have the needed technical skills and equipment, and men with the right mental and physical aptitudes. He began a rigid selection process, which included exhaustive psychological testing. Beckwith explained that two years would be needed to accomplish the selection, training, equipping, and validating of his new force. In the meantime, the Army created "Blue Light."]

Our preparations were about to pay off. In June 1977, our team, ODA-594, was just coming back from Skull Valley Utah, where we had been tasked with testing the security systems at the weapons testing and storage facility there. We had jumped into the desert, evaluated weaknesses, penetrated undetected, then casually entered the NCO club, bought a case of beer (which you see us drinking in the photo below) and then notified the Air Force security of our presence.

Coming home, we jumped into Fort Bragg but right away, as we landed in the Salerno DZ and were gathering up our parachutes, a jeep drove out to me. I was told to have someone else turn in my parachute; I was to report to the 5th SF Group HQ building and report to Colonel Mountel immediately.

Image 152. A plaque commemorating ODA-594's
successful penetration of the security systems of the Utah
Test and Training Range (with the NCO club beer).

There, Colonel Bob "Black Gloves" Mountel (he was
known for smoking a pipe and for always seeming to
have a pair of black leather gloves), Commander of 5th SF
Group, explained to me that he had just been given command to form a new unit specifically for 'Direct Action.'
This was a departure from the original intent of Special
Forces. SF was created to train foreign troops to defend
their own country. This SF unit would not be training others. They'd be doing special operations themselves. This
new unit was called 'Blue Light' and was under the 5th
Special Forces Group. Blue Light was an interim counterterrorism unit, while the other counterterrorism unit
(eventually known as Delta Force) could be funded, recruited, equipped, trained, and certified fully operational
over the coming two years.

There in his office, Colonel Mountel gave me a list of the Green Berets that he was thinking about assigning to the teams. On the list of 12 for my team, none of the other 11 were from ODA-594. I immediately informed him, "Sir, I know some of these people, but I already have an A-team. Why would I want 11 guys who have never worked together, when I have a team that already operates as close as a family?"

Colonel Mountel listened to my rationale and honored my request and for that I'm thankful. ODA-594 was one of the original A-teams picked for Blue Light, which had about 70 people in total. This included Earl Bleacher, Joe Lupyak, Kenny McMullin, and Elmer Adams, who were involved in the Son Tay Raid. I remember Lt Colonel Cincotti, Major Evans, Captain Carlin, Rob Mountal, Mark Boyatt, Jimmy Blair, Ron Brown, Brad Sheffer, Larry Kramer, Lowell Stevens, and Virgil Palk. Over the coming weeks, all of our training was now done at Mott Lake, about 25 miles southwest of the main garrison area of Fort Bragg.

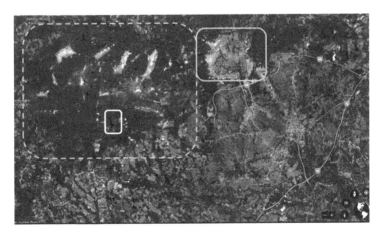

Image 153. This Google Earth image shows Mott Lake (in yellow) on the ranges (dashed line) to the west of the main post at Fort Bragg (the solid green rectangle).

Snipers were attached to each team. Attached to ODA-594 were Sgt 'Tiny' Young (another friend from the Son Tay Raid) and Sgt Jim Lally. They were outstanding marksmen. Some of our ranges had mockup buildings and we'd place balloons in a window of a building to represent the bad guys. From 300 yards, the snipers would shoot the balloons with us suspended by rappelling gear just outside that window (maybe only 18 inches from the path of the bullet). Then, within a few seconds, an explosion of charges we'd set would take down the door and we would enter. Live-fire exercises like this were the only way to prove that we could handle a hostage rescue scenario of this sort.

Image 154. An artist's rendering of the types of tactics and equipment we might choose to use in a hostage situation.

We were heavily focused on pistol firing with all the emphasis on close-quarters combat. Over the weeks, we settled on the M1911 .45 cal pistol. One contingency we trained for was for actually taking a shot on a terrorist who was holding a hostage closely in his arms.

In the fall of 1977, we went to Tampa, FL, and practiced taking down various types of aircraft. We developed techniques for eliminating terrorists from various aircraft from the Boeing 707 to the Boeing 727, 737, and 747. We stayed at the Holiday Inn at the airport, chosen because it was very near to the aircraft parking area where the aircraft were provided to us. The old airport terminal was no longer in use. Aircraft maintenance experts were advising us on all options for how to devise an entry plan. We'd train only after midnight so that we would not cause any concern among the civilians. The aircraft were parked well away from anyone not involved. We'd train until the sun came up.

The 747 was the easiest one to enter. The landing gear well had panels that we disassembled to infiltrate the interior. All the other three types of airliners required us to go through a door or a window. We studied scenarios like the Israeli Defense Force's raid on the hijacked aircraft at the airport in Entebbe, Uganda, which had taken place just the year prior. We also studied lessons from the Munich Olympics terrorist event of September 1972. We learned how to pose as airport employees such as baggage cart drivers, loaders, refuelers, airplane lavatory servicers, interior cleaners and food replenishers, etc.

Image 155. The old terminal at Tampa (the gray-surfaced aircraft parking area on the lower right) was a perfect place to practice scenarios of a parked airliner taken by terrorists.

The commander of Special Forces, Major General Jack Mackmull, spent a lot of time at Mott Lake monitoring our training with Colonel Mountel. We had a lot of high-ranking visitors, military and civilian.

[We now understand why. There was a significant conflict of philosophies. One faction of commanders wanted this new tasking (counterterrorism) to be within the structure of the Special Forces. Another faction of commanders held that this tasking should be apart from the rest of Special Forces and should be under the direct command of the Chief of Staff of the Army. Blue Light reflected the former. Delta Force was the latter.]

Image 156. General Mackmull had visited me and my team in the first week that he was commander of Special Forces. He explained that the prior commander had advised him, "Get to know Jakovenko." My first message to him, "If you want to know what's really going on, don't ask the guy pointing to the chart. Ask the guy <u>holding</u> the chart." During his entire tenure, he'd often stop in to get my opinion. I had immense respect for him.

We put on so many demonstrations for dignitaries that it started to feel like a dog and pony show. This breeds cynicism. In the back of our minds, we started to suspect that all the credit was somehow gonna go to what we called "Charlie's Angels."

So, by early 1978, our opinion of the "other guys" started to sour. At one point, the Army Chief of Staff came to Fort Bragg and, after watching demonstrations by Delta Force and then by Blue Light, asked, "So, do we have two separate units doing the same role?"

It was frustrating. Our leaders were being told to defer to a unit that's still in its development phase hoping to achieve some future certification to begin operations. All this while we were the ones actually holding down the real-world counterterrorism tasking, ready and certified now. We started to take note of how very small our training budget was, compared to the scenario exercises we believed we needed to be running through. We were using duct tape to hold 2x4s together on our range targets, while we saw Delta getting a million dollars for their new gym facility and workout equipment.

One day in August of 1978, toward the end of one of our Blue Light official formations at Mott Lake, we were told to report to Building 5 at Smoke Bomb Hill. There, Colonel Beckwith gave us a briefing in which he offered us the opportunity to join Delta Force. He acknowledged, "You have been doing some good training. You have a good reputation."

But then he said that we would have to go through the normal selection process and screening phase just like every other candidate. "All of you who are interested in becoming a part of Delta Force, please remain here in the auditorium to give us your name and we'll begin the process."

I believe the entire Blue Light team walked out. We felt it was just so disrespectful. Not one stayed and signed up for Delta Force that day (though, later on, a few did end up eventually spending some time in Delta Force).

Delta Force had been put through its initial certification exercise in the summer of 1978 and the handwriting was on the wall. Blue Light was disbanded in August.

[Delta Force would eventually be fully certified and officially operational in November 1979.]

In March 1979, my name showed up on the promotion list for E-9. I'd known that I had a chance for promotion, but I didn't expect it. I'd never been to the Sergeant Major Academy and assumed that would have sealed my fate. Sergeant Major and Command Sergeant Major are both E-9. I'd have been satisfied being an E-8 (Master Sergeant) team sergeant until I retired.

Immediately, I received orders to become the Company Sergeant Major for Charlie Company, 2nd Battalion, 5th SF Group, replacing Sergeant Major Jim Sweeney. Jim had been in the thick of battle in the Korean War when he was captured as a POW of Kim Il Sung's North Korean communist army. He was retiring after 30 years of service. What an honor to receive the standard from this battlefield warrior and carry it forward. I had the great benefit of working under Jim those years when he was our Company Sergeant Major, and I was Team Sergeant of ODA-594. Two major principles he taught:

1. Never forget that officers command and noncommissioned officers lead.
2. Take care of the enlisted troops; they have the crucial job, and they'll get it done.

The Iran Hostage Crisis

On November 4th, 1979, the American embassy in Tehran, Iran was overrun, and 52 Americans were taken hostage. 5th SF Group's area of operations at this time included the Middle East. (As an example, I later earn my Jordanian Parachutist Wings with the Jordanian Special Forces.) 2nd Battalion, Charlie Company's area of operations included Iran. In fact, some of our teams periodically operated inside Iran, including time inside the embassy, during their exercises with the Shah's Special Forces.

Charlie Company (comprised of six A-Teams) was raised to Real-World Alert status and went into isolation at Camp Dawson, WV, to prepare for possible deployment to Iran. We were issued Target Study folders and exercised in small unit tactics and urban marksmanship for hostage rescue. We developed a tentative plan to infiltrate the American Embassy in Tehran.

Throughout November and December, we decided upon weapons and approaches. We trained with the intel that we were given and waited for further authorization. Our reporting structure was under the 5th Special Forces

Group with a dedicated organization of commanders and planners. Our company was outstanding, prepared to go in if called upon.

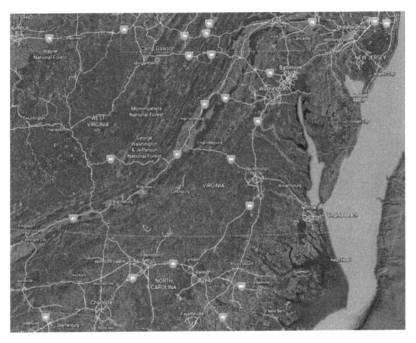

Image 157. Camp Dawson (see the red marker) is cloistered away in a remote river valley only an hour (by helicopter) west of Washington DC.

Every day, P.T. was at 5am. In early December, we had blizzard conditions. One morning, I awoke to find that the snow was falling, and the wind was howling. I couldn't see more than 25 feet. Our company commander was up and asked my opinion about P.T.

I said, "It does look bad, sir, but I really think we should have P.T. I can make it short. This'll be more psychological than physical."

I woke the team sergeants and told them, "P.T. At 0500 hrs in field jackets, watch caps, gloves and boots."

At 0500 sharp, the company was formed up in the parking lot as normal. We usually did about an hour of P.T. We started with a run. I said, "Stay close together."

No one asked how far we'd be running. (Usually, it was two miles or more.) I ran them less than a mile and came back to the parking lot. We formed up in four columns, spread out for ground exercises. (By now, there was about a foot of snow and the blizzard was worse now than before.)

We did some pushups.

We did about 50 flutter kicks.

We did 25 Hello Lil Darlings.

Then I put everyone back on their feet. I thanked them all and told them to clean up and get some breakfast.

Not one of those troops bitched. I was proud of them.

I went upstairs in the bay area, got some coffee, and looked out the window. I could see where each man had been, doing flutter kicks. More than 60 impressions in the snow (sort of like snow angels) lined up in ranks and columns. Each one represented a real-life fighting man, a guardian angel on duty come rain or snow. I called the Company Commander. I wanted him to see this.

I stood there, proud of these soldiers. It was a sign from the good Lord. Charlie Company was ready to sacrifice, without complaint. They would accomplish any mission given to us.

When the middle of December came, the National Command Authority took a different posture. We were on call and could be called back if the situation worsened, but there was less urgency.

…and we were never called upon.

By early January 1980, we were brought back to Fort Bragg. Back at Bragg, I found out that I'd received orders to PCS (permanent change of station) to Guam on a family-accompanied, two-year tour as Sergeant Major for the ROTC detachment at the University of Guam. Having a young family, I accepted the assignment.

And then, on April 25th, the news was completely depressing. A raid to rescue the American hostages in Iran had failed and ended in catastrophe at Desert 1.

[Remember that it was in November of 1979 (while we were preparing at Camp Dawson) that Delta Force had achieved operational certification. The mission had been given to Delta Force.]

The analysis of Operation Eagle Claw is now history. We have great respect for Delta Force and all the men of Operation Eagle Claw. They did everything that was asked of them.

37

Guam

1980

It was in mid-January 1980 that I left Charlie Company (2nd Battalion, 5th SF Group) and turned my focus to our family's move to my new assignment at the Department of Military Science, University of Guam. The commander there was LtCol Dave Swanson. He was Infantry, Ranger-qualified, and a highly decorated Vietnam veteran. On the phone, LtCol Swanson was eager to get quarters for my family. My report date would be February 2nd, 1980.

On January 15th, with my wife (at the time) and our two sons, Jason (4) and Jamie (1), we set off in our 1976 Plymouth Volare station wagon and passed through Idaho (a glimpse of the past) arriving at a guest house at Fort Lewis in late January. I processed into 4th ROTC Region HQ (this region included the western states and the entire Pacific) and cleared post.

The flight was long, with a layover in Hawaii (a glimpse of our future). Guam is part of the Northern Mariana Islands. Some important battles took place here on (and then launched from) the islands of Saipan and Tinian to end the war with Japan. LtCol Swanson met us at the airport in Agana, the capital of Guam, helping us clear customs.

The island of Guam is really described by two halves. There's the north half, which is Anderson Air Force Base and a south half, which is under the Navy.

We settled in. My wife started playing softball on a women's league. Jason and Jamie joined the swim team. All was good.

Image 158. Jason in Guam and the infamous Airborne tattoo.

Guam's congressman, Antonio Won Pat, was a member of the House Armed Services Committee. Congressman Won Pat wanted to have an Army ROTC program at the University of Guam. (The last name is two words, 'Won Pat.') We had many students interested from the Mariana Islands. It became a congressional mandate with millions of dollars attached. The mandate stipulated that the first commissioning of a graduating class of at least fifteen second lieutenants must be done by the spring semester of 1982.

The LtCol had been working on recruiting cadets. He had some ROTC cadets at levels MS1 (Military Science freshmen) and MS2 (sophomores). What we needed was MS3 and MS4. Our approach to these was to find cadets with prior service who had a few years of college. LtCol Swanson had been a professor of military science at the university of Hawaii for five years. He knew all the ins and outs of recruiting students for ROTC. Sgt 1st Class Frank Guerrero and I went recruiting at the Army Reserve Center and National Guard. We also talked to all the high schools who had junior ROTC programs.

Everything came together well over the next few weeks. A few more officers joined us as assistant professors.

Some of the classes we taught:

- Small unit tactics
- Patrolling
- Map reading
- Survival skills
- Marksmanship

The ROTC program kicked off in high gear, thanks to Congressman Won Pat and Governor Calvo of Guam and the President of the University of Guam.

But what really made this program a success was the dedication of the cadets. They had the motivation and leadership to help each other succeed. I learned first-hand the cadets' dedication and will to prevail.

We attended the 1981 ROTC Advanced Camp at Fort Lewis, Washington. This is a six-week Advanced Camp held during the summer between junior and senior year. This camp permits cadets to put into practice the principles and theories they have acquired in the classroom. It also exposes them to Army life in a tactical field environment.

This being for the 4th ROTC Region, we had representatives from all the western states and Hawaii and, for the first time, Guam. The six weeks was very competitive. Awards were given for best performances of each event. The most prestigious award was the "Warrior of the Pacific" award. It was given to the university with the highest cumulative score from all the graded events throughout the six weeks.

This was six excellent weeks. They were good. Really good. Their performance gave notice to all universities that the University of Guam ROTC would be back next year.

My tour there ended in February 1982, when I received orders back to Fort Bragg to be the Sergeant Major for Charlie Company, 1st Battalion, 5th Special Forces Group.

In early May, I was settled fully back into Special Forces life. My group was in the field, deployed to Greece. We were working with the Hellenic Army's Raider Forces, (Greek Special Forces) in the mountains near the Bulgarian border.

Image 159. We regularly jumped into major exercises.

A helicopter came to our base camp and an American officer tracked me down with a message that I was invited (and approved) to attend the commissioning ceremony for the University of Guam—the first ever. He explained that the cadets had asked Congressman Won Pat to advocate for the Army to approve flying me from Athens to Guam.

I wish I could have gone. I'm so proud of them. But I'm the Sergeant Major in the middle of a real-world, major international exercise. Knowing that LtCol Swanson and Sgt 1st Class Frank Guerrero were still there and would have that connection with the original cadets, I made a very difficult decision that I simply could not leave at that time.

Well, in July, they were back at Fort Lewis, Washington, at the 1982 ROTC Advanced Camp, this time with males and females, juniors and seniors. They were sharp. They carried themselves with great pride. And the Warrior of the Pacific award went to…the cadets from Guam!

In the late summer of 1982, I received a letter from Congressman Won Pat letting me know how proud he was of the great honor that the Guam cadets brought back to their island, the Warrior of the Pacific award.

Throughout the years I have kept in touch with some of the cadets who were commissioned in 1982, even now, four decades later. I'm happy to have certificates and awards from those years proudly listing their names. Years later, I was honored to receive a call from one of the graduates letting me know that they were naming their newborn son after me. My tour with the University of Guam ROTC program is one of my most cherished memories.

In July 1984, I was assigned to a unit based in the Washington DC area called the SPSA (Special Project Support Activity). We'd still live at Fort Bragg, but I'd travel. We were two-man 'cells' (a lieutenant colonel and a sergeant major), sent all around the Special Forces community.

- We did the testing for the 'Double X cell canopy' parachute. This was about a month at the Yuma Proving Grounds in Arizona. It was a concept where SF HALO jumpers could take a person who was not parachute qualified into a tactically difficult location attached to us using a tandem (2-person) harness.
- We did some high altitude jumping with the newest type of free fall parachute.
- We tested certain diving equipment at SF Underwater Operations in Key West.
- We did some underwater recovery testing from Eglin AFB in Florida.

Image 160. On a C-141 at Pope AFB for a 14,000-
foot jump. Note the altimeter on my wrist.

Image 161. One of our HALO jumps from a C-141.

Image 162. The SPSA was a cool gig, testing out new equipment and procedures. In this 1985 photo, I'm at Fort Bragg's Sicily Drop Zone.

38

The CIA

1985

Now it was 1985 and I ran into some of my friends from prior years who'd served with me in Special Forces, but who had seemed to disappear. They wouldn't tell me anything outright, but clearly, they were working with a certain government agency whose HQ may or may not be located in the Washington DC suburb of Langley, Virginia. Knowing that I had 25 years of service and could retire, they asked if I would consider joining their government agency. The pay would be three times what I was making as an E-9.

I had dealt with people in this agency over my career (and that experience had often been negative). But, talking with my old friends, it now sounded interesting. I agreed to apply. They said, "You'll be contacted." (No time or date given.)

I was busy in my job, full time Active Duty. A few months went by, and I'd forgotten about the idea. I received a thick manila envelope with an application for employment with the CIA. It took a lot of time to complete and included a lot of psychological test questions. I filled it out and sent it off.

Again, weeks went by. Then, I got a call from a very professional-sounding lady by the name of Bernice who scheduled me for an interview. She told me to check in at a certain motel in Tyson's Corner, Virginia, on a certain date and there I would get further instructions. I arrived and called the number provided. A very professional-sounding man by the name of Bernard told me to come to the Langley headquarters. I processed through security and was taken to my interview. I met the chief of paramilitary operations and saw a number of my friends from Special Forces, so many that it felt like a reunion. One was from Blue Light days. A few were from 5th SF Group days. I knew I would enjoy working with these guys.

I was told, "You'll be contacted." (Again, no time or date given.)

And again, several weeks went by. I received another thick manila envelope. More detailed questions, personally specific to me,

- Questions about my place of birth in a Soviet republic,
- How many times per day do you urinate,
- What homosexual acts and/or sex with prostitutes have you had,
- List all the illicit drugs you've ever taken,
- Questions about my family members and their activities,
- What have I been doing since the day I was born…

I filled it out. I sent it back.

About a week later, in July 1985, I received a call from Bernice, and she scheduled me for a polygraph test. It was a very hot summer day when I checked in at the same motel and called Bernard. He said he'd call me the next day with instructions.

The next morning, after breakfast, I get back to my room and the phone rings. The man tells me to go upstairs to the room directly above mine. I knock, and a couple of agents wearing ties are there unpacking a small suitcase with what looks like recording equipment.

I'm gonna be spending the next eight hours connected to the polygraph, answering questions. Right before they hook me up, they're sitting right behind me, kinda in the dark. They ask me, "Is there anything else that you did not fully explain on the psychological paperwork?" What a question.

I feel compelled to tell them that there was a time after a patrol with the Montagnards. They would pass around a pipe that I'm pretty sure was probably some kind of opium. It had an immediate effect, making you mellow. It was their common practice. (Interestingly, as soon as we would ever give them menthol cigarettes, they would far prefer those and would skip the pipe for as long as they had menthols.)

The agents wearing ties put a strap across my chest. It has electrodes. They put some more on various places.

The interview does not seem encouraging. It's the way the operator is asking the questions. And he keeps going back to the *same* questions. At times, it becomes a hostile interview, almost like an interrogation. They specifically use the word "hostile" to try to belittle me and it does kinda piss me off. To me, it seems like they've declared me a hostile subject, implying that I'm holding back, like I'm lying.

I was told, "You'll be contacted." (No time or date given.)

I went back to Fort Bragg thinking, *Maybe I don't want to work for these folks.*

So, I was surprised when I got a call from Bernice, "Since you're over 40, we need to give you a certain type of physical examination." She scheduled my next trip to the motel at Tyson's Corner.

On the motel room phone, Bernard tells me my physical will be at 1pm at a certain suite at the Watergate Hotel. "We need you to have a fleet enema."

"I don't know what that is."

He explains that any drug store clerk would know where they are.

At a drug store along the way, I ask the clerk. She says, "Aisle 2."

When I arrive at the Watergate Hotel, it's around 11:30am and real hot. I have a lot of time to kill. I locate the suite and then find a bar where I could get a cold beer and some lunch. I distinctly remember having a wiener schnitzel with sauerkraut. After another beer, I head up to the office. They take my name and explain that this will be a lower tract examination. "Did you do the enema?"

"I have it right here."

"What?!" The doctor rolls his eyes and says, "You were supposed to have done your enema this morning at the motel before you came here." He distances himself from the screwup, "They've done it again!"

He asks with a hopeful tone, "Did you eat today?"

I tell him about my breakfast—my *huge* breakfast—and all that I had for lunch.

In a huff, the doctor says, "Get the keys to the men's room from the receptionist, do the enema, and then come back."

"I've never had an enema before."

He says, "It's easy. Just follow the instructions on the box."

Now, let me tell you that the Watergate is a *very* swanky hotel. I unlock the Men's room to find it's an executive bathroom, real fancy. I'm standing at the sink, reading the instructions. I can see that "It's easy" was not a true statement.

1. 'Fill the bag with water. (The chemical powder is inside.)'
2. 'Shake thoroughly.'
3. 'Lie on your side or back…'

I begin. I'm standing at the sink, filling the bag with water. The long hose is hanging down with a tiny little clip at the business end. I think to myself, *I hope no one comes in. Maybe my key is the only key.*

All of the sudden, I hear someone unlocking the door!

In walks a gentleman. Somehow, it doesn't take long for him to realize what I'm doing. He makes a very hasty exit and gives me a weird look.

I decide that I'll use the last stall. Let's start with a dry run. I close the toilet lid and lie on my back on the commode. I lift my legs and my feet are up against the door. Nice and stable…positioning is everything…I can keep my balance…

Suddenly, the door is unlocking again, but at this point, I got it all under control. No sweat. I just relax and wait it out.

The person comes in the bathroom and goes about their business, none the wiser.

Finally, the coast is clear again. I'm now ready. I drop my pants. It's go-time.

I prepare the tip of the spear and commence insertion. Balance. Position. I got this. A little further…hold! Delicately, I hold the bag up. I remove the clip. The liquid flows readily—a cold rush. Within seconds, my lower tract explodes!

Shit!

This cleanup is gonna require more than just toilet paper.

So, with my pants down around my knees, I open the stall door and shuffle to get a ton of hand towels. I wet them in the sink and then go back into the stall. Someone is unlocking the door. And then someone else. *Great, now everyone is trying to use this damn bathroom.* I have to wait it out. I was really pissed.

Eventually, I am finally alone again and I'm able to finish up. Washing my hands, I imagine a Watergate Scandal on the front page of the Washington Post:

Special Forces Sgt Major Caught Performing 'Enema' at The Watergate Hotel. Claims the CIA Told Him to Do It.

Do you think the agency would disavow ever knowing me?

I walked back to the doctor's office and found the receptionists laughing. One said she'd lost a bet that I would not come back.

Well, I did finish the examination. But I ultimately decided that I was not going to retire from the Army to work for an agency as ass backward as this.

In late 1986, I got orders to become the Sergeant Major at the WESTCOM Special Ops support detachment at Fort Shafter, Hawaii, and my wife told me straight up that she was not going to go with me. Instead, just a few days later she gave me separation papers and told me she wanted a divorce.

Even though I could see it coming, nothing tears at your soul and emotions like a marriage breaking up, especially when it involves children. Losing your house, your car, and all the material things, is nothing compared to losing your children. Putting them in the middle of a divorce is devastating. You start to doubt yourself. I thought, *Am I destined to always lose in family life?* When I looked at Jason (11 years old at the time) and Jamie (8), I couldn't keep the tears from my eyes. It felt like 1967 (my first divorce) all over again.

I would handle it differently this time. I went to personnel and cut an allotment for $1500 per month for the support of my sons. I created an automatic withdrawal for the mortgage payment for the house. I'm not giving up my sons.

On a frigid morning in late January 1987, 3am, it was time for me to go. I had to catch the plane to my next assignment. I had to say my goodbyes to my sons. Jason awoke even as I entered his room. I kissed him and we hugged. My heart was breaking. I woke up Jamie, kissed and hugged him. I started to cry. "Goodbye. I'll always be there for you."

Between the frost on my truck and the tears in my eyes, I could barely see to drive. I was leaving 13 years of marriage with the clothes on my back, my duffle bag and two suitcases. I let all my emotions go. I asked, *"Why, Lord?"*

I slowly started to drive, trying not to make too much noise as I'd shift gears. Later, Jason would tell me he remembers the sound of my truck leaving and that he started to cry, knowing I was gone and would no longer be there during the nights.

As the sun rose, I arrived at my first stop, Fort Belvoir, Virginia. I spent that day and the next clearing my assigned unit, SPSA, and said my goodbyes. I'm amazed at how many dedicated people there are supporting Special Forces in accomplishment of their mission.

Then I headed further north to Lakehurst, NJ. This was the Department of the Army, Receiving, Issuing, Storage and Shipping Activity ("DARISSA") at Hangar #5,

Lakehurst Naval Air Station. It was a very secure facility supporting storage, staging, and movement of special operations equipment.

I cleared DARISSA and then spent a few days with my parents, who lived only 10 miles away. It was a very special time with my parents, and I found it hard to say goodbye. I explained that this was my last tour and that I would retire at my 30-year mark.

Pop was 84 and mom, 71. They didn't own a car. They still spoke broken English and were still here on their green cards after 37 years of living in America! But they were so thankful for the USA and always said, "If heaven is half as good, we won't be disappointed."

I put my truck in for shipping at the port of embarkation in Bayonne, NJ, and took a taxi to my hotel at JFK Airport and departed the next morning for Honolulu.

As I stepped off the plane, I was met by Master Sgt Elmo Adams, an old friend from the Son Tay Raid days back in 1970. Elmo helped me get my bags and explained that the detachment was holding a 'welcome aboard' party for me that afternoon at one of the estate clubhouses.

My orders assigned me to HQ Western Command, Support Detachment (Special Operations) at Fort Shafter. I was replacing a good friend of mine. We'd served together in 5th SF Group. While I had the SCUBA team in Charlie Company, he'd been on the SCUBA team in Bravo Company. Since he was already gone, I didn't have the opportunity to hear from him about the detachment and my responsibilities. Elmo gave me a quick briefing and I'd get to meet with the detachment commander in the coming day or so.

I was a little beat from the trip, but glad to meet most of the detachment members and their wives. We stayed late into the evening and got acquainted. Elmo drove me to a small cottage that would be my temporary home until I met with post housing to find out where my permanent quarters would be.

I processed in the next day and found that I would receive a housing allowance to live off base. I rented a two-bedroom condo right across from Waikiki Beach, less than 10 miles from Fort Shafter. Elmo let me use his old car until mine would arrive in about two weeks. I settled in.

It was not hard to take. Every evening, I'd sit at the bar at the Hale Koa (a military-only hotel) on the beach, watching the most beautiful sunset in the world.

The detachment commander explained that the mission was to support WESTCOM (US Army Western Command) for all special operations coordination in the Pacific Rim. WESTCOM's 3-star general lived here at Fort Shafter. Our detachment coordinated training exercises as far away as Thailand and was the liaison for all Army special operations forces that operated in the Pacific. We also had a counterterrorism cell that provided training and briefings for WESTCOM.

Attached to our detachment was a target acquisition group that maintained target folders for some of the Special Forces units. Sometimes, we had a Reserve civil affairs and psyops (psychological operations) unit operating out of our facility.

We were located in a WWII tunnel inside a mountain. It was totally secure with special access requirements. It had all the comforts of a headquarters. We had the highest security classification and a limited access roster. The detachment was top heavy with rank. We had a Colonel, six

Lieutenant Colonels, five Majors, and only four Captains. On the enlisted force were three E-9s (Sergeants Major), a Master Sgt, two Sgts 1st Class, three Staff Sgts, and four Sergeants.

I had a good working relationship with the detachment commander. I respected him, and he always respected my opinion.

But early on, it was pretty clear that we were not working in harmony as a unit.

It took a couple of months of observation to put my finger on it. I listened to the enlisted folks and had some conversations with officers. Each of us had our areas of responsibility and too often, we fell into 'Every man for himself,' or 'My project is more important than your project.'

I scheduled a meeting with the detachment commander to talk about it. I told him, "We're admin, and we're acting like it. Most of us are from Special Forces Groups or Airborne units, but we're not acting as we would in operational units. I guess I'm used to working as a team."

The commander listened and he agreed with me.

We didn't train together. I brought up the fact that we didn't ever have P.T. as a unit.

Even though most of the officers and senior NCOs were jumpmaster qualified, they never performed the jumpmaster or drop zone duties. It always fell to the same two or three individuals to pull all the responsibilities for our airborne training ops.

We had weekly clean-up details such as grass cutting, police call, trimming the bushes, and sweeping the entryway to the tunnel but these details were always being pulled by the lowest enlisted (who were NCOs) and it would take the whole Friday to do it. I recommended that the commander have us do these as a detachment. Not only would it be faster, but it would also build teamwork and pride in our unit.

So, we had a detachment meeting and announced we would be having P.T. as a detachment. I would run the P.T. program and rotate other members to run P.T. I would schedule a few rucksack marches with a 30-pound rucksack.

Also, everyone that was master- or senior-parachute qualified would now be conducting jumpmaster duties after they attended a jumpmaster refresher training given by me.

Finally, we would now take every Friday afternoon to clean up, and details would be done as a detachment.

The new policy went into effect and was supported by almost everyone in the detachment. A few officers and enlisted were resistant. The Colonel took care of the officers; I took care of the enlisted.

The lower ranking people were happy with the changes—especially one, a Sergeant who had been doing most of the jumpmaster duties. In the performance of her jumpmaster duties, she was one of the most outstanding I'd ever seen. She gave me my jumpmaster check (JMPI) for my first jump with the detachment. When she gave the jump commands, she put people out of the aircraft right on the release point. She spent four years in the 82nd Airborne Division before coming to special operations. Her name was Sergeant Sandy Pressel.

I don't really know why, but our detachment had enough Special Forces dive equipment to equip an SF SCUBA team. There was a designated SCUBA locker in the tunnel, and I performed the inventories and maintained the inspection logs. It was always ready if needed.

Image 163. The Army life is the life for me!

Captain Kilgore was our detachment's dive officer. He was also a NAUI-certified divemaster (National Association of Underwater Instructors) and taught civilian SCUBA at a dive shop called Down Under Divers. Captain Kilgore recruited me to help him teach the shop's two-week SCUBA course. I was a PADI-certified divemaster (Professional Association of Diving Instructors) and had 19 years of experience as a combat swimmer, qualified in both open circuit (SCUBA) and closed-circuit (oxygen re-breather) rigs.

A Navy chief also taught with us at the SCUBA shop. We stayed pretty busy. I would work with the students who had difficulty in some aspect of the SCUBA class. As long as a student truly wanted to learn, we'd always let them recycle to the next class without charge until they qualified as a novice class SCUBA diver.

I talked to my sons almost every week. They wanted to spend the summer with me in Hawaii and we agreed to let them come to Hawaii when school let out. I sent them each a round trip ticket. They would come at the end of June (this was 1987) and stay until late August.

We had the *best* times of our lives. It was truly a dream. 12-year-old Jason learned to surf, and he qualified as a NAUI Novice Diver. 9-year-old Jamie loved the boogie boarding. The two months flew by, and it was time for them to go back to Fayetteville. I hated to see that day come.

As I watched the plane lift off, I felt like I'd lost a part of me. My condo and my heart were empty. Everywhere I looked I saw the boys. In each room, there was something of theirs. Jason's surfboard that a friend gave him. Jamie's boogie board. I felt alone. I wouldn't see them for a long time. That night, I couldn't stand to be in the room with so many warm memories. I went to the Hale Koa, sat watching the waves, and liberally applied the anesthetic. That evening the sunset was not the same. I shuffled back to the condo and was greeted by...

...silence.

40

New Purpose

1987

But God saw my sorrow. He made my grief short. The next month, September, Jason's mother called. She said Jason was out of control to the point that she was thinking about putting him in a reform school.

Before she even finished the sentence, she heard me say, "I'll take him! He can live with me here in Hawaii. As a matter of fact, I'll take them both."

She said Jamie was doing fine and that he wanted to stay with her and would understand if Jason were to live in Hawaii. So, we agreed that Jason would come to Hawaii to live with me.

I had new purpose in my life. I went to personnel and started the paperwork to have my son join me as my direct dependent. Jason arrived and plopped right into 7th grade in the local school.

His mother called within days. She explained that Jamie now realized that he didn't want to be apart from Jason. Before she even finished the sentence I said, "I'll take him!"

Immediately I went to personnel and applied for on-base housing at Fort Shafter. In less than two weeks, Jamie arrived and there was a four-bedroom house for me on Radar Hill, where all the E-9's lived with their families. It had a view of Pearl Harbor and the USS *Arizona* memorial. Now, my sons expressed some disappointment that we would move out of the condo at Waikiki. That's understandable from the viewpoint of boys who love the beach, but Fort Shafter was a more secure place to raise kids, with a better school situation. Full time active duty, with two sons living with me, I was like a lot of single parents in the military who somehow find a way to make it all work... and I was blessed. I didn't have much in the way of furnishings, so the housing people filled my quarters with all new rattan furniture and got me special permission to keep the furniture until the end of my tour.

A new detachment commander, Colonel Meeks, took over and I got along with him well. He often asked me to accompany him to meetings at Camp Smith or WESTCOM headquarters and I noticed that he always wore long sleeve shirts with his uniform. Everyone else wore the short sleeve shirt.

Well, at P.T. one day I saw that he had an Airborne tattoo on his right forearm. I must admit that I'd never seen a Colonel with an Airborne tattoo. Sharing how I related to his situation, I told him the tale of my Airborne tattoo. I recommended that at this point, he should just let it show proudly. He seemed to appreciate my story.

He invited me to a get together at his quarters with the officers in our detachment and their wives. He said, "You should bring your lady friend."

"Colonel Meeks, do you know who my lady friend is?"

He said, "No, but I'm sure she must be a special lady."

"It would be an honor for us to attend, but I wonder if some of your officers and wives might not approve. My lady friend is your admin NCO, Sgt Pressel."

He smiled and said, "She's a fine choice. Don't worry about the officers. My house, my invitation. I'll take care of any concerns."

Sandy and I went and had a good time.

In November of 1987, the boys and I had our first Thanksgiving. Sandy helped us make it a big traditional dinner with all the trimmings. We then put up a real Christmas tree. Jason and Jamie really liked Sandy. She didn't take any nonsense from them, and they respected her. Life was good.

During this time, I was sometimes back in Southeast Asia, working in Thailand with 1st Special Forces Group with their annual Cobra Gold exercise. I spent a few weeks in the Philippines with Philippine Special Forces for the Balikatan international special ops exercise. In March 1989, I visited Colonel Nick Rowe. Colonel Rowe is a legend in the Special Ops world. He was the chief of the US Special Forces advising the Philippines counter-terrorism efforts. His life was continuously under threat. In his armored limousine, he brought me to his house and his wife cooked a wonderful meal for us. He was interested in hearing about some of our common friends we'd known in Special Forces over the decades.

Less than a month after I left, the terrorists finally succeeded in assassinating him.

[Colonel Rowe was a POW in Vietnam from 1963 to 1968, he is one of only 34 who ever escaped from their captivity, detailed in his book, *Five Years to Freedom*. He was assigned to the JUSMAG Philippines (Joint US Military Advisory Group) as chief of the Army division providing counter-insurgency training to the Philippine Army against the New People's Army, the communist uprising that threatened to topple the government. In February 1989, Colonel Rowe had intel that the NPA was planning a major terrorist act. My visit in March was to coordinate our support. But on April 21st, 1989, his armored limousine was ambushed at 7am with automatic weapons on a street in Manila by the NPA.]

I represented WESTCOM at his memorial service at Fort Bragg. Colonel Rowe was an outstanding soldier and an officer to be respected. He is what Special Forces is all about.

My friend Command Sergeant Major Sidwell was the Command Sergeant Major of WESTCOM. He was at the

30 year point and his retirement date was set. I myself was coming up on 29 years. I could tell that he was not ready to retire from his beloved Army. I felt the same way. But he said it's his time to get back to those hills of West Virginia. "I've been gone too long," he said.

I was in charge of arranging one last parachute jump for him. The deputy commander of WESTCOM, Major General Lightner, would be jumping with him. I coordinated with the riggers and scheduled a CH-47 Chinook helicopter.

On the day of the jump, I helped set up the drop zone and then gave the MACO briefing (Marshalling Area Control Officer) there. I told General Lightner that I had a special treat for him. I introduced the jumpmaster, a young sergeant who had spent four years in the 82nd Airborne. "She is one of the best jumpmasters I've ever come across, Sgt Sandy Pressel."

Image 164. Sgt Sandy Pressel is in the
front row, toward the center.

Image 165. Stock photo of a static line jump from a Chinook.

Image 166. Stock photo of a static line jump from a Chinook.

After the jump, General Lightner said, "That was the best jumpmaster procedures I've ever seen."

A few days later, it was the sad day when the old soldier, CSM Sidwell, the Command Sergeant Major of WESTCOM, was retiring. They had a formal dinner for him with awards for his faithful service of 30 years. Among the many who came was the WESTCOM Commander, Lt General Bagnal, and many of his senior staff, including those of other services. The place was packed, all in formal uniforms, I in my white uniform. I thought white, with all those gold stripes, looked sharp. I was asked to speak at the ceremony. I could reflect on his honorable career, with both of us having served many years in Special Forces. I knew he was not ready to retire and when my time came up to honor this old Green Beret, I stepped up to the microphone.

A hush comes over the hundreds of people in the room, with everyone waiting for me to say something. "What an honor it has been for me to serve with Command Sergeant Major Sidwell."

[I almost say that he was not ready to retire and that the Army and its soldiers still need his leadership. He is a soldier, not a politician.

Instead, I choose the following words.]

"To honor this Special Forces soldier for his service to our country, I dedicate the following." I reach into my coat pocket and take out a small harmonica and play the tune for "The Ballad of the Green Berets."

Command Sergeant Major Sidwell, at the head table, stands up at attention before I've even finished the first verse, his wife rises by his side. This has not been rehearsed or planned. Soon, a half dozen officers and their wives are standing. Lt General Bagnal stands. Then the entire audience stands at attention.

["The Ballad of the Green Berets" rose to #1 on the pop charts in 1966, written and performed by a Special Forces soldier, Sgt Barry Sadler, a tribute to the past, present, and future Special Forces, especially those who gave their lives in the defense of our country.]

As I finish, I see tears. Command Sergeant Major Sidwell thanks me. Between the Command Sergeant Major and me, I could have not paid him a greater tribute.

Now, it felt like the right time for me to retire. I always said, "The first 20 years are what you have to do. Anything over 20 is what you want to do." I went to the Personnel Office. The personnel NCO, who happened to be someone that I had taught in civilian SCUBA, worked with me to come up with a plan that would have me retire from my beloved Army December 31st, 1989, with 29yrs, 1 month and 7 days of service.

For my last jump, Sandy was there.

Image 167. On the occasion of my retirement,
getting to jump with Sandy. Wow!

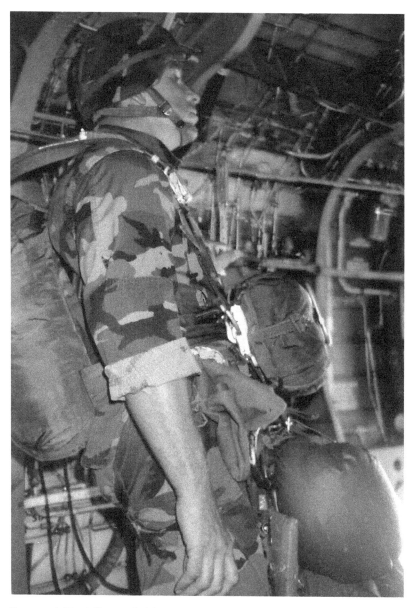

Image 168. All good things must come to an end. Full combat
gear. Clearly, it's a bittersweet day.

Combat ready

Sgt. Maj. Vladimir Jakovenko, U.S. Army Western Command
prepares for his last career jump.   Photo by Spec. Jeffrey A. Hackle.

Image 169. The Army newspaper at Fort
Shafter covered my retirement jump.

The detachment commander put me in for the Legion of Merit.

…I almost didn't get it. The story starts like this. "One Friday night, at the NCO club…"

…my buddies and I are meeting up for a little celebrating. Sandy and I are seated at a bar in an area of the club that is away from the crowd. It's quiet, with just a few men and women, not packed with people. A Samoan band is playing. The club downstairs has their own band and is the place for the dancing (and the fighting). Usually, whoever is downstairs will stay downstairs. If you just want a calm evening, you'll stay upstairs.

Well, I'm at the latrine down the hall and as I exit to return to our table, I stop to talk with a couple of other friends from our detachment. Sandy comes down the hall. She's looking for me.

She says, "There's about to be a fight. Three drunks came upstairs into our bar. They sat down next to me, and I told them that my date is sitting in that seat. The one drunk smartass said, 'He must be very small.' So now, he's got my drink and they're making comments to the women. A Sergeant Major from the tunnel, who was in uniform tried to talk them into leaving. One of the drunks picked up *my* drink and said, 'I'll leave when I finish this drink.'"

I start walking to the bar, and I say, "Yep, there's about to be a fight."

As I enter the room, I decide to knock out the biggest one. He's sitting at the bar. Since the barstools are the swiveling type, I spin him around and hit him, putting him to the floor. I turn to take on the other two, who are on me pretty quick. My old friend Elmo Adams jumps in to help, and he gets knocked into the drum set, making a huge crash. (He ends up with about 8 stitches.) One of the two other guys sucker punches me and I was so mad that it didn't take me long to land punches on each of the two remaining guys. The Samoans in the band come over to restore peace. By this time, the bouncer of the club (who happens to be an old friend of mine) says, "Get out of here. The MPs are coming."

Sandy and I go to my quarters. It's after midnight. I have a swollen lip and a puffed-up eye, but the three drunks were in worse shape, last I saw them.

I look out the back window of my house. I can see the club from my quarters, and there's an MP car coming up the hill toward us.

Sure enough, there's a knock at the door. "Sergeant Major, were you at the club tonight and in a fight?" (Like my face wasn't proof enough.) "Would the two of you come to the station with us, please?"

They didn't cuff me. Sandy and I walked into the station and immediately we see the three troublemakers.

I say, "Hi. How you guys doing?"[21]

In his office, the investigator tells me, "An assault charge is being leveled against you by these gentlemen (the three drunks). Do you hold a rank in martial arts, by any chance?"

"No."

"Well, these gentlemen say that you had them in some sort of eye-gouging martial arts technique."

---

21   This is a bar fight to be particularly proud of. Righteous indignation.

After I tell him what happened, the investigator explains that all the witnesses say that the three came in looking for trouble. (They found it.) After an hour or so, no further action was to be taken. There would be no charges. Sandy and I were free to go.

I did receive the Legion of Merit and we held the award ceremony at the tunnel with the detachment.

Image 170. Colonel Meeks (proudly displaying his Airborne tattoo) awards my Legion of Merit.

Image 171. With Sandy for my retirement.

November 3rd, 1989, was one of my saddest days. Sandy and I were standing at the departure gate for the flight that would take the boys and me back to the mainland. Sandy would be separating from the Army in a few months and it

felt like a long time to be apart. I told Sandy, "If you'll have
me, I would be honored to be your husband for the rest of
my life." When she accepted my proposal, we could not let
go. My sons got on each side, trying to comfort me. It felt
like I was leaving a part of me.

I wrote to Sandy every day. Before we knew it, it was
Christmas 1989. My folks loved having me and the boys
living with them for that season.

I was hired right away with DynCorp, the contractor that
operated DARISSA in Lakehurst, NJ. A number of people I
knew from my SPSA days worked there. I was a weapons
supervisor. I had an outstanding crew with five gunsmiths.
We customized weapons for Special Operations.

On New Year's Eve, I celebrated with my friends, many
of whom I'd known for years, at the VFW in Lakehurst.
At midnight, as "Auld Lang Syne" played, I realized that
I was now a civilian. It's important for me to describe for
you the feeling in that moment. It was the same feeling a
lot of us had coming back from Vietnam. In the late 60s
and early 70s, we were alone and felt like no one really
cared, so we kept it to ourselves and tried to just blend in
with the general population.

But at that moment, a certain elderly lady noticed me.
Likely, she had seen that look in others at the VFW over
many years. She made a point to share my last moments
as a soldier and made sure that those around me knew the
significance. They hugged me and said, "Thank you for all
you've done for us and for our country."

In January, the boys and I moved into a house, and I sent
photos to Sandy. I wrote her a special letter for Ground Hog
Day, happy for the passing of the last holiday we'd be apart.

The last two weeks seemed the longest, but in mid-March I was driving to the Philadelphia airport to pick Sandy up, one of the happiest days of my life. Snowy, freezing cold, nasty weather, it may as well have been the Fourth of July as far I was concerned. Five of the longest months of my life, and there she was! We made up for lost time in hugs and kisses. We were together again and would never part.

Sandy and I traveled to Trotwood, Ohio, for me to meet her family and to ask her parents' blessing for us to marry. Asking permission from her father was my greatest fear (maybe more so than being in a firefight). Sandy's father was a WWII veteran of the Navy, and he then worked for General Motors. We really got along well. They immediately treated me like part of the family. They were church-going and God-fearing. They worked hard for everything and raised six children (Sandy has two sisters and three brothers) in a home filled with love. I have a deep respect for them.

We had a church wedding on September 1st, 1990, with Sandy's pastor officiating. It was a beautiful ceremony, and our military friends came from as far away as California. I asked the pastor if we could have "Amazing Grace" played after we were pronounced husband and wife, and all agreed it was a beautiful conclusion. Later, we gathered at the hotel with our military friends telling stories well into the night.

When DARISSA moved to Kentucky, we moved with the job. As the years went on, our family grew. As of this writing, I have a saint of a wife, four sons, a daughter, six grandchildren, and three great grandchildren. John was a Marine and then retired as a police captain. David retired from working for the State of NJ. Jason retired as an Army CW3. Jamie worked in construction but passed away in 2021 (for a parent to bury their child—there's nothing sadder). Katelyn is thriving as a therapist in an addiction counseling practice.

Images 172, 173, 174. (l-r) John, David, Jason, Jamie, Katelyn, Sandy, and Jake.

Image 174a. The Jakovenkos at the Fort Bragg SF induction ceremony.

41

Soldiers

In January of 2024, I received call from Colonel James L. "Hawk" Holloway. He informed me that I'm being inducted into the Special Forces Distinguished Members of the Regiment. This is at Fort Bragg (now named Fort Liberty) in 'The White House,' at the JFK Special Warfare Center with the ceremony being held in the JFK Auditorium. It's the very stage on which, 54 years earlier, Bull Simons called for volunteers to go with him on his "moderately hazardous mission." This headquarters is at the epicenter of induction and training for all Special Forces. Today, a huge statue of Bull Simons is there, inspiring all trainees as they walk from building to building. Inscribed on the base is 'SON TAY RAID, NOVEMBER 21, 1970.'

But before that, back in 2002, I received a call from "Ranger" Brown. I hadn't seen him since his retirement almost 20 years prior. We'd known each other since the 173rd LRRP in Vietnam in 1966. We spent over an hour talking about the old days. Then he said that he and other members of the 173rd were nominating me for the US Army

Ranger Hall of Fame. I thanked him, but I didn't feel like I'd done anything that others hadn't done. They did nominate me, and I was inducted into the Ranger Hall of Fame in 2003.

Let me close with a memory from the Ranger Hall of Fame induction ceremony at Fort Benning in 2003. I felt as honored as if I'd been elected to the highest office. I was being recognized by soldiers I'd served with in war and in peacetime. I was proud, not of my rank or of any achievement. I was proud to be a *soldier*. It is such an honor to be called a soldier by other soldiers. I accepted the honor, not for myself but as a representative of all those others that I've talked about in this book, some named and some unnamed. This is part of what it means to be a soldier. You always depend upon and respect fellow soldiers.

On stage there in the huge Marshall Auditorium at Fort Benning's main headquarters building, I told one last story. It was about something that happened during my first physical after retirement. The doctor noticed that, for the first time in my life, there was found a serious medical problem. My heart had the condition Atrial Fibrillation. Again, I'd never had it before. I'd always been perfectly healthy. The good doctor was very concerned and was describing my options. But to me, it was immediately clear what had happened.

I told him, "Doc, there's nothing you can do about it. My heart broke when I left the Army."

Image 175.

Messages for Our Current
Generation
from the Life and Career of Jakovenko

(Cliff Westbrook's observations)

Under Jakovenko's leadership, not one of his team members was ever lost in battle.

We need more Jakovenkos. We must recruit and retain more like him. Sure, we need to develop a certain number of polished, soldier-statesmen, diplomatic Command Sergeant Majors. But we must also ensure we have plenty of Sergeant Majors who are gladiators. That goes for all other ranks as well.

Cossacks (among whom were Jakovenko's ancestors) were fierce and in many ways exemplary fighters in European wars. It's in his blood. To create an army, you must develop men and women of Spirit, Skills, and Combat Experience. We must find people with his kind of Spirit and then nurture it.

Spirit Spirit is an act of your *will*, your freewill actively choosing a noble, submitted life. People humbly choose to submit themselves to something greater, despite the fact that it entails great sacrifice. Call people to a noble cause and that Spirit will identify itself, already existing in their DNA.

Skills For those who respond to that call with "Here am I," offer them the tools of war and train them in their expert use. 'Skills' pertains to the *mind*, sharpened and readied for their assigned tasks.

Combat Experience More than anything else, Combat Experience is for the benefit of your *emotions*, to steady them and to mature them.

You must have all three (Spirit, Skills, and Combat Experience) to succeed in battle, but how can you prepare your untested soldiers in 'combat experience'? War games, maneuvers, and exercises are not enough.

[If you think I'm going to say, "street fights," then you're starting to figure out Jakovenko—but I'm not going to say it. And I'm not going to say, "bar fights," though you certainly learn something about yourself in those situations. You must already know yourself well if you are to prevail in that split-second when the Siberian Tiger lunges.]

Michael D. Echanis (CIB, Bronze Star, Purple Heart) was a legend in martial arts and unarmed combat. As a civilian, he was hired to teach 'H2H' (hand-to-hand combat) for Special Forces at Fort Bragg's JFK Special Warfare Center starting in 1975 and for SEAL Team 2 at Little Creek, Virginia, in 1977. He was hired as an advisor to Nicaraguan President Somoza's military in their fight against the communist Sandinista guerrillas. (Echanis eventually dies in a military plane crash in that conflict in 1978).

Echanis knew something about fighting and he had something to say about Jakovenko. While Jakovenko's team, ODA-594, was on a counterterrorism field exercise in Puerto Rico in 1977, Echanis was involved with their team as a civilian contractor/instructor. The Puerto Rican commandos asked Echanis and Jakovenko to go up against each other, no-holds-barred, in a hand-to-hand combat demonstration. It was one of the few times Echanis was brought to bay. Each man punched, wrestled, and kicked with unbridled ferocity. Jakovenko eventually succeeded in putting a choke hold on his opponent that ended the bout. Mike Echanis's summary assessment of Jakovenko was, "He is one of the toughest men I've ever seen!"[22]

Do we want more Jakovenkos? Yes, we want more Jakovenkos.

Image 176. This photo was taken right after the one-on-one fight. Echanis is in the foreground and Jakovenko is just over his right shoulder. In the background are the Puerto Rican commandos.

---

22   This story is from Greg Walker in an article he wrote about Echanis for The Sentinel, Special Forces Association Chapter 78. See the Bibliography.

As recently as the September 2023 edition of *Army Magazine*, a combat-seasoned officer, Major Wayne Heard, pointed this current generation of officers to "legends like Jakovenko" as the kind of soldier that our military needs if we are to win wars. Major Heard called Jakovenko an "NCO that helped shape this officer."

The greatest benefit of **Combat Experience** is the fact that it can dampen irrational emotion. This is far from being a science. **Spirit** is clearly an art, not a science. **Skills** has numerous parts and the only part of Skills that can be reduced to a science is that which relates to the technology we have at our disposal. The other parts of Skills relate to the arts of leadership, administration, persuasive communication, and personal mental discipline.

A grey-bearded combat veteran, John McAllister Schofield, described the counter-intuitive challenge of the art of war. "The discipline which makes the soldiers of a free country reliable in battle is not to be gained by harsh or tyrannical treatment. On the contrary, such treatment is far more likely to destroy than to make an army. It is possible to impart instruction and give commands in such a manner and such a tone of voice as to inspire in the soldier no feeling but an intense desire to obey, while the opposite manner and tone of voice cannot fail to excite strong resentment and a desire to disobey." We are talking about an <u>art</u>. It's an art that needs be taught and passed down through generations.

Leo Tolstoy challenges the soldier to play their role with a confidence in the inevitability of God's will being done. As horrendous as your experience may end up being, a life lived seeking to do the Right thing is the life that is worth living.

We must have confidence in eventual victory. Carl von Clausewitz lists faith as one of the 'Chief Moral Powers' of an army. Immanuel Kant, the 'dean of all the philosophers,' told us that sound reason and logic lead us to the conclusion that there exists God and his sovereignty over the arc of human events, including war. But battle is less academic, it is more feeling. Tolstoy's summary is "Success never depends—and never will depend—on position or equipment or even on numbers. It depends upon the <u>feeling</u> that is in me and in him and in each soldier."

So, we need to steady and focus the soldier's nerves with perspective. **Combat experience** is the source of that perspective, and it is delivered through *generations*. Untested soldiers need to have combat veterans serving beside them. Let those who have been there be mingled in amongst, train with, and serve alongside the inexperienced.

What qualifies as 'combat experience'? This may hurt some feelings, but there is an answer, and that answer is this: Enemy rounds landing beyond you. When you realize that you are within the range of your adversary, your perspective changes. You know it could have been you. This change in your perspective may not be noticed by the outside world. To them you may still seem cocky. But, having been there, deep down, you now know that you are not in control. You know that it's not your abilities that kept you alive. The word 'lucky' is commonly used, but it's just a silly word that really doesn't mean anything. Luck is not a thing. Luck is just the absence of an unhappy event. 'Not your day to get hit' might be a more accurate way to put it. For the vast majority of people on any battlefield, today will not be 'your day to get hit.' On any given battlefield, the vast majority of those within range will never be touched by enemy fire. And yet, the sound of a 105mm Howitzer or a 106mm Recoilless Rifle is far more persuasive than 107 scientific, statistical studies telling you how extremely low are your odds of getting killed in battle. In the moment, your strength will be summoned from the duty to your fellow soldiers, all of whom are depending on you.

Combat experience convinces you that you can make decisions without waiting for further instructions. You can execute your part of the plan steadfastly, knowing that it's not about you. Your responsibility is not to worry whether you live or die even as men all around you perish. Yours is to carry out your mission to the best of your ability. This is what Clausewitz called military virtue. Our country's highest honors and deepest gratitude are conferred upon people with this character.

Knowing that you were a candidate for a bullet—knowing that, but for the grace of God, a round could have reached you—is life-changing. It adds a quality to your demeanor and your words that will aid you and your fellow soldiers the next time that you choose to step onto contested ground.

Younger generations will need that from you as they take that step with you. It's not how well you tell the stories. It's not that you're perfect. It's not about being brave or being a hero. It's about them knowing the fact that you've been there, experienced the reality, and yet you're willing to go again. Seeing that quality in you complements the sense of gratitude and duty that first stirred their heart and yours to serve in the profession of arms.

Image 1. The Cossacks of Ukraine, the ancestors of Jakovenko. (Painting: *Reply of the Zaporozhian Cossacks*, by Ilya Repin) In this painting, the Cossacks are writing a vulgar, contemptuous letter to the Sultan of the Ottoman Empire, Mehmed IV, in 1676. It is their reply to his ultimatum that they must submit to him. "Za Porozh" translates "from beyond the rapids," referring to the area around lower Dnieper River in Ukraine. Led by Ivan Sirko (center, smoking a pipe), they replied with sarcasm, insults and profanities and in this painting, they are adding more and more vulgarities.

THE END

Index

Glossary

.50 cal	A Browning M2 "fifty caliber" machine gun
ATL	Assistant Team Leader
ARVN	Army of the Republic of Vietnam (South Vietnam)
C-ration	"Meal, Combat, Individual ration"
CIB	Combat Infantryman Badge
CIDG	Civilian Irregular Defense Group (South Vietnam)
D.I.	Drill Instructor
D.P.	Displaced Person
DZ	Drop Zone for parachutists
EIB	Expert Infantryman Badge
IRF	Immediate Response Force
JMPI	Jumpmaster Parachute Inspection
KP	Kitchen Patrol
LAW	Light Anti-tank Weapon
LBE	Load Bearing Equipment
LLDB	Lực Lượng Đặc Biệt Quân Lực Việt Nam Cộng Hòa, ARVN Special Forces
LRP	Long-range Patrol (often a squad of roughly 10 soldiers)

LRRP	Long-range Reconnaissance Patrol (typically six soldiers)
LZ	Landing Zone for helicopters
MACV-SOG	Military Assistance Command, Vietnam, Studies & Observations Group
MEDEVAC	Medical Evacuation
MOS	Military Occupational Specialty
M.P.	Military Police
MSL	Altitude above Mean Sea Level
NVA	North Vietnam Army
ODA	Operational Detachment-Alpha (a Special Forces A-team)
PLF	Parachute Landing Fall
P.T.	Physical Training
RTAFB	Royal Thai Air Force Base
RON	A camp in which you will Remain Over Night
RTO	Radio Telephone Operator
S.A.S.	The British Army's Special Air Service
SF	Special Forces
SFG(A)	Special Forces Group (Airborne)
SITREP	Situation Report
SOP	Standard Operating Procedure
Spec 4	US Army Specialist E-4 rank
TACAIR	Tactical Air Support
TOC	Tactical Operations Center
VC	The communist Viet Cong army working in South Vietnam
WIA	Wounded in Action

In Appreciation

We greatly benefit from the magnificent body of work that Colonel John Gargus, USAF (retired), has bestowed for the benefit of future generations. His seminal book, *The Son Tay Raid: American POWs in Vietnam Were Not Forgotten* is the most authoritative history of the Son Tay Raid.

We are sincerely grateful for the help of the following people reviewing the manuscript and providing their critique and contributions.

Nick Seaward, Ph.D., Lt Colonel, USAF (retired)

Erick Wikum, Ph.D.

Ron Wiley, Ph.D.

Phil Clayton, J.D., Colonel, USA (retired)

Tres Westbrook, J.D.

Nate Haas, Lt Colonel, USA (retired)

Reed Cundiff (Thank you for the stories and details you contributed!)

Larry 'Red' Cole (Thank you for the stories and details you contributed!)

Terry Buckler

Stephanie Westbrook

And very special appreciation to Sandy Jakovenko for her hundreds of hours of scribing and reviewing and making this possible.

Thank you,

Jake and Cliff

Bibliography

Gargus, John, Col USAF, ret. *The Son Tay Raid: American POWs in Vietnam Were Not Forgotten.* College Station: Texas A&M University Press, 2010

Schemmer, Benjamin F. *The Raid.* New York: Harper & Row, 1976 (Updated 1986)

Buckler, Terry and Westbrook, Cliff. *Who Will Go: Into the Son Tay POW Camp.* Charleston SC: Palmetto Publishing, 2020

Clausewitz, Carl (translated by J.J. Graham). *On War.* Produced by Charles Keller and David Widger, 2006, https://www.gutenberg.org/files/1946/1946-h/1946-h.htm.

Dix, Drew *The Rescue of River City.* Fairbanks AK: Drew Dix Publishing, 2000

Ellis, Lee, & Godek, Greg. *Captured by Love: Inspiring True Romance Stories from Vietnam POWs.* FreedomStar Media, 2023

Guenon, William A., Jr., Maj USAF, ret. *Secret and Dangerous: Night of the Son Tay POW Raid.* East Lowell MA: King Printing Company, Inc., 2002

Harris, Carlyle S. "Smitty", Col USAF, ret. *Tap Code.* Grand Rapids MI: Zondervan, 2019

Heard, Wayne. "NCOs that Helped Shape This Officer". *Army Magazine*, Volume 73, Number 9, September 2023, page 7.

McRaven, William H., Adm USN, ret. *SPEC OPS: Case Studies in Special Operations Warfare: Theory and Practice*. New York: Ballentine Books, 1995

Meyer, John Stryker. *Across the Fence (Expanded Edition)*. Oceanside, CA: SOG Publishing, 2018

Meyer, John Stryker. *SOG Chronicles: Volume 1*. Oceanside, CA: SOG Publishing, 2018

Plaster, John, L. *SOG: The Secret Wars of America's Commandos in Vietnam*. New York: Penguin Group, 1997

Rowe, James Nicholas. *Five Years to Freedom*. New York: Presidio Press, 1971

Rutledge, Howard and Phyllis. *In the Presence of Mine Enemies*. Grand Rapids: Baker Publishing, 1973

"The Legacy of Valor: The 335th Assault Helicopter Company-'Cowboys, Falcons.'" The Vietnam Helicopter Pilots Association, 2022, https://museum.vhpa.org/companies/335ahc/335ahc.shtml. Accessed 23 April 2023.

Tolstoy, L.N. (Translated by R. Edmonds). *War and Peace*. Baltimore: Penguin Books, 1957.

Waldron, Thomas R., LtCol USAF, ret. *I Flew With Heroes*. Lexington KY, 2019

Walker, Greg. *Battle Blades: A Professional's Guide to Combat/Fighting Knives*. Boulder, CO: Paladin Press, 1993.

Walker, Greg. "Hwa Rang Do's Immortal Warrior – The Untold Story of Michael D Echanis". *Black Belt Magazine*, August 9, 2013.

Walker, Greg. "Wounded Warrior-Part Two." *Sentinel* of Special Forces Association Chapter 78, August 2022, https://www.specialforces78.com/wounded-warrior-part-two

Holy Bible, New International Version. Biblica, 2011.

Image Sources

Cover & Jacket images:

A. American Ukraine Flag: www.uspatriotflags.com/ products/usa-ukraine-friendship-flag-made-in-usa/

B. Dominican Republic: https://thetimes-tribune. newspapers.com/image/531521503/?clipping_id= 122669336&fcfToken=eyJhbGciOiJIUzI1NiIsInR5c CI6IkpXVCJ9.eyJmcmVlLXZpZXctaWQiOjUz MTUyMTUwMywia WF0Ijox NjgxMzIwMDc3 LCJleHAiOjE2ODE0MDY0Nzd9.0jFjcU_RHU etx3eeYSJDM-BKIoPw1ZQM268b8FiiC3U

C. Blue Light: https://sofrep.com/news/blue-light-americas-first-counter-terrorism-unit-part-4/

D. War Zone D: https://arsof-history.org/articles/v5n2_mike_force_page_1.html

E. 173rd, LRRP: https://www.google.com/url?sa=i&url= https%3A%2F%2Fwww.yiaco.com%2Fthumbnailsq% 2F%3Fk%3DT-1-E-58-LRP-LRRP-K-Co-75th-

F. Eagle Flights: https://www.stripes.com/special-reports/ eagle-flights-prey-on-fleeing-viet-cong-1.494252

G. Combat Swimmers: https://external-preview.redd.it/ oT_7vz9MHQdBNwfo9cV5mVDZ-GLhEqsoCsQ9Y

ga5pi8.jpg?auto=webp&v=enabled&s=c6b4d748f965
efd05b04ac5f7ff4df5894c55db9

H. Jakovenko, Hall of Fame: https://www.Benning.army.
mil/infantry/artb/rhof/photos/1114-csm_Jakovenko.jpg

Interior images:

1   Cossacks of Ukraine   https://upload.wikimedia.
org/wikipedia/commons /thumb/7/79/Ilja_
Jefimowitsch_Repin_-_Reply_of_the_Zaporozhian_
Cossacks_-_Yorck.jpg/1920px-Ilja_Jefimowitsch_
Repin_-_Reply_of_the_Zaporozhian_Cossacks_-_
Yorck.jpg By Ilya Repin - The Yorck Project (2002)
10.000 Meisterwerke der Malerei (DVD-ROM),
distributed by DIRECTMEDIA Publishing GmbH.
ISBN: 3936122202., Public Domain, https://com-
mons.wikimedia.org/w/index.php?curid=158198

2   Starved peasants, Kharkiv   "File:GolodomorKharkiv
.jpg." Wikimedia Commons. 28 Jan 2023, 03:35
UTC. 23 Apr 2023, 15:22 <https://commons.
wikimedia.org/w/index.php?title=File:Golodomor
Kharkiv.jpg&oldid=728384460>.

3   Soviet Union Famine   "File:Famine en URSS
1933.jpg." Wikimedia Commons. 28 Nov 2022,
05:04 UTC. 23 Apr 2023, 18:34 <https://commons.
wikimedia.org/w/index.php?title=File:Famine_en_
URSS_1933.jpg&oldid=710391055>.

4   Girls at Donbas Mine   "File:RIAN archive 21733
Komsomol appeal.jpg." Wikimedia Commons.
26 Mar 2022, 06:21 UTC. 23 Apr 2023, 18:38
<https://commons.wikimedia.org/w/index.

php?title=File:RIAN_archive_21733_Komsomol_
appeal.jpg&oldid=644137788>.

5   Operation Barbarossa   "File: German-tanks-
     advancing-towards-Soviet-village-during-
     Operation-Barbarossa-October-29-1941.jpg."
     Encyclopædia Britannica . April 23, 2023. https://
     cdn.britannica.com/98/228398-004-A7772664/
     German-tanks-advancing-towards-Soviet-village-
     during-Operation-Barbarossa-October-29-1941.
     jpg?s=1500x700&q=85

6   Family photo in Berlin.   From the author

7   Occupied Germany   https://schoolhistory.co.uk/
     wp-content/uploads/2022/01/Berlin-Blockade-2-
     300x168.png

8   Letter from his father   From the author

9   Avro York aircraft   https://upload.wikimedia.org/
     wikipedia/commons /8/83/Avro_York_-_Wunstorf
     _-_The_Berlin_Airlift_1948_-_1949_HU98413.jpg

10   The Hanover School   From the author

11   USS Sturgis refugees   https://www.unhcr.org/
     spotlight/wp-content/uploads/sites/55/2020/12/
     RF148968_25526-720x475.jpg

12   Manifest Bremerhaven   https://www.ancestry.com/
     family-tree/person/tree/185332566/person/
     382424012622/hints

13   New York City   https://assets1.cbsnewsstatic.com/
     hub/i/r/2011/10 /22/a8afd8fb-a643-11e2-a3f0-
     029118418759/thumbnail/620x465/e1e266c2550
     cc03791130f5c6c4fb774/statue_of_liberty_2496255_
     fullwidth.jpg

14 Arrival at Ellis Island https://www.ancestry.com/ imageviewer/collections /7488/images/NYT715_ 7918-0202?pId=3026386274

15 Ashton ID https://railfanguides.us/stations/id / 2AshtonID1977a.jpg

16 Mother & Son From the author

17 Jersey City street https://www.google.com/url? sa=i&url=https%3A%2F %2Fwww.pinterest.com% 2Fpin%2F545850417333598601%2F&psig=AOv Vaw3hi6EoscVzH_ede6PnJ08U&ust=1654523775 808000&source=images&cd=vfe&ved=0CAwQjRxq FwoTCPjLkMK7lvgCFQAAAAAdAAAAABAI

18 TV, radio, camera https://www.google.com/ url?sa=i&url=https%3A%2F %2Fwww.reddit.com% 2Fr%2Fgaming%2Fcomments%2F7mv934%2Fcuph ead_on_a_classic_television_from_1953%2F&psig= AOvVaw0WlrSLeipa0xQn0lyl0dx3&ust=16545266 15155000&source=images&cd=vfe&ved=0CAwQjR xqFwoTCNitpYzGlvgCFQAAAAAdAAAAABAf

19 Map of Jersey City Created by C.Westbrook using Google Maps

20 Slapstick https://img1.etsystatic. com/019/0/7115795/il_570 xN.498536389_5wxu.jpg

21 The Frogmen movie ! https://media-cache. cinematerial.com/p/500x/ ylg1dyqn/the-frogmen- movie-poster.jpg?v=1456342405

22 Battle Cry movie https://i.pinimg.com/originals/0a/ ab/7d/0aab7d03 124d2ec8be559b3cafab6f6f.jpg

23 Up Front movie https://www.imdb.com/title/ tt0044173/media viewer/rm3682222592/

24 The Ike Jacket From the author

25 Green Beret, no Flash   From the author

26 250-foot towers   https://lh3.googleusercontent.com/ p/AF1QipPzhD34lA a7hPD3wkJmot7GeWSbVh1ec -HLXdhv=s3808-w3808-h2144

27 Corcoran jump boots   https://www.snipershide.com/ shooting/attachments /image-jpg.7433980/

28 Static line from a C-119   https://ruudleeuw.com/ images/c119/mayher-c119-swift_strikeII-1962.jpg

29 501ˢᵗ Infantry Regiment   https://i.pinimg.com/ originals/9d/91/a3/9d91a3 ebc863b88805a729ff 1de7407a.jpg

30 Geronimo   https://en.wikipedia.org/wiki/501st_ Infantry_Regiment _(United_States)#/media/ File:501-Parachute-Infantry-Regiment.svg

31 Castro & Khrushchev   https://www.thenation.com/ article/archive/the-cuban-missile-crisis-at-55/

32 Mermite cans   http://cdn9.dissolve.com/p/ D378_22_592/D378 _22_592_0004_600.jpg

33 Camp Mackall Airfield   From the author

34 Camp Mackall Airfield   From the author

35 Tyrone Adderly   https://arsof-history.org/icons/ Adderly.html

36 Ranger School mountain   https://www.Benning. army.mil/Infantry/ARTB/5th-RTBn/content/PDF/ Welcome-Packet.pdf?12NOV2021

37 Dominican Republic   https://history.army.mil/html/ bookshelves/resmat /dom_republic/CMH_Pub_93-5- 1(Maps_and_Charts).pdf

38 Santo Domingo   https://history.army.mil/html/ bookshelves/resmat/dom _republic/CMH_Pub_93-5- 1(Maps_and_Charts).pdf

39 InterAm Peace Force   https://upload.wikimedia.org/ wikipedia/commons /thumb/3/31/Honduran_soldiers% 2C_first_troops_of_Inter-American _peace_force %2C_arrive_to_assume_peace-keeping_duties_ and_to_render_emerg_-_NARA_-_541976.tif/ lossy-page1-1000px-Honduran_soldiers%2C_first_ troops_of_Inter-American _peace_force%2C_ arrive_to_assume_peace-keeping_duties_and_to_ render_emerg_-_NARA_-_541976.tif.jpg

40 Santo Domingo map   https://rc.library.uta.edu/uta-ir/bitstream/handle /10106/11153/Beshel_uta_ 2502M_11646.pdf?sequence=1&isAllowed=y

41 Recoilless Riffle   https://static.wikia.nocookie.net/ vietnamwar/images/b/b0/Rcl106lat2.jpg/revision/ latest?cb=20120502235106

42 CIB Dominican Republic   From the author

43 Troops, Santo Domingo   https://media.gettyimages. com/photos/American -troops-of-the-82nd-Airborne -Division-issue-food-and-water-to-picture-id1227731687?s=2048x2048

44 A 'Mule'   https://www.historynet.com/wp-content/ uploads/2015 /08/Ask_Marines_Dominican_MHQ.jpg

45 Bien Hoa airfield   https://upload.wikimedia.org/ wikipedia/commons /thumb /d/dc/Lockheed_U-2_ at_Bien_Hoa_1965.JPG/1280px-Lockheed_U-2_at_ Bien_Hoa_1965.JPG

46 Bien Hoa Army post   https://scontent-atl3-1.xx.fbcdn. net/v/t39.30808-6/233733496_4297278756975008_ 1493236240584671643_n.jpg?_nc_cat=103&ccb= 1-7&_nc_sid=8631f5&_nc_ohc=jQn3GJyDfTsAX-4zIL4&_nc_ht=scontent-atl3-1.xx&oh=00_

AfAPdBkHr-3_pE44maIBCP7b-dbX9Kqa2SMK vcF-dQfxoA&oe=63634A6B

47   Eagle Flights https://www.stripes.com/special-reports/eagle-flights-prey-on-fleeing-viet-cong-1.494252

48   University Quarry https://nebula.wsimg.com/ 7c68d1745d0ddb30b8 e09 bfd55ac54b7?AccessKey Id=E883D7F0A92E197D224D&disposition=0&allo worigin=1

49   SUMPCO https://www.history.navy.mil/content/ history/museums /seabee/explore/online-reading-room/tregaskis-photographs/tregaskis-31-45/_jcr_ content/body/media_asset_697820863/image.img. jpg/1485811872212.jpg

50   Starlight Scope http://www.1stbn83rdartyVietnam. com/Artillery_Info /Tools_of_the_Trade_Photos/ AN_PVS-1_Scope_Schwartz.jpg

51   Song Be https://upload.wikimedia.org/wikipedia/ commons /2/2d/Southvietmap.jpg

52   Cowboys https://museum.vhpa.org/companies/ 335ahc /images/335thAHC1966-67.jpg

53   Falcons https://i.ebayimg.com/images/g/8FMAAOS wB09YNOcF/s-l640.jpg

54   Choppers at Ben Cat https://www.flickr.com/photos/ 13476480@N07 /52273832835/in/photostream/

55   Choppers at Ben Cat https://www.flickr.com/photos/ 13476480@N07/522 73832895/in/photostream/

56   Last Chance https://www.flickr.com/photos/ 13476480@N07/5227 3833230/in/photostream/

57   UH-1Ds at Ben Cat https://www.flickr.com/photos/ 13476480@N07/5227 2371777/in/photostream/

58   Paratroopers at Ben Cat   https://www.flickr.com/ photos/13476480@N07/5227 3365298/in/ photostream/

59   Sniper road at Ben Cat   https://www.flickr.com/photos/ 13476480@N07/5227 3832685/in/photostream/

60   In the Song Be River   https://www.flickr.com/photos/ 13476480@N07/5227 2371867/in/photostream/

61   M26 Grenade   https://upload.wikimedia.org/wikipe-dia/commons /7/78/M-61Grenade.jpg

62   M26 Grenade   https://www.lexpev.nl/images/ m26seriedoorsnede.jpg

63   War Zone D   https://upload.wikimedia.org/ wikipedia/commons /1/16/III_CTZ_May_to_ September_1965.jpg

64   Viet Cong tunnels   https://web.mst.edu/rogersda/ umrcourses/ge342 /Cu%20Chi%20Tunnels-revised.pdf

65   The Plain of Reeds   https://d3i71xa-burhd42.cloudfront.net/ee9f583a762 d9ac618b9e0eccd0912e1ed0cc0b2/3-Figure1-1.png

66   173rd LRRP   https://www.inkace. com/173rd-airborne-brigade-decal/

67   Nha Trang   http://www.therossjewelryCompany. com/pic-ntair.gif

68   5th SFG gate   http://www.therossjewelryCompany. com/nt-5th-gate.gif

69   Project Delta   http://www.Vietnamgear.com/ vgphotos/ProDelta.jpg

70   Recondo School   https://upload.wikimedia.org/ wikipedia/commons/4 /40/Entrance_to_the_ MACV_Recondo_School%2C_Nha_Trang%2C_ March_1969.jpg

71 Team 4   From the author

72 Grease Gun   https://upload.wikimedia.org/ wikipedia/commons /8/89/M3-SMG.jpg (By Curiosandrelics - Own work, CC BY-SA 3.0)

73 Soldiers running to Huey   https://battleofiadrangvalley. weebly.com/uploads /1/3/7/1/13716742/4069184_ orig.jpg

74 Jakovenko in camo   From the author

75 Map of Saigon coast   https://geohack.toolforge. org/geohack.php?pagename =Bearcat_Base&params =10.835_N_106.96_E_

76 Larry "Red" Cole   From the author

77 Moya and Cundiff   Photo credit: Co Reentmeister, LIFE Magazine.

78 O-1 Bird Dog   https://www.cybermodeler.com/ aircraft/o-1/images/o-1_title.jpg

79 .30 cal machine gun   https://weaponsystems.net/ system/703-Browning%20M1919A6

80 .50 cal machine gun   http://www.military-today. com/firearms/m2.jpg

81 82mm mortar   https://www.ima-usa.com/products/ original-Russian-WWII-m1941-82mm-82-pm- 41-display-mortar-dated-1942?variant=26168664517 #mz-expanded-view-1093643669701

82 M18 Smoke Grenades   https://inertproducts.com/ wp-content/uploads/2020/05 /M18-NATO -Smoke- Grenade-GROUP-PHOTO-Inert-Replica-OTA-2900- copy-1.jpg

83 Huey w purple smoke   https://commons.wikimedia. org/wiki/File:NARA_111-CCV-349-CC43096_ Smoke_grenade_identifies_landing_zone_for_

101st_Airborne_UH-1D_carrying_brigade_
commander_Operation_Cook_1967.jpg

84 Huey w .50 cal & soldiers https://www.google.com/
url?sa=i&url=https%3A%2F %2Fwww.pinterest.
com%2Fpin%2F311311392971388989%2F&psig=AO
vVaw3Wt8ScTBeyJxBv6LDE4Y-Q&ust=1669244420
571000&source=images&cd=vfe&ved=0CAwQ jRx
qFwoTCPCKsZvywvsCFQAAAAAdAAAAABAD

85 Phu Loi https://www.68thahc.com/Photos_Old_04/
Saigon _area_map%20from%201st%20AB%20
web%20site%20%20ed.jpg

86 Staff Sgt Jakovenko From the author

87 Unarmed combat From the author

88 Raider School From the author

89 Zip gun https://www.thefirearmblog.com/blog/
wp-content/uploads/2019/03/keyzipgun1959.jpg

90 Key West https://arsof-history.org/articles/images/
v3n1_key _west/p1_main.jpg

91 Emerson Mk6 http://www.therebreathersite.nl/
10_Semiclosed rebreathers/Images/Emerson/
Picture15.jpg

92 Emerson Mk6 From the author

93 Vietnam map Nha Trang https://arsof-history.org/
articles/images/v3n1_team _effort/400/map_sf_
deployment.jpg

94 Kontum Army Airfield https://upload.wikimedia.
org/wikipedia/commons/5 /51/NARA_111-CCV-20-
80856_Aerial_view_of_Kontum_airfield_1967.jpg

95 Dak Seang on map https://vvaveteran.org/32-1/
images/dakto_map.gif

96 Dak Seang photo https://upload.wikimedia.org/ wikipedia/commons /thumb/7/76/Dak_Seang_ Special_Forces_Camp_aIrfield.jpg/1280px-Dak_ Seang_Special_Forces_Camp_aIrfield.jpg

97 Dak Seang paved runway https://www. daktomemories.com/uploads /1/3/4/7/134791198/ hinhanhlichsu-dakseang1_orig.jpg

98 The Montagnards https://www.historynet.com/wp-content/uploads/2019/02/v-960x640-8.jpg

99 Dak Seang trenches https://www.daktomemories. com/uploads/1/3/4/7 /134791198/pinimg-dakseang-60c3b7af6d18f4eb177df1864508b44c_orig.jpg

100 Dak Seang shooting range From the author

101 Dak Seang runway run From the author

102 Dak Seang mortar high From the author

103 Claymore Mine https://www.historynet.com/wp-content/uploads/image /2012/MH/09%20SEP/ HandTool.jpg

104 Fougasse https://upload.wikimedia.org/wikipedia/ commons /thumb/c/c8/Flame_Fougasse_as_battle-field_expedient.jpg

105 Recoilless Rifle https://upload.wikimedia.org/ wikipedia/commons /1/16/NARA_photo_111-CCV-556-CC38290.jpg

106 Flechette http://1.bp.blogspot.com/_oC8TwXe4PF0/ SU x1Qsm4oOI/AAAAAAAAPQ/1z3hv5bZcqo/ s1600/FLECHETTE.gif

107 The Dak Seang club From the author

108 Crossing a river From the author

109 Dak Seang mortar low From the author

110 The John Wayne Tower From the author

111 Cigarette   From the author
112 Dak Seang May 1970   https://upload.wikimedia.org/
     wikipedia/commons/ thumb/c/c2/Dak_Seang_Special_
     Forces_Camp%2C_May_1970.jpg/1280px-Dak_
     Seang_Special_Forces_Camp%2C_May_1970.jpg
113 Departing Dak Seang   From the author
114 Dak Seang C-operation   From the author
115 PRC-25 radio   https://geographicalimaginations.
     files.wordpress .com/2014/10/the-new-rto.jpg
116 General Flanagan   https://static.wikia.nocookie.
     net/military/images /3/3a/EdwardMFlanaganJr%
     28LTG%29.jpeg/revision/latest?cb=20181108215405
117 Colonel Bull Simons   https://www.usmilitariaforum.
     com/forums /uploads/monthly_03_2016/post-4101-
     0-77483900-1458404327.jpg
118 M79 grenade launcher   https://qph.cf2.quoracdn.net/
     main-qimg-a25961df77fb55a0c32541dbebeda256-lq
119 M60 machine gun   https://www.historynet.com/wp-
     content/uploads/2022 /03/M60-General-Purpose-
     Machine-Gun-Vietnam-Gregory-Proch-1200x772.png
120 Barbara   https://www.airandspaceforces.com/
     Image/Magazine Archive/PublishingImages/2018/
     October%202018/1018_Son_Tay_002.jpg
121 Greenleaf   http://sontayraid1970.com/wp-content/
     uploads/2018 /12/13.-Son-Tay-Raid-Photographs.pdf
122 Blueboy   http://sontayraid1970.com/wp-content/up-
     loads/2018 /12/13.-Son-Tay-Raid-Photographs.pdf
123 Redwine   http://sontayraid1970.com/wp-content/
     uploads/2018 /12/13.-Son-Tay-Raid-Photographs.pdf
124 Aux Field #3 barracks   From the author

About the Authors

Image 177. Jakovenko was inducted into the Ranger Hall of Fame in 2003 and the Special Forces Hall of Fame in 2024. His name is engraved on the Ranger Memorial at Fort Benning, the site used for Fox News' special America's Top Ranger which follows the Army's Best Ranger Competition. Born in the Donbas region of Ukraine under the Soviet terror of Josef Stalin, his family escaped from the Soviets and then from the Nazis to arrive at Ellis Island. He enlisted at 17, and his 30-year career encompassed Rangers, Special Forces, land combat, underwater operations, HALO infiltration, Long-Range Reconnaissance Patrols, the Blue Light counterterrorism unit, the Son Tay Raid...tell you what, you'll hear some of the stories tonight at the NCO club.

Image 178. Cliff Westbrook is the co-author (with Son Tay Raider
Terry Buckler) of Who Will Go: Into the Son Tay POW Camp.
A 1988 graduate of the US Air Force Academy and a pilot of
the B-1 bomber, Cliff is the son of Clyde "Neal" Westbrook,
the Aircraft Commander of *Lime 2* during the Son Tay Raid.
As a member of the Son Tay Raid Association, Cliff has
interviewed numerous Raiders and helped gather the historical
behind-the-scenes facts, including a complete compilation
of the radio channels (air & ground) recorded during the Son
Tay Raid. He partners with veterans to tell their stories for
the benefit of future generations. Contact him to help capture
your veteran's story. Email: cliffwestbrook88@gmail.com.

.